Praise for *Discovering the City of Sodom*

"Dr. Collins is a meticulous archaeologist who isn't afraid to challenge traditional assumptions about the location and fate of the Bible's most mysterious city—Sodom. This riveting account of Dr. Collins's fascinating journey and discovery has contributed a unique body of knowledge that surpasses anything published on the subject. I don't know of a more convincing case for Sodom's long-awaited identification."

—Joseph M. Holden, Ph.D., president of Veritas Evangelical Seminary
and coauthor of *The Popular Handbook of Archaeology and the Bible*

"'Welcome to Sodom' signs are absent—so has Steven Collins found the place? Latayne Scott imaginatively tells how Collins concludes it is Tall el-Hammam, east of the Jordan River, arguing vigorously from biblical texts, geography, and his discoveries at this large site. Archaeology's slow processes come to life in this vivid narrative."

—Alan Millard, Emeritus Rankin Professor of Hebrew and
Ancient Semitic Languages, The University of Liverpool

"This lively volume provides the compelling story of the (re)discovery and excavation of an important biblical-period site, combining personal experiences, archaeological evidence, and discussion of biblical texts. Even if one does not see eye to eye with the authors' interpretations on the identity of the site and relationship to specific parts of the biblical narrative, the enthusiastic description of the story of the study of this site and related issues makes it a great read!"

—Aren Maeir, professor, Bar-Ilan University, Ramat Gan, Israel,
and director of the Tell es-Safi/Gath Archaeological Project

"*Discovering the City of Sodom* is sure to create discussion, conversation, controversy, and enjoyment among lay and scholarly communities alike. Collins carries the reader on a journey through the Bible's ancestral tales of sacred obedience, decadent lust, and apocalyptic destruction, uncovering impressive archaeological remains of a sprawling metropolis possibly used by the biblical writers as their geographic setting. This is a book not to be missed in the debate over the Bible's role in archaeological studies."

—David C. Maltsberger, Ph.D., professor of religion,
Wayland Baptist University

"In this book, Collins provides the most complete discussion to date of all of the relevant biblical texts. The most compelling part of the book is Dr. Collins's argument for locating Sodom northeast of the Dead Sea, rather than farther to the south as many have assumed. Much of the skepticism about the historicity of Sodom over the years has been conducted in an archaeological vacuum. Now, with the excavations of Tell el-Hammam and Collins's extensive presentation of the historical, geographical, and archaeological data, we now have a better material basis for further discussion."

—Robert A. Mullins, Ph.D., professor of archaeology and Old Testament,
Azusa Pacific University

"The intrigue and biblical/historical detective work in this book thoroughly captivated me."

—Chris Fabry, author of ECPA Best Fiction winner *Almost Heaven*

DISCOVERING
THE CITY OF
SODOM

THE FASCINATING, TRUE ACCOUNT
OF THE DISCOVERY OF THE OLD TESTAMENT'S
MOST INFAMOUS CITY

Dr. Steven Collins and
Dr. Latayne C. Scott

HOWARD BOOKS
A Division of Simon & Schuster, Inc.
New York   Nashville   London   Toronto   Sydney   New Delhi

Howard Books
A Division of Simon & Schuster, Inc.
1230 Avenue of the Americas
New York, NY 10020

First Howard Books hardcover edition April 2013

HOWARD and colophon are trademarks of Simon & Schuster, Inc.

For information about special discounts for bulk purchases, please contact Simon & Schuster
Special Sales at 1-866-506-1949 or business@simonandschuster.com.

The Simon & Schuster Speakers Bureau can bring authors to your live event. For more information
or to book an event, contact the Simon & Schuster Speakers Bureau at 1-866-248-3049 or
visit our website at www.simonspeakers.com.

Designed by Davina Mock-Maniscalco

Manufactured in the United States of America

10 9 8 7 6 5 4 3 2 1

Library of Congress Cataloging-in-Publication Data

Collins, Steven.
    Discovering the city of Sodom: the fascinating, true account of the discovery of the Old
Testament's most infamous city / Dr. Steven Collins and Dr. Latayne C. Scott.
    volume; cm
    Includes bibliographical references.
    1. Dead Sea (Israel and Jordan)—Antiquities. 2. Sodom (Extinct city) 3. Bible. O.T. Genesis
XVIII–XIX—Criticism, interpretation, etc. 4. Bible. O.T.—Antiquities. I. Scott, Latayne Colvett.
II. Title.
    DS110.D38C65 2012
    939.4'62—dc23   2012029038

ISBN 978-1-4516-8430-8
ISBN 978-1-4516-8437-7 (ebook)

DR. COLLINS:

For Danette, the love of my life

DR. SCOTT:

*I dedicate this book to the servant-hearted people of
the Mountainside Church of Christ in Albuquerque, New Mexico. I
signed the contract on this book when my husband, Dan,
had been hospitalized and lay unconscious with a profoundly severe case
of Guillain-Barré syndrome in the intensive care unit for four weeks.
During the following four months of his hospitalization
at Presbyterian Hospital, Specialty Hospital, and Health South
Hospital, he received extraordinary care from the dedicated medical and
management personnel at those fine facilities. Throughout those long
months and the subsequent period of his recuperation at home,
the Mountainside congregation, along with family and other friends
across the country, provided everything—housing, transportation, funds,
food, encouragement, and respite—to "hold up my arms"
so that I could write this book. Without them, and the inestimable support
of son Ryan Scott and daughter Celeste Green and their families,
the writing of this book would have been impossible.*

Contents

PART ONE: Land of Facts and Fables

PART TWO: Right Place, Right Time,
Right Stuff: The Science of Tall el-Hammam

Foreword

THE DESTRUCTION OF THE CITIES OF THE PLAIN—SODOM, Gomorrah, Admah, and Zeboiim—is proverbial. The events described in Genesis 19 are so well known that anyone with minimal knowledge of the Bible is familiar with the dreadful destruction by fire and brimstone that God brought on these "sin cities." Paintings have been made of Sodom's overthrow, books written, and movies made.

When, in 2009, Dr. Steven Collins asked me to help him with the recording of the architectural remains of a site that he believed to be Sodom, I was very skeptical about the possibility of finding any vestiges of this city of infamy. A key verse in the New Testament, Jude 7, indicated that the destruction of the Cities of the Plain was an example of annihilation by eternal fire. So—my reasoning went—how could one expect to find any traces of them?

There was no shortage of theories as to the location of these cities, but in my view, none of them held water, particularly the one that associated their destruction with the formation of the Dead Sea! It is clear from the text of Genesis 14, where "slime pits" or sinkholes are mentioned, that the Dead Sea already existed before the destruction of these cities that was witnessed by Abraham from afar. Such sinkholes appear when the water level of the Dead Sea is very low, as it is today. These areas, where the ground has collapsed, were seen for the first time in 2009 and they are getting larger every year. Geological research has shown that today's low level of the Dead Sea is comparable to what it was at the time of Abraham. Most of these sinkholes are found in the area of Qumran, the likely location of the Valley of Siddim. It was in similar sinkholes that the "kings" of the Cities of the Plain fell.

Much of nineteenth-century scholarship put these cities to the northeast of the Dead Sea, whereas later researchers proposed a southern or eastern location. Bab edh-Dhra and Numeira are sites on the east side of the Dead Sea that have tentatively been identified with Sodom and Gomorrah, although the communities that lived in these sites, excavated in the 1960s and 1970s, never existed simultaneously. And the search goes on. Even as recently as 2011, a Russian-Jordanian team mooted a proposal to search the bottom of the Dead Sea with a submarine for these doomed cities.

Hearing Professor Collins's explanation of Genesis 13:1–12 and visiting the site of Tall el-Hammam forced me to rethink the whole question of the location of Sodom and Gomorrah. These verses make it quite clear that the Cities of the Plain, the Cities of the Kikkar—the vast circular expanse at the southern end of the Jordan River—must have been located east of Bethel/Ai, that is, northeast of the Dead Sea. The eastern part of the Kikkar can clearly be seen from this location. Having worked at the site of Khirbet el-Maqatir, which has been identified as Ai, for seven seasons, I can vouch for this. Even today, the eastern Kikkar is a well-watered plain with agricultural crops growing abundantly in the middle of winter. There can be no doubt that this region corresponds to the description of the area that Lot gazed on from Bethel/Ai and to which he was fatefully lured.

Because the Jordan Valley has long been a military zone, archaeological research had been severely restricted up to a few years ago. After the signing of the peace treaty between Israel and Jordan in 1994, Dr. Collins used this newly created opportunity to explore the Kikkar and search for archaeological sites that may correspond to the biblical description of the

Cities of the Plain. What he found was astounding. In this archaeological terra incognita, more than a dozen Bronze Age sites were identified, the largest of which, Tall el-Hammam, is being excavated by him and his team.

Not only is Tall el-Hammam one of the largest Bronze Age sites in the whole of the Middle East, but nowhere else have I seen such a thick layer of destruction, with collapsed walls, burnt debris, and dramatic skeletal remains, all inside a meter-thick layer of ash. The destruction of this ancient city was complete, and interestingly, other adjacent Bronze Age sites have a similar archaeological profile, showing that they suffered a similar fate.

After this total overthrow in the Middle Bronze Age, Tall el-Hammam was never rebuilt as a city, although there is evidence of later building activities during the Iron Age, about seven hundred years later. The archaeological remains therefore were not buried beneath many layers of civilization, but were found immediately below the surface. In 2012 the remains of a large gate were uncovered. As this book describes so poignantly, finding the Gate of Sodom, described in Genesis 19:1, was at the top of Professor Collins's wish list. Undoubtedly, the main and only gate of Tall el-Hammam has been found. If indeed Tall el-Hammam is Sodom, then this is the place where "Lot sat in the gate."

Dr. Collins is well aware of the difficulties involved in identifying this site with Sodom. Many will agree with the location, but the date of the final destruction is problematic for some. Typically, Professor Collins does not shrink from dealing with this problem and confronts it with his characteristic forthrightness. He believes that his site is in the right place and in the right time. As I see it, the location of Tall el-Hammam corresponds indeed to the biblical location of Sodom. For me, the identification of Tall el-Hammam with Sodom ticks all the required boxes but one—the time of its destruction. Instead of rejecting the identification of this singular site with Sodom on this point only, I suggest that this unticked box of the accepted chronology needs closer examination.

This book is the intriguing account of Dr. Collins's personal research into the location of the Cities of the Kikkar, particularly that of Sodom. Even if you still have some reservations, as I have, it is a compelling story of the discovery of a site that, more than any other, corresponds to the place of the cataclysm described in the early chapters of Genesis.

Dr. Leen Ritmeyer
Archaeological Architect
Cardiff, Wales

Preface

ONE OF THE MOST VIVID STORIES OF THE OLD TESTAMENT IS the tale of Sodom and Gomorrah in Genesis 18–19. Sodom and Gomorrah, two of the five "cities on the plain" adjacent to the Dead Sea, were steeped in wickedness, and the Lord was determined to destroy them. The Lord was willing to change his mind if Abraham could find at least ten honest people in the towns, but alas, he could not, so "the Lord rained on Sodom and Gomorrah sulfur and fire from heaven, overthrowing those cities and all of the plain" (Genesis 19:24–25).

For centuries most folk who rooted their faith in the Bible took this and the other stories of the patriarchs at face value. But with the flood of new discoveries in the Near East in the 1800s, such as the decipherment of Egyptian hieroglyphics and Babylonian cuneiform, which provided access to a vast sea of ancient Near Eastern literature, widespread skepticism began to emerge in biblical criticism by the end of that century. Adherents of this skepticism, sometimes called "modernists," tended to see the Bible as mostly pious poetry—beautiful and of high moral value, but with little or no historical basis. The patriarchal narratives, including the story of Sodom and Gomorrah, were seen as compositions to foster ethical behavior, but certainly never really happened.

With the growth of scientific archaeology in the Holy Land in the early 1900s, biblically oriented scholars, especially Americans, began to react to this cynical approach to the Old Testament. One of the most articulate of these new scholars was the famous William Foxwell Albright, whose magisterial excavations at Gibea (1922) and Tell Beit Mirsim (1933–36) demonstrated a surprising correlation between the biblical narratives about the kingdoms of Israel and Judah and the "Iron Age" archaeological data. More digs in Israel by other scholars—again, mostly Americans—began to reveal the lifestyles of the local inhabitants during the earlier "Bronze Age," and Albright, among them, suggested that the life situation of the Old Testament patriarchs and their spouses—Abraham, Sarah, Isaac, Jacob—as described in the Bible fit very well with the facts on and in the ground brought to light by excavations.

This was such an exciting prospect that there began a great rush to find new Bronze Age sites to explore—particularly those with possible biblical connections. It was in such a hope that the Jesuits of the Pontifical Biblical Institute in Jerusalem, led at first by Father Alexis Mallon, S.J., began to excavate Tuleilat Ghassul in Transjordan from 1929 to 1938, on the Kikkar of the Jordan, the circular plain just north of the Dead Sea—the area that in his mind was the correct location of the biblical Cities of the Plain. Father Mallon was convinced at first that what he found at Ghassul was evidence of the destruction of Sodom and Gomorrah, but what they had uncovered was, as a matter of fact, not a Bronze Age site, but one from yet another period earlier, the Chalcolithic. However, they recognized that nearby sites, such as sprawling Tall el-Hammam, were covered with Bronze Age pottery sherds. Unfortunately, the untimely death of Father Mallon and the onset of European hostilities kept the Pontifical Biblical Institute from pursuing what might have been a wonderful discovery.

When pursuing the question of the historicity of the Sodom tales, there are two ways of proceeding. One would be to seek evidence that the events actually occurred as narrated in Genesis. The other would be to leave that possibility perhaps open, but to search for a site whose destruction would have been the *basis* for such a narrative. For example, were the writers familiar with certain ancient ruins (tells or talls), the location and destruction of which suggested an etiological or explanatory story: "How did such places and destruction come about? It must have been . . . ," etc. Many archaeologists maintain that Jericho, for example, was indeed destroyed, but not exactly at the time of Joshua; however, because it was laid waste in the area of sites that Joshua actually did destroy, it also became part of the Conquest narrative.

In either approach, it is necessary to find a site that would explain the origin of the Sodom narratives, and just possibly one that produces evidence that the narration as it appears in the Bible may not be disconnected from historical reality after all. This is what the authors of this book have done. Among the several sites or collections of sites that have been proposed for the notorious Cities of the Plain, which includes Sodom as its nucleus, Collins's proposal of Tall el-Hammam as this very place is convincing indeed. The evidence that the Tall el-Hammam Excavation Project (TeHEP) has brought to light, and which Professor Collins marshals to demonstrate the correlation between Tall el-Hammam and the biblical narrative, must now enter the discussion as offering by far the strongest candidate for the site of Sodom. The way Collins and Scott present the material is itself a delightfully deepening series of discoveries that mirrors the process of an archaeological excavation itself.

As the one who has curated the Ghassul material in Jerusalem at the Pontifical Biblical Institute for more than forty years and who has constantly encountered the trays of Bronze Age sherds that Mallon had picked up at Hammam, I am both pleased and excited to see what has become the trajectory of the artifacts I have lived with for so long, now made clear by TeHEP's wonderful work on the eastern Kikkar and the authors' cogent analysis.

William J. Fulco, S.J., Ph.D.
National Endowment for the Humanities Professor of Ancient
   Mediterranean Studies
Department of Classics and Archaeology
Loyola Marymount University
Los Angeles

An Important Note about Terminology

TERMINOLOGY IS ALWAYS CHANGING IN THE WORLD OF ARchaeology as old terms give way to newer, often more accurate ones. Reflecting that, this book uses the word *tall* to refer to an occupational mound, instead of the word *tell*. The book also reflects the most up-to-date names of archaeological periods and the scholarly designations of BCE and CE instead of BC and AD. Also, for ease of reading, most diacritical marks have been removed from foreign words. The place name "Tall el-Hammam" is sometimes referred to as "Tall al-Hammam" on certain maps from the Jordanian Geological Survey, as this is the spelling typically used in Jordan.

PART ONE

Land of Facts and Fables

ONE

Down from the Jordan's Source:
The Setting for Sodom

To UNDERSTAND THE ROLE OF THE ONCE-GREAT CITY-STATE of Sodom, you must visualize where it is in relation to the rest of the history of the Semitic people in whose land it lies. Though the recent discovery of Sodom seemed to come out of nowhere, it has been in the same place for thousands of years. It must take its proper place on both maps and timelines of Bible events.

It often surprises those who love the Bible when they learn that most of that book's events took place in a footprint smaller than the state of New Jersey. Excepting the sojourns of biblical people in Egypt and captivity in Babylon (and of course the travels of the apostles after the time of Jesus), practically everything biblical happened in an eight-thousand-square-mile skinny rectangle that transects the so-called Fertile Crescent, which stretches from the Arabian gulf to the borders of the Nile River in Egypt.

Once a year, Albuquerque, New Mexico–based Trinity Southwest University conducts an archaeological study tour of the Holy Land, crossing back and forth over the fortified but nonetheless amicable borders between Jordan and Israel to see the most significant sites. The grand prize of the tour is a look at Tall el-Hammam—biblical Sodom—over the last days of the tour, of course. But all of Holy Land history, all of the Holy Land itself, is as knitted together as the souls of David and Jonathan. And the lifeblood of the Hebrew people's history is the river in its heart, and the logic of its story follows the great Jordan River south to the Dead Sea. To understand biblical history you must follow the Jordan—whose very name means "descent"—as it makes its way through the geography of biblical history.

The narrow rectangle of the Holy Land is split, quite literally, right down the middle by the profound valley of the Jordan River. Unlike the upside-down Nile, the Jordan runs north to south through an area called the Great Rift. This long, deep fissure, formed in antiquity by the shifting of adjacent tectonic plates, stretches from Turkey all the way to the Serengeti Plain in Africa. Its once-suboceanic past is revealed by its mountaintops, which are here and there crusted with fossils that even today crunch underfoot.

In the Holy Land, this Rift's northern border is defined by the Lebanon Mountains and the iconic Mount Hermon, the "grey-haired mountain" whose summit marks the border of modern Israel. Its fifty-foot drifts of snow have inspired psalms, such as the one that compares fellowship to "the dews of Mount Hermon." The same snow provides one source of the Jordan River's headwaters and is perhaps the site of the Transfiguration of Jesus, where he communed with Moses and Elijah (Mark 9:2–5).

(How did the apostles know the identity of those two long-dead men when they saw them with Jesus? a guide asks, and then allows guesses until the right answers appear: Moses by the great light coming from his face—Exodus 34:35—and Elijah by his bald head and excessively hairy body—2 Kings 1:8.)

Northern Israel is a thin, vulnerable place, a bruised and bloodied fist that jabs toward its menacing neighbors. Even if there weren't fortified fences, anyone could see the borders of Israel: just as Egypt is the gift of the Nile, Israel is the gift of drip irrigation. Just across Israel's barbed-wire borders, where the green ends and the brown begins, lie both Lebanon and Syria and the reasons for bomb shelters in every kibbutz; the signs on the roadside tell you not to walk past the shoulder because there are mine-fields there.

Visitors try to digest the reality of still-active land mines in a civilized country. They ponder the irony of mosques in Israel and the contradiction of its population of 12 percent of Muslims, whose Quran-reading children take part in the Israeli army's compulsory service for all its young citizens.

This is a place millions have dreamed of visiting since they heard the Bible stories of childhood. Proportionally, more come here from non-English-speaking countries than not. The popular tourist sites are a Babel—or perhaps, a Pentecost—of groups, huddled in semicircles as they listen to discourses in their native tongues by hoarse and earnest tour guides with waving arms.

American groups contain all types of people. On one extreme are people like the middle-aged Arkansas farmer who tries to figure out how to anchor on his head the little yarmulke with the blue Star of David that he's just bought from a vendor (and whether or not he should rock back and forth as he prays, as he sees the black-coated Hasidic Jews do). On the other side of the scale is the chattering group of schoolgirls who have been sent here with the hope that old sacrednesses will rub off on them and stick to their clothing when they return to the malls and MP3s of their lives. Somewhere in the middle are the pious families and the young couples who haul their unwitting children from site to site and try to take notes and photographs and videos of every important thing.

And in Israel, every site is an important thing. There is no other place on earth about which so many uncounted libraries have been written. It's surely the most documented eight thousand square miles on earth.

Some tourists are lured by the churches and mosques built over most of the familiar places: the Temple, the Nativity, the Holy Sepulcher, and the holies of other assorted holies. But a tour specializing in Israel's archaeology disdains everything Byzantine and newer ("Second century AD, huh? Move on!") and takes the pilgrim first to the fount of every blessing, the bubbling-up emergence of the Jordan River's pristine waters from the very ground at a place called Tel Dan. Here is a lush habitat for birds and salamanders and fish that climb waterfalls, a place where dew and moss drip from everything.

Under excavation and deteriorating in the sopping air at Laish (Tel Dan) down the road is a mudbrick gateway, with perhaps the oldest arch in existence—through which Abraham may have passed on his route from Haran to his inheritance in Canaan (Genesis 12:4–5). Literally a few steps away are the stone foundations of a gateway where kings of his Israelite descendants sat centuries later, arbitrating disputes among the people. Gateways such as this do not always endure, but their stone foundations usually do. Perhaps that is why the idea of a gateway and heaven have become tied together in people's minds.

Adjacent to it is Caesarea Philippi, the place where Jesus pointed up to a gaping mouth of a cave into which pagans threw human sacrifices to Pan—perhaps subdued by hallucinogens still discernible in excavated ancient drinking vessels. Here Jesus brought his disciples on a six-day journey out of their way, to this place of decision. Here he told his disciples that what he would build, the open heart of a church, would not be a matter of flesh and blood, would not be overcome by such things as this gate into hell (Matthew 16:13–20).

The river falls precipitously a few miles downstream into the Sea of Galilee (or Tiberias, as it's also named in the Bible). Tourists ride in loaded barges across it and eat basketfuls of the grilled St. Peter's tilapia (named after that apostle's famous eureka of a coin in the jaws of one of these mouth-breeding fish, as recorded in Matthew 17:24–27). Later, everyone gawks at the recently found "Jesus boat," a wooden fishing vessel from the first century improbably preserved in Galilean mud until its discovery and restoration just a few years ago.

It isn't Jesus's sailing ship, though, because he didn't own anything. In modern terms, he would have gone to Hertz Rent-a-Boat when he needed one.

On the northwest shore of the lake is Capernaum, one of three cities cursed by Jesus. Yet that same city was extraordinarily blessed when he healed a servant of the man who built its synagogue. This man, a Roman centurion, possessed and immortalized what Jesus called "astonishing" faith (Luke 7:1–10).

A Christian guide points out the exact middle of the tiled floor. All ancient synagogues are perfect squares, he tells visitors, like God spreading himself over the four corners of the earth. Look here, he says, this is where Jesus would have stood to read. This synagogue floor is much more modern than in Jesus's day, but the floor from his time lies beneath this one. People go and stand next to that spot, wanting proximity, fearing usurpation lest they crowd out his memory.

The archaeological tour doesn't go to Nazareth, for there is little ancient to see there. Instead, the visitors look out at what Jesus would have seen from there: a breathtaking landscape that would have been his history book. There everyone could see Mount Tabor's unmistakable mammary profile, the fitting setting of the story of the extraordinary heroine Deborah when she and Barak conquered the king of Hazor (Judges 4). The sight of Mount Carmel, across the valley, evokes the telling of the fire from heaven that ignited Elijah's waterlogged firewood and sent the pagan priests running in terror, history's first cutters, still dripping blood from their self-inflicted skin-slicing (1 Kings 18).

Then the guide points out Sepphoris, a neighboring city not mentioned in biblical texts but that was a bustling building project during the teenage and young adult years of Jesus. His father Joseph, the guide explains, was a *tekton,* a word whose meaning can include the concept of a carpenter but more probably meant a builder or artisan, perhaps even a stonemason. How many times, as the guide points out, did Jesus speak of stonework, of cornerstones, capstones, foundations, towers? (See Matthew 24:27 and elsewhere.)

Then he tells of a recent discovery in close-by Nazareth, under what is called "the trench of St. Joseph," of a *mikva* or ritual bath found only in the homes of wealthy Jews. The question arises: Were Joseph and Son successful regional construction experts? Did Jesus give up a successful career and comfortable lifestyle to become a hounded itinerant rabbi?

No archaeological tour of the Holy Land is complete without several days in Jerusalem. No matter from which direction you come to that city, you always come up, because it's a mountain in a valley-bowl surrounded by hills. Though situated in the world's most overdocumented country, this is the most disputed real estate on the planet, its very soil in a constant and intractable tug-of-war between Muslims and Jews and Christians.

It's as if all of history is distilled and concentrated here so potently that no one wants to share it. Everywhere are ruins and buildings under excavation. The Israeli government's commitment to archaeology is more than just a scientific endeavor; it's the Jewish nation's attempt to confirm an entire history that a Muslim world would deny ever existed.

The repatriation of Jerusalem by non-Arabs, the Arabs say, is just a repeat of the Crusades.

Remembrance is the key to salvation, Jews say; forgetfulness leads to exile.

The Witnesses

THE OLD CITY OF DAVID excavations bear witness to a Jewish past: Gihon Spring, David's water shaft, Hezekiah's Tunnel, and Warren's Shaft, the Siloam Pool.

People emerge with the story on their shoulders and heads, green with moss, from the newly excavated sewers through which the rich people of Jerusalem attempted to escape the Romans in 70 CE.

The uncovering and restoration of the house of the high priest, in whose courtyard the prisoner Jesus stood, verifies.

The Garden of Gethsemane, the once-smoldering Hinnom Valley, Herod's palace, the Mount of Olives, all testify.

And of course the retaining walls of the temple, with massive stones of over a hundred tons each, thirty feet long, unmoved for more than two millennia from the place where Herod's workers placed them and today without even a razor's width between them, mutely communicate an implacable story.

On the archaeological tour, a bearded man with close-cropped gray hair points up to where he has discovered features hidden for millennia. This is Dr. Leen Ritmeyer and the Temple Mount is his adopted homeland, his real estate, and he is the unquestioned expert on this site of all sites. In fact, many of the reconstruction drawings in Jerusalem's museums and drawings on government-sponsored tour signs in the city are by Ritmeyer. He is a recorder of archaeological data, the extrapolator of it, interpreter of new discoveries such as the famous trumpeting sign on the Temple Mount. He is legend to non-Arab archaeologists and at the same time a persona non grata, banned from the Muslim Dome of the Rock and its surrounding precinct.

The modern city of Jerusalem is a jumble. Viewed from the outside, its very topography exemplifies and illustrates the contradictions of Israel. It is peaks and valleys, inclusions and exclusions, history and future, one side moistened by the Mediterranean and heavily wooded, the other cracked, dry desert.

The desert. The Hebrew word for desert is the same as the word for hearing. Throughout its history, people went to the desert to listen: Jesus "shoved" by the Holy Spirit (as the *koine* Greek of Mark 1:12 describes it) into desolate places to hear the voice of Satan, the apostle Paul then tutored by Jesus whispering in the winds of the Arabian dunes (Galatians 1:12–17). Both were heirs of the legacy of Old Testament prophets sent into sandy exile, where they too heard voices from beyond this world.

There is little of archaeology in the desert places of Israel, but its few sites are stark and memorable.

Qumran, of course, is the essence of the speaking of the desert itself, which divulged in 1947 the long-silent Dead Sea Scrolls. These famous documents were written (it is supposed) by Essenes who built their desert community in homage to parchment and what could be immortalized on it, intentionally facing library and scriptorium east, to get rid of moisture.

Ritmeyer concurs, saying that he can't begin any of his architectural drawings in the Holy Land until the sun comes up and dries the paper.

He taps with his foot the crust of the unique sandy soil that closes itself up and sheds water. No wonder the scrolls survived the ages in their clay jars. Could there be more of them? Perhaps the desert might still have muted voices waiting to speak.

Near the southwestern shore of the Dead Sea towers its most iconic desert symbol of Jewish nationalism, Masada, the fortress/palace city of Herod. Still visible from its breath-catching heights are the outlines of the camps of an entire legion of Roman soldiers who over a six-month period built a huge siege ramp up to the captured fortress to try to kill more than 900 occupying Jewish men, women, and children.

Rations alone for the legion would have totaled more than $36 million in modern currency. What was the great threat? Was it to Roman pride, losing a garrison because its guards, who thought it impregnable, were careless?

Centuries before the Romans, King David once ascended and secreted himself on the heights of Masada, as 1 Samuel 23:14 indicates when it speaks of his hiding in a "stronghold" in the Judean desert. But his favorite desert hideout from the wrath of King Saul (1 Samuel 24:1) was the lush slit in the Judean hills, the lovely and surprising En-Gedi. At its summit is a concave of caves, with a dagger of light and water into its heart, its legendary spring. It's a wonder that David would leave that place of peace and beauty to try to rule over a contentious nation that, after his son's death, would never again be united.

Secrets of the Waters

BUT THE DESERT IS FAR from the heart of Israel, because its lifeblood is in the Jordan. This river meanders so much that if it were straightened out, it would be twenty miles longer. Its fords and falls cache some of the best stories in the Bible. The patriarch Jacob crossed over it and its tributary (Genesis 32:22); an entire nation in exile walked dry-shod over its damp and dammed-up riverbed to claim its inheritance beyond the ruins of the walls of Jericho (Joshua 3:14–17). It delineated the border between some of the tribes and their brothers. Here Jephthah killed the Ephraimites (Judges 5:12–6), Gideon lay in wait for the Midianites (Judges 7:24), and Solomon's foundries of brass seethed (1 Kings 7:46). Atop its waves two prophets walked (2 Kings 2:8, 14); at its banks Elijah performed two miracles (2 Kings 5:14, 6:6). The river isn't just source and border, it's cleansing too: in its depths Jesus himself submitted to baptism (Mark 1:9). From that point on, he crisscrossed its shores during his entire teaching ministry.

The river is the distillation of a nation's history; it is life. But like all earthly life, it begins to slow and amass the ills of earth, until it reaches its own death in the Great Salt Sea.

On the western shore of the Dead Sea, Israeli ingenuity has recently made fruit trees grow in the pebbly and boulderous lime-caked sand, little outposts of green vigor in this lifeless place. Nearby, the desiccated cliffs seem so imposing, yet so fragile that they would crumble under the fingernail of God.

The Great Salt Sea lies in its own crusted coffin, seeming to have pushed its heels up against an impassible barrier on its south side. It reaches the lowest point on earth—thirteen hundred feet below sea level—as the Jordan ceases to erode, becomes muddy and morbid and turgid, and is finally trapped in its own dead-end rut.

But its depths hold secrets: at its lake bottom, it's another twelve hundred feet below its own surface.

It is incredibly salty, not because it has no outlet (many other lakes have no outlet and yet have fresh and sparkling water), but because its surrounding rock strata are laden with anhydrous chloride salts that leach into the water until its molecules can absorb no more. Then, until more seasonal water flows from the river into the lake, the laden water waits patiently to capture more salt.

Its many names reflect people's theories about it. Jews of Jesus's day called it Lake Asphaltitus because it had for centuries spit up little black chunks of asphalt from deep deposits. But earlier in Genesis it was called the Salt Sea, or the Sea of the Arabah, or the Eastern Sea (which makes perfect sense if you lived between it and the Mediterranean). But to most people, it's best known as the Dead Sea.

Do you want to know the level of that body of water in antiquity? It fluctuated. During the Bronze Age (around the time of Abraham and his descendants, before they went to Egypt), and during the Roman period, and then during the Byzantine period and the Middle Ages, it looked almost exactly as it does today in the twenty-first century.

The level of the lake has never been lower than it is now, not since humans have lived here. Therefore, there isn't the remotest possibility that there are hidden cities beneath its brackish surface. Sodom and Gomorrah aren't there. Not now, not before. Not ever.

The waters have secrets to divulge, perhaps. But if you're going to look for the famous Cities of the Plain, the site of Sodom, its sister city Gomorrah, and the others, you'll have to look somewhere else.

Dr. C's Dilemma

The characters within the following section were developed to represent the differing opinions on Sodom and are not based on any actual individuals.

It was two weeks into a three-week archaeological study tour of the Holy Land in 1996 that Dr. Steven Collins began to feel a bit uneasy.

Perhaps, he thought, it was the hair-raising journey the day before. The tour bus had wrenched everyone's stomachs and equilibriums as it clung to a precipitous road long ago scraped beside the Wadi Qelt's sun-bleached southern edge. Or maybe it was the still-fresh memories of the fact that in that very ravine just a year before, two Israelis had been gunned down by fighters from the Palestine Liberation Organization in broad daylight.

"Are you sure we're safe here?"

The question came from Peggiann Hoffman, who'd brought up the recent shootings just as they arrived at the parking area to walk down a sloping stone and asphalt walkway. "My guidebook says this isn't a safe place to travel alone." She brushed her limp platinum hair out of her eyes.

"And we aren't alone, dear, are we?" Her husband, Chuck, struggled to hold the shoulder bag of books the couple took everywhere. He was trying to stuff more brochures into its pockets and sighed. Here nearly at sea level he could breathe easily, though the dry air was nothing like what he was used to at home in Florida. "There are twenty of us, and we have Dr. C, of course."

Steve, "Dr. C," grinned at them. He'd been leading tours like this for years, and he never grew tired of it. Though repeated visits to ancient sites had made them familiar to him, as familiar as his own home state of New Mexico, each time he came back to the Bible lands it was with the same enthusiasm and freshness of the first time.

What had become more predictable than the beloved sites and landscapes was the way that each study tour's group of participants always seemed to settle into strata as distinct as the layers in an excavation. At the beginning of each tour, there were shy people and brash people and knowledgeable people and awestruck people. But as day after day together passed, it was no longer personality types that he noticed, but how they viewed what they saw.

Take Chuck and Peggiann Hoffman, for instance—probably the wealthiest ones on the tour, at least from the way they talked. Peggiann didn't buy postcards and trinkets at the tourist shops; she bought jewelry, good jewelry. And Chuck, a financial analyst, managed to let it "slip" early on that he had just sold "one of the stock portfolios" to help with "archaeological" research.

Dr. C had cringed as Chuck continued: the "research" he spoke of was by what Dr. C would call "a romping, stomping pseudo-archaeologist" who had claimed he'd discovered everything from Noah's Ark to Sodom and Gomorrah to the Ark of the Covenant. Many good-hearted people like the Hoffmans thought that at last—at last!—the scientific world would believe the Bible.

To the contrary, every legitimate archaeologist in the world knew this untrained guy with a camera and an overactive imagination was a fraud. But hoping against hope, these people believed. And donated.

There were others on the tour who wanted to believe in that kind of hopeful visual verification, even in spite of Dr. C's gentle attempts to turn conversations to more reputable findings. After all, they'd joined this tour because the Bible gave them something to trust, something to believe in.

Later, aboard the bus, Dr. C heard a gasp of appreciation as the travelers saw, through the lush grove of olive and palm and cypress trees, the startling, bright turquoise-blue dome of the fifteen-hundred-year-old St. George Monastery. The ancient building's beige walls seemed to extrude from the limestone canyon walls.

Khaki. Dr. C liked that color. In fact, he'd been known to wear khakis under his academic robes at graduation ceremonies.

"Now, what are the legends about this place?" The voice of Robert Pinkerston rang out. He was used to raising his voice above crowds: as an Episcopal youth minister, he'd shepherded noisy kids through cultural events and service projects until his hair and patience had worn thin. He'd settled into local ministry until his wife died two years ago, and now rounding the corner with two bad knees toward his sixties, he was enrolled in Trinity Southwest University as one of Dr. C's distance-learner doctoral degree students. The two men had butted heads in a good-natured way both in emails and in person when he'd come to Albuquerque for classes, because Robert knew what he'd been taught in seminary, and he knew that the only way to reconcile the Bible to the real world was to make sure everyone understood he didn't think the Bible was *as* real as Dr. C said it was.

Dr. Collins on-site at Tall el-Hammam.

A valuable and edifying book, to be sure. For Robert, even a beloved book. But like most "higher critically" educated intellectuals—for so he saw himself—he believed the documents of the Bible to be the earnest, faith-filled literary attempts of people who wanted to help build the faith of others; true in their principles but not really something a modern thinker would regard as history. Build faith with good stories: that always worked for Robert.

Dr. C smiled. "There are legends associated with this place," he said. "Some people believe that Joachim, the father of the Virgin Mary, was here when an angel announced that he was going to father a child," he said.

"That's Catholic stuff," Peggiann said under her breath, and Dr. C continued on, raising his voice above the roar of gushing water that, like the monastery, seemed inexplicably to spring from the canyon rock itself.

"But a lot of documented history, too. Built in the fifth century CE and destroyed by Persian invaders two centuries later—but the recon-struction wasn't finished until 1900 or so."

There were more oohs and aahs from people catching sight of the monastery, which looked as if it had been superglued into the cliff face. To the east, through a slit in the wadi, the haze over the distant Jordan Valley would soon give hints of the mountains that rose above the Hashemite Kingdom of Jordan.

Dr. C walked along with the tour members, taking satisfaction from the delighted expressions on the faces he saw, and caught up with his old friend Dr. Eugene Mason. A retired mechanical engineer, Eugene had a pleasant face that could reflect any positive emotion except humor, a quality he apparently thought extraneous to any analytical thinking. And above his head, he would ruefully admit.

"You didn't mention that some people think that this is the site where Elijah was fed by the ravens," Eugene said. "But probably no reason to say that; there's no proof."

Dr. C nodded. Of all the people on this tour, Eugene and he saw things the most eye to eye, as far as their view of the Bible was con-cerned. "Find it in the dirt, see how it matches the text," Eugene often said. From his point of view, if you couldn't find some documented proof that Elijah was here, in this very place, all the ravens and tradi-tions in the world wouldn't make it worth a mention.

And in his opinion, the same went for every single site in Jordan and Israel.

The group walked into the monastery's modestly decorated interior and Dr. C watched Peggiann and some of the other women shudder as they looked at skulls neatly stacked there. "Those are the priests killed by the Persians I told you about," Dr. C said.

One woman who wasn't shuddering was Dr. Beth Neal, another of Dr. C's students, an outdoorsy, practicing emergency room physician from Toronto. She squatted next to a glass coffin where a mummified man's body lay, dressed in the regalia of a Russian priest of the 1800s. His prominent teeth gleamed white against his age-browned skin. Beth's black ponytail bobbed up and down as she looked at the top and sides of the transparent surface. Undoubtedly she was making mental notes about the preservation of the human body in an arid climate like this. Her slacks might be wrinkled and she'd slap every pocket in them and her traveler's vest looking for the eyeglasses that perched on her head, but she was all about keeping track of ideas and details.

Later that night in Jerusalem, the group seemed subdued. They'd hiked four miles through the cavernous, dusty wadi after their visit to the monastery, and their dinner was quiet—and short. The next morning, Abu-Yusef, the bus driver who'd driven for Dr. C during several previous tours, stood patiently waiting in the hotel lobby as the tour group gathered.

"I can't even pronounce the names of the places we're going today and tomorrow," Peggiann said, holding an itinerary up in front of her and trying to wrangle some of the names. "Tell Gezer, Beth Shemesh, Azekah, Lachish, Ashkelon, Beer Sheva, Ein Avdat." Some of the other women laughed. She looked at her husband, who was trying to extract himself from the straps of two black bags crossed across his chest.

"But Petra—you'll like Petra," he said.

"Isn't that where they filmed that scene from one of the Indiana Jones movies?" Robert asked, in his loud, come-to-order voice. "The pink walls, all carved out of the side of a cliff like St. George Monastery?"

"Much more dramatic than the monastery," said Eugene Mason. He was the only one other than Dr. C who had seen it before, but his comment was swamped by Peggiann's excited squeals.

"Sodom! Day after tomorrow is the day we go to Sodom!" She pulled a book out of one of the bags her husband held in his lap. She pointed to a photograph in it. "See, sulfur balls. We'll see them, won't we?" Without waiting for an answer, she pointed to another photograph in a book written by the adventurer who was the Hoffmans' hero. "Pillars of salt like Lot's wife. And we'll see these melted canyon walls, from the fire and brimstone, right?"

Dr. C shifted uncomfortably. He didn't want to dash her hopes. There was an awkward silence.

"Everyone knows those cities are underneath the Dead Sea," said Dr. Neal abruptly. "So how could we see them at all?"

Beth hardly ever spoke, and her words had a hint of challenge in them. The burgundy frames on her round, oversize glasses sliding down her nose and her straight-cut bangs made her look like a precocious child with weathered skin. "I mean, every reputable archaeologist, from W. F. Albright on, thinks they're in those shallow waters, right? And aren't some Russian archaeologists planning to do some diving expeditions to document it? So we're just going to the Sodom *region*, isn't that right?"

"This tour is all about education and learning new things," said Dr. C evenly. "We're going to two archaeological sites, Bab edh-Dhra and Numeira. There are burn layers in the excavation that some archaeologists say make them good candidates for two of the famous Cities of the Plains—maybe Sodom and Gomorrah" (see Map 1).

To his right, Eugene Mason nodded. On this they agreed. Eugene had read some of the professional literature, and the two sites "had their charms," they concurred.

"No need to disagree," said Robert, the peacemaker. He stood with his arms outstretched in the middle of the group, enjoying the attention as he looked around at them. "It's the lesson we should learn about God's power over nature. From a theologian's point of view, you have to believe that those stories were just made up, years after the fact, to explain why that area south of the Dead Sea is so"—he struggled for a word—"so dead?"

Everyone laughed. They'd been in and out of some desolate places for the last two weeks, much unlike the lush landscapes in which most of them made their homes and lived their lives. They began boarding the bus.

Abu-Yusef leaned with the sole of one foot against a bus tire. Dr. C went and stood beside the driver. "Ready for another ride?" he asked. He felt closer to this generous middle-aged Arab man than to anyone on the tour.

"The lady with the ponytail? She is right about Sodom being under the Dead Sea," Abu-Yusef said. "The Quran has the story of Ibrahim and Lut, and my family lives here for centuries. We believe Allah made the Dead Sea to cover up the evil cities."

Dr. C put his hand on his friend's shoulder. "Just get us to the border. We'll have an adventure no matter what we see!"

That night, after tours of sites that Peggiann called "the unpronounceables," Dr. C sat alone in the fading light of an evening that filtered through the curtains of his modest hotel room in the Israeli city of Arad.

He pushed the worn fabric aside. His window overlooked dun-colored buildings and hard-angled architecture that symbolized the resolve of a place that stands sentinel over wastelands. Beyond the city lay the Negev, an arid wilderness more desolate than the Mojave Desert of his early childhood, and more incised and featureless than the grassless expanses and mesas of his homeland of New Mexico.

He leaned forward in the creaking chair for a long look at the great beige expanse of dusty ridges beyond it. Tomorrow he would lead a group of people he'd grown to like, who respected and trusted him, on a short journey east beyond the Dead Sea to desolate Bab edh-Dhra, a place some biblical scholars called Sodom, and to Numeira, which was identified as its sister city, Gomorrah.

He stretched his neck from one side to the other and wondered about the two sites with their layers of ash and other evidences of a fiery destruction. That fit. But there were problems with the chronology, he knew. Perhaps something in a coming excavation would resolve a five-hundred-year disparity between when the Bible said that the cities were destroyed and what the archaeology showed. Surely they could be reconciled.

Start with the text, he told his students. Always start with the text. In this case, he held in his hands the only ancient text in existence that described Sodom, the single source that claimed to be witness of its events.

He wanted to look at everything with new eyes. He thought about the Hoffmans and Robert and Eugene and Beth, and even his bus driver, Abu. Each one believed something different about cities whose locations no one could prove.

Start with the text. He opened his Bible to Genesis 10–19 as if it were a letter describing an event he'd missed and would want to know about.

The first time he read it, he shook his head.

The second time he read it, he closed his Bible and sat for a long while thinking.

The third time he read it, he studied the key words in it, again looking at the familiar passage as if for the first time.

He read in Hebrew of a great city of Sodom located on a "bread-disk" in the well-watered Jordan Valley. The original language spoke of a fertile breadbasket, a circular setting.

A place that was as lush as Egypt's ever-green Nile Valley, and as prolific and luxuriant as the very Garden of Eden.

He found himself pacing with anxiety. He prided himself on the accuracy of his tours and his research. For six seasons he had been a field supervisor at the Khirbet el-Maqatir excavation, possibly the site of biblical Ai, defeated by Joshua, and had made reasonably sure that before he put his endorsement behind that discovery, it matched up with where the Bible said it was.

But what he was reading now in Genesis, alone in his hotel room, was shocking to him. He felt dread, the dread of learning you've been wrong about something.

The Bible described a Sodom located in a place completely unlike the two windswept ruins near the southern shore of a salt-laden and sterile body of water that some archaeologists had been calling Sodom and its satellite-town, Gomorrah.

That Dr. C had been calling Sodom and Gomorrah.

What he read in Genesis went against what most archaeologists, Bible scholars, *and* mapmakers had insisted on for more than one hundred years.

What he read, if true, would shed light on one of the most enduring mysteries of all of ancient civilization.

He refused to believe—had all his life refused to believe—the easy-going Robert Pinkerstons who say that geography and other details don't matter because the Bible is only a collection of made-up stories written to promote a particular theology and boost national pride.

All his professional career, it was easy for him to dismiss the claims of crackpots and their fanciful explanations of sulfur balls and swirling geological marls. Now, not just because of the ignorance of people who make those claims, but because the location was wrong, all wrong.

He realized that if the Bible was indeed reliable in its geographical descriptions, it meant that even educated and well-read people like Beth Neal—and the archaeologists and experts they depended on for their information—were wrong.

It meant that the dearly held stories told by the very inhabitants of the land, passed on for generations and as sacred to them as scripture, were wrong.

It meant that his friend Eugene, who trusted him and studied his writings and came on his tour, was wrong—because Dr. C had been wrong.

He realized that, if what he read in the Bible, the same Bible he'd read all his life, could be verified in the reality of pottery and artifacts, in earth and excavation, it would turn the study of the Bible lands upside down.

It would shake up the bones of every archaeologist he knew and put him in the category of the crackpots if he said it and couldn't prove it.

It would cause skeptical people to think about and perhaps even read the Bible differently.

He knew this could cost him everything financially. It could cost him friends and professional associates.

Truth, he thought to himself, is the best friend of all.

By now the room had gone dark except for a desk lamp that shone on his Bible.

Dr. C drew a deep breath, read the passage one last time, and set aside his plans for his life.

TWO

Coming to Tall el-Hammam

THE WONDER OF TALL EL-HAMMAM, THE SITE OF THE MIGHTY ancient city of Sodom, isn't that it exists, for it has stood for thousands of years, hulking and dominant just eight miles from the Dead Sea in what is now known as the Hashemite Kingdom of Jordan.

The wonder is that it has escaped the notice of most Bible-focused archaeologists, all but virginally untouched for most of the one-hundred-plus years that modern archaeology has existed.

It is certainly not invisible, no Shangri-la perceived only by enlightened eyes. A traveler would observe that from its foothills it is actually one of many; yet first among peers, a giant among the mounds or "talls" along the western edge of the foothills of the Transjordan Highlands.

It has been hiding in plain sight of those who, for no good scientific reason, didn't just summarily cross it off a list of candidates for Sodom.

In fact, in the last century, practically no one had put it on the list in the first place.

As one travels up through the mountains and crags that huddle around Tall el-Hammam, it's at first indistinguishable, at least in hue, from the dun-colored Kafrayn Dam across the road and the sagging slopes of runoff-sliced hills all around. From that vantage point, everything from here to the east is beige and taupe and light brown and tan and off-white.

In contrast, the blocky fields of squat little banana trees blare green. They are watched over by their owners on nearby hills; and in the case of Sodom, six brothers' houses overlook the brilliant emerald of their cut-leaf trees, each one bearing the only crop of its lifetime: not-yet-yellowed fingers all pointing up like hands grasping for the sun.

Towering above the fields, Sodom looks as natural—and upon observation, as designed and processed—as a huge anthill that has erupted from the earth, once of the earth and now in it. As with an anthill, too, almost nothing grows on its higher slopes, perhaps in tribute to the fact that its desolation speaks of upheaval and transport and other times, of a hidden history revealed, of secrets and threats and dread.

Tall el-Hammam, upper tall, looking west, with the well-watered Kikkar of the Jordan spreading out from its base.

Once you are within its mighty walls, both hot and cool springs are now in the open, anchoring a spot of luxurious foliage, home to Sodom's abundant little green frogs.

Every rock on this mud mountain was hauled up there, from the small ones to the great boulders that formed foundations for immense walls. Some haven't seen light for four, five, six thousand years. Even the mud itself, decomposed bricks, came from somewhere else.

Along the approach to the site from the east, in the foothills of tortured sandstone, sits a knee-high, room-sized pile of pottery sherds from seven years of archaeological excavation. But these are the discards, the pieces of pottery that weren't important as "diagnostics."

Around the other side of the great mound you can bend downward and make out human bone fragments, protruding like compound fractures through the skin of a balk, one of the vertically cut sections of the excavation.

These aren't tombs. They were dwellings for the living. And the people whose remains lay blasted and scattered here were not gathered to their fathers with respect and ceremony. They died suddenly in their own private places and kitchens, as they ate and drank from the pottery vessels whose sherds now surround them.

Jordan, the Home of the Biblical Site of Sodom

A MAP OF THE HASHEMITE Kingdom of Jordan, the home of Sodom, reveals it to be a bedfellow to Israel, backing the spine of its entire western border up to the Jordan River, which gives it its name. On a map, its roads are knotted veins and arteries around its central city, Amman. Eventually the clot loosens and sparse highways meander west, or drip down to the tourist spots on the shore of the Dead Sea where dates grow with water ten times saltier than other plants can stand, and every other living thing drinks purified water or lives in soil repeatedly washed to leach out the minerals.

Then, on either side of those massive, life-numbing waters, are the places and sights that contrast with Sodom, that by the descriptive friction between them define Sodom. What the Dead Sea is, Sodom is not. What the desert is, Sodom is not. And yet they were part of both the backstory and the aftermath of what happened to Sodom, in the record of a kingdom left behind in the buildings and artifacts they used.

Every visitor should come to the Dead Sea at night the first time. Going down into the valley of deadness, every driver tap, tap, taps his brakes. A persimmon-colored moon looks like a hand cupped to the sky, asking for rain. Across the water, the lights of Israel flicker.

Water bottles cringe and collapse. Everything inclines toward and yields to the loss of altitude. In the distance, the hotels are outposts of green and fluorescence along the shore of the great silver lake.

In daylight there is more to see, but away from the water, everything is dusted in sand. The most famous ancient site in southern Jordan, indeed in all of Jordan, is Petra. Unfortunately the Bible omits notice of it and the name of its builders, the Nabateans. That rosy-pink city lay long hidden in a cleft of rock and forgotten for millennia, but now attracts everyone from movie producers to hundreds of thousands of tourists a year whose breath is taken away by its unexpected beauty. For many, Petra defines the ancient world of Jordan.

Other than those rose-colored facades and the few modern cities, everything in Jordan comes off three color palettes. There's the green-green of banana fields and dusky-green of the country's twelve million olive trees; there's earth in all its variations of one sand-shade to another; and there's the wild micropalette of human occupation, with houses painted colors from glaring white to Pepto-Bismol pink, with trucks sporting psychedelic murals on their cargo panels, with intricately patterned rugs slung over roofs and porch walls and secured against the searing wind's power by plastic lawn chairs whose legs span exactly the distance to act as giant clothespins.

Though many of the homes are luxurious inside, what a Westerner would regard as their yards are concessions of defeat to the enemies of grit and wind. Black plastic garbage bags and little white shopping bags balloon in the breezes and hang in thorny tree branches. And almost every home in the countryside looks like an insect bristling with multiple antennae of rebar from its roof.

Jordanians call the rebar a sign of hope: everyone builds a bottom story and then says, "I hope I get an inheritance, I hope my daughter marries a rich man, I hope my business deal goes through so I can build a second story on this house."

Traveling on one of the oldest highways in the world still in use, the King's Highway that runs from Aqaba to Damascus via Amman, is an adventure even on the paved main roads that follow its route in the twenty-first century. Somewhere between Petra and the Dead Sea is where Moses asked the Edomites if he could pass through with his horde of exiles, and the Edomites' refusal ostensibly cost the Israelites a great deal of distance and trouble (Numbers 20:14–21).

Or maybe not. Shortcuts in Jordan take exactly the same amount of time as the long way. Jordanian guides often concur when they can't get their tour bus microphone switches to work, and then remember to speak with the "on" button in the "down" position: "Everything is backwards in Jordan."

The small towns all look alike, with the ubiquitous Muslim versions of the neighborhood bar that serves thick black coffee. On nearly every corner are the aluminum cases outside shop doors that contain rotisseries of what Tall el-Hammam excavation crews call GSC—"greasy spinning chickens."

Anywhere near the highway is a dangerous place for pedestrians, who are fair game for any motorized vehicle, and people hurry across with wide eyes and robes streaming out behind them. A Mercedes-Benz bus just barely misses a truck with a hand-painted tailgate that reads "NI55AN" and careens from side to side in what is nervously referred to as "surfing Jordan."

The Muslim call to prayer wafts out over the sound of honking horns, shouting vendors, and the near-shouts of "normal" Jordanian discourse. Here the mosques and minarets range from the colorless and austere to some that have strings of blinking neon lights not unlike those on the coffee shops.

Yet there are areas with high percentages of Christian believers, too, such as Madaba, where one in five of its residents is a Christian. It even has a mosque named "Jesus the Son of Mary."

In Madaba is a rare, nonancient attraction: the St. George Greek Orthodox church, whose fifteen-hundred-year-old mosaic floor was discovered during a restoration in 1884. There in the tiles is the oldest map of the Holy Land in existence, even showing still-identifiable features of Jerusalem and other sites.

Most exciting of all for those who seek Sodom and Gomorrah in the details of that tiled depiction are two mosaic "cities" right where the Bible says they should be—in the Kikkar of the Jordan, though, unfortunately, the writing on the Madaba Map identifying them has been lost.

The sixth century CE Madaba Map showing the location of Zoar (3). In this orientation, left is north. Note that no cities are represented in the area south of the Dead Sea. Because this is primarily a map of famous biblical sites, the two city representations (1 and 2) northeast of the Dead Sea are, logically, Sodom and Gomorrah, although the captions are missing.

Compared with Israel, Jordan has many fewer biblical sites and the distances between them are great, but that's because the nation of Israel went west across the Jordan under Joshua's command and for the most part, from that time forward, lived on the other side of the river.

Mount Nebo, where God showed Moses a panoramic view of the Holy Land (Deuteronomy 34:1–3), is all caliche and rough rocks, accessible via a stomach-coiling ride up a sand-scrubbed and lurching road. Even more remote is the seeming road to nowhere that ends at the edge of the Arnon Gorge, where the ruins of Aroer (Deuteronomy 2:36) teeter on the edge of the remote bottom of the precipice.

The site of Dibon is remarkably unassuming given the spectacular nature of a basalt slab found there. On it, an inscription that was broken into pieces in modern times to increase its marketability was nonetheless reassembled and includes the name of King Omri, confirming the narrative of 2 Kings 3:4–5 in the Bible.

Then there is Makawer (Machaerus), the site where John the Baptist was incarcerated (Matthew 14:3) until his head was sent by courier to Herod Antipas's wife, Herodias, at a party going on in the palace upstairs. His captors had dragged this man, whose bones were made of insect shells and whose veins ran half honey, along these skidding stones and slammed him into one of the many caves that dot the slopes of the hill below the fortified compound. Though Roman walls still stand atop the prominence, these caves are history without the ruins, an enclosure of emptiness that says more than edifice.

These are desolate desert places where even broad-leafed cacti slump and shrivel. Goats quick-step from shade to shade, even in the winter. Water is so precious here that Jordan's pipelines bear bullet holes where bedouin, who camp in sprawling gray tents with plasma televisions inside, make their own impromptu utility connections to water their flocks.

To come back up the eastern side of the Great Salt Sea from its southern end along the cliffs is to be sandwiched between two deaths. On one side are the rugged sandstone cliffs whose very curves grasp and rasp the eyes. On the other side is a lifeless body of water. Travelers in this area have always gone north, because there is only more bleak death to the east.

Just as everyone goes up to Jerusalem, so everyone goes up when moving away from the lowest spot on earth, the Dead Sea. The Kikkar of the Jordan, the breadbasket of the Jordan Valley, lies just north of the Dead Sea. Here the Jordan River has overflowed its banks annually and the alluvial soils for millennia have washed down from the mountains, forming in antiquity some of the most fertile soil in the region (see Map 2).

This is the place that Moses described as "well-watered, like the garden of Yahweh, like Egypt" (Genesis 13:10).

The site of Sodom, whose modern name is Tall el-Hammam, is easy to find on any map (see Map 7). Look a few miles north and east from the Dead Sea on a highway map—or Google Earth—for the Kafrayn

Dam and see how the road in front of it is forced to make a sharp curve to go around a large object. That object is the ruin-mound of Sodom. It commands the landscape—and even meteorology. It can be snowing in Jerusalem and in Amman, and be 60 degrees Fahrenheit on Tall el-Hammam. The Kikkar has, in fact, its own microclimate.

Just over one kilometer north lies Tall Kafrayn, a smaller site. Tall el-Hammam is surrounded by many such "daughter" communities, and there is evidence of other smaller, ancient hamlets in the immediate vicinity. That's the first cluster. Continuing along the highway for about ten kilometers you arrive at Tall Nimrin, the second-largest site on the eastern Kikkar. Next on the route, one kilometer away, you come to two "twin" sites, Tall Mustah and Tall Bleibel, separated only by a wadi. That's the second cluster.

This is significant: two large ancient cities with associated satellite villages, two tight clusters separated by about six kilometers as the crow flies.

Not only that, Tall el-Hammam, the site of biblical Sodom, is surrounded on its eastern side by the largest sacred landscape, or sacrescape, in the region—covering several square kilometers and aggregately larger even than Stonehenge. Dotting that sprawling megalithic landscape are more than five hundred bench-like stone dolmens, what is left of fifteen hundred of them, each formed in antiquity by the deliberate placement of a large horizontal stone on top of three or more vertical ones. Tall el-Hammam researchers Dr. Steve McAllister and Dr. David Maltsberger have documented the precision of the astronomical alignments of these dolmens, which are arranged to designate equinoxes and solstices marking the southern and northern drifts of the sun as it hits the earth.

They aren't tombs, though many of them shelter the reburial of individual bones. In ancient times, perhaps at each equinox and solstice celebration—four times a year—families or clans of Sodom's pious inhabitants would select a token bone from the burial cave of their ancestors (where, like many in the ancient world, they put new corpses atop old

Dr. C with one of Tall el-Hammam's hundreds of still-standing dolmens. The Hammam Megalithic Field includes not only dolmens, but also menhirs (standing stones), stone alignments, henges, and stone circles, all signaling the cultic sacredness of the area. It is the largest such assemblage of megalithic structures in the Levant.

family bones so that when people died they were literally "gathered to their fathers") for use in a solemn ritual. Probably bearing torches and gathering within the sacrescape of dolmens and standing stones, they commemorated the passage of seasons with rites involving the bones and small vessels containing olive oil and grain. In fact, Tall el-Hammam excavators have uncovered as many as forty-five such ceremonial vessels in a single dolmen chamber, along with human bone fragments.

Unlike many other active archaeological sites, Tall el-Hammam isn't fenced, but it's certainly guarded. It's surrounded on three sides by banana fields and residences, and its frontage on the road that runs alongside has the buffer of a little complex of buildings: a small home and outbuildings owned by a frenetic, white-haired man named Abu-Ahmed; a white-washed mosque; and a unique graveled parking lot.

The parking lot was leveled and packed down by Trinity Southwest University's Tall el-Hammam Excavation Project, and during the digging seasons the excavation's equipment is housed—and protected—there and inside the mosque building itself. This may be the only mosque in the world with a Christian who has a key—and full access—to it.

Abu-Ahmed runs out its front door with greetings for visitors and embraces and kisses for old friends. There is a great deal of pantomiming and arm waving and laughing. Abu-Ahmed's English is brisk, confident, and sometimes incomprehensible.

The wily, wiry little man has installed a great swing on which two or three people can step up and stand, and he grabs a visitor and they swing back and forth. Another visitor he takes by the hand and leads to the back of his house; they return with the visitor's arms full of oranges and limes Abu-Ahmed has picked from his trees and given to him.

More than once, Abu-Ahmed put up a big tent and brought in a kind of upside-down chicken-and-rice dish—*maglooba,* Arabic for "upside-down"—and other traditional foods to feed the entire excavation crew. His heart is great; his pride in the discoveries taking place literally in his backyard is boundless.

The hospitality, though, does not extend to other foreign visitors who come unannounced. One afternoon as the excavators were temporarily away from the site, they got a call that Abu-Ahmed had intercepted a group of Chinese tourists who were trying to climb up to the top of the mound. Abu-Ahmed had the terrified group cornered and was throwing small rocks at their feet, just as his ancestors have done for millennia to correct the course of wayward sheep.

The ascent on foot up Tall el-Hammam has very little of the romantic or dramatic until the steepness begins to reveal what must have been the great mound's utter inaccessibility in ancient times. Pitiful, desperate tumbleweed-like plants cling to its inclines, and dislodged stones roll with increasing velocity down its slopes.

Thousands of years after the event that defined it, Sodom still carries the sense of a killing field. Even on its surface areas that have covered the great destruction, it's a pockmarked and ravaged site. Though the excavations have "opened" less than 1 percent of the tall, more than 30 percent of it has Bronze Age and Iron Age ruins exposed at the surface.

Tall el-Hammam has an upper and a lower city; the upper is one hundred feet higher and less than half the size of the lower, larger part of the site. Enormous trenches raised by war machines during the Six-Day War with Israel rut the surfaces of the upper tall. Sometimes the best the excavators can do is salvage work after the twentieth century's ravages.

Other holes spring up overnight: a team of "night diggers" can sink a twenty-foot shaft between dusk and dawn, looking for the gold that many Jordanians believe was hidden in this area after the Ottomans left. But invariably all they find is mudbrick and more mudbrick. Often, tired excavators wonder if they might save a lot of time by putting a sign in Arabic, "Possible gold here." They are sure they'd come back in the morning to exploratory holes or "soundings" ready-made.

In the course of seven seasons, project surveyors have marked off more than thirteen thousand six-meter-by-six-meter (twenty-foot by twenty-foot) excavation squares, but only about eighty of those squares have been opened, and most are still in progress. It's hardly a raw, virgin tall after seven seasons of excavation.

And the tall has aged many who've sought her secrets, because it isn't just about excavating squares or cataloging finds. The business of excavation in a foreign country requires ongoing work away from the dirt: raising the money, finessing the politics, analyzing the data, publishing the reports, engaging the critics, and attracting the volunteers to get the job done year after year.

But the finds have been rich: though no precious metals have yet come out of the excavations, pottery sherds representing all or part of more than forty thousand separate vessels have been brought out of the soil. The "diagnostic" sherds (primarily datable rims, handles, bases, and decorated body sherds) have been registered, and the rest go to the discard pile, or "pottery dump," back at the site. One square yielded an altar with five chalices and a broken figurine, all Iron Age 2, from the time of the Israelite and Judahite kings. Another produced a highly detailed steatite seal of Hyksos design from the second half of the Middle Bronze Age. All are, of course, the property of the Hashemite Kingdom of Jordan. For purposes of study and publishing, certain artifacts may be "loaned" to the archaeologists who excavate them, clean them, categorize them, and record every detail of their discovery, appearance, and context.

Danette Collins doing drawings and paperwork in Square UC.28J, Season Three.

Anything can be underfoot at Tall el-Hammam. One moment you can be walking on the massive stones from an Iron Age gate and its cobblestone plaza. A few steps farther and there is the clink of pottery from the time of Abraham.

A visitor nearly stumbles over some barbed wire left from twentieth-century military activity. "That's Iron Age, too," someone says. The visitor bends down to look but catches herself and begins to laugh.

Very little is left alive on Sodom. Pale walking-stick insects blend into the sand behind them. An odd, fleshy green fruit hangs from wistful tree branches. Large and inviting, this "Sodom apple" the size of a cantaloupe is as empty as a dried gourd.

"Watch your step," a veteran of the digs announces. "Keep an eye out for the 'five-step' Palestinian viper. Five steps after it bites you, you're dead," he says. Someone asks if any of the excavators have ever been bitten, and he tells the story of a digger who sat on one and lived to tell the story. Then he tells the story of the Jordanian worker who was recently hospitalized from snakebite. Everyone looks down as he walks.

Tall el-Hammam means "hill of the hot baths." For many years in the late twentieth century, though, few were brave enough to document it, because part of the site was reportedly overspread with land mines. Not until 2004 did members of the Tall el-Hammam excavation team walk over the entire tall, including the area of vegetation around the springs. There were no warning signs or fences, so they concluded that since 1996 the area had been swept clear of mines by the Jordanian military (a fact confirmed by the Department of Antiquities)—and double-checked by the many local herds of sheep and goats whose owners may have wondered about the ancient curse of Sodom.

On the tall, the flies are annoying and everywhere. They don't usually bite, though. They're looking for something recently alive to eat.

On the other hand the visitors, like blowflies, are looking for signs of the dead. And they're everywhere. More than four hundred "saddle"-type grindstones have been found scattered across the tall's surface, showing that multitudes of people grew and ground grains here. Digging in, the excavations reveal a "red"-plastered palace with secrets to divulge. Elsewhere there's a large Roman bath, forty meters on a side, which has led to conjecture about whether in New Testament times Tall el-Hammam was one of Herod Antipas's vacation palaces. One burial spot uncovered a headless corpse that has caused more questions. There are mysteries everywhere.

It's the architecture that makes the tall remarkable. Made of stone, the Iron Age building foundations from the days of Solomon and later are interesting, but they say little about the destruction that kept the bustling city in the middle of a fertile valley completely abandoned for seven hundred years before that time.

At the time of Abraham, the Middle Bronze Age, Sodom was about one-half monumental or administrative buildings, and about one-half residences, all made of mudbrick on stone foundations. If you want to know what the homes and buildings look like, just look at pictures of Taos Pueblo in northern New Mexico. That's Middle Bronze Age–style architecture, still in use today.

Huge size? Ten of the City of David would have fit inside Sodom's city walls, with room to spare. Stability? For more than twenty-five centuries this great, two-tiered city was the impregnable Rock of Gibraltar to this valley—the center of a powerful city-state.

One sign of its solidity is that, unlike many other excavated sites in the Near East that reveal "layer cake" strata of new buildings and cultures, this site has few such layers up through the time of Abraham. For example, dwellings weren't replaced—they evolved. The same houses, the same buildings, were continuously inhabited for hundreds of years. When entirely new structures were built, previous ones were purposefully "condemned" and covered with "engineered fill." But in general, you lived in the house your great-great-great grandfather lived in. If walls weakened and collapsed, you rebuilt the ancestral home just as it had been before, on the same footprint. The mudbricks might be brown or yellow or tan, depending on the source of the mud. But the floor plan rarely changed. This was stability. No wonder the city seemed so secure, so safe.

There must have been a sense of Sodom's invincibility in the Middle Bronze Age, when people like Abraham and Lot knew this city. Its towering height gave it a visual vantage point. There is no indication that it was ever destroyed by a military enemy. Somewhere between 150 and 200 *million* mudbricks formed a rampart around it that made its great height virtually unscalable. With a 35-degree incline and covered over with a smooth layer of dried clay, no human being or beast could climb up it without great, hunched-over, vulnerable struggle.

This rampart is quintessential Middle Bronze Age in the same way a '57 Chevy is an icon of its time: distinctive, nothing like it before or since.

But on Sodom there are areas that tell a remarkable story. There are places on the mound where no one ever rebuilt after a catastrophic event destroyed it. Not in the Iron Age, not later, not ever.

The soil is powdery, nasty with burnt things in it. Sometimes you can smell ash still, thousands of years later.

Some of the dirt is gray with crushed cinders and ash. If rain has fallen on it, it becomes crusty and impermeable, plaster-like.

There are places where mudbricks didn't just fall down, they turned red or became pottery-like from heat. Even some of the underlying foun-

Danette and Dr. C standing atop the Middle Bronze Age defensive rampart that surrounds the upper city. It is constructed of tens of millions of mudbricks.

dation stones show evidence of severe burning. Across the site are pieces of pottery that look like dime-a-dozen Bronze Age vessels on one side, but when turned over look like glass or green lava bubbled up from the molecules of clay.

There are skeletal remains that lie as they fell, wrenched and contorted. There's human bone-scatter all through the final-day ash: human beings who blew apart before they fell.

The view from the summit of Tall el-Hammam is breathtaking. In the distance is the Jordan River channel, and closer is the luxuriant green of the fields between its banks and the great mound. It was fields and homes and nomad tents all the way to the river in Abraham's day.

And what you can see from here: At the 12:00 position, there's Tall Jericho. There right at 11:00 is Jerusalem. At 10:00 there's Bethlehem. At 9:00 there's Hebron. And at 1:30 are Bethel and Ai, where Abram and Lot looked toward Sodom. You can look back, eyes sweeping from the Dead Sea to all these important sites, from this height.

The landscape demands a question: can you read the Bible without geography, without tying its words to the earth on which its events occur? Certainly if it is the Word of God, it can't be dependent on its every reader being an eyewitness or a visitor to the Holy Land.

While some may assert that the Bible is autonomous, timeless, and above even the cultures in which it occurred, if its events happened, they happened somewhere.

The ground itself gives up its secrets.

And here, at Sodom, the rocks cry out a catastrophe.

THREE

The Chronicles of the Kikkar

Some of the volunteers helping at Tall el-Hammam during one season are a team of Jordanian teenagers who began their few days at the site with outright hostility. Before they began excavating, one of them (apparently spokesman for all) asked, "Why are you coming to our country to find all our gold and take it back to America with you?"

Only after a week of excavating are they seemingly satisfied that there's more gold in the surrounding villages than there is in the ground at

A group of Season Six volunteers and staff. During an eight-week excavation season (Jan./Feb.) at Tall el-Hammam, it's common to have volunteers from four to five continents of the world.

Sodom. They learn that the real "gold" is the enlightenment of unearthing the past—their true national treasure.

Heading the excavation, of course, are professional archaeologists—American, Jordanian, and international. But the hands of an archaeological dig are the support staff and volunteers: teenagers and families and couples and even men and women "of a certain age"—and of a certain necessary agility.

It's hard, dusty work, kneeling in increasingly deep square trenches, going backward into the layers of time. Excavators sweep away pebbles and dirt from every piece of brick, bone, pottery, and metal that begins to surface. But that's just the beginning for any discovery—whether it's just a random piece of a broken pot, an exciting detail such as a previously unseen bull motif on a potsherd, or a rare piece of bronze. Each significant find is photographed as its surroundings are meticulously brushed aside and carried topside in buckets. Then workers wash and label and analyze and catalog each meaningful object.

Lunch is a welcome break from the physical labor. Today there's reddish sauce and goat meat heaped on a huge platter with the ever-present olives and hummus and foot-high stacks of the staple of Jordanian life: thin, steering-wheel-sized breads still steaming from the griddle.

In cultures around the world, from the beginning of civilization, disks of bread are the mainstay of diets. A Mediterranean would call it a pita, a Mexican a tortilla, an Indian, naan. Here in Jordan, people eat what their ancestors for thousands of years have patted out and rolled out and baked and grilled—what was called a *kikkar* in ancient times.

In Hebrew, *kikkar* has many meanings. It can mean a circular, flat bread, or a disklike piece of metal such as a coin or metal ring, or a spreading, circular area of land.

Perhaps the workers who stop for lunch at Tall el-Hammam, people who tear the stretchy, satisfying bread with their teeth, don't see the irony of the fact that they're eating kikkars in the middle of, well, a geographical kikkar—what the Hebrew of the Bible in Genesis calls "the Kikkar of the Jordan" (see Maps 7 and 8).

The Great Rift through which the Jordan River runs is often so precipitously deep that there are few places where passage across it was safe or easy in ancient times. But coming from the Transjordan plateau, one such ancient road was a major trade route, and ran at the base of Tall el-Hammam, just across from Jericho, through the Kikkar.

In humankind's early days after the worldwide catastrophe recorded in ancient Flood narratives, Noah's descendants became families that banded together to form clans, and clans to form tribes. Here in the rift valley as elsewhere, people developed tools for tasks and strategies for survival. Perhaps after someone discovered that the clay daubed inside a basket became a rock-hard container when the straw burned away, people made clay into indispensable cooking pots and dishes and cups and storage jars and transport vessels.

People discovered that you could keep ciphers on this soft clay and it would dry, leaving a permanent record. Their descendants in Sumer began to write on clay tablets with symbol-shapes that over time evolved into cuneiform script, made with impressed wedge-marks that people all over the Near East embraced and used.

Clay's versatility burgeoned with humanity's imagination. People used it in religious ceremonies, lit their homes with oil in clay lamps, and some even buried their dead in pottery.

Many an ancient clay container still bears the fingerprints of its creator. Most important of all to archaeologists, Near Eastern pottery styles became the hatch marks on humanity's timeline, with distinctive designs and shapes and methods of formation for every age in which human hands created it (see Archaeological Ages chart).

Chalcolithic in the Kikkar

IN THE ERA CALLED THE Chalcolithic ("copper-stone") Period, increasing refinements in pottery that had distinctive features, such as pierced lug handles and ropelike decorations, paralleled a new awareness of community. Settlements sprang up in the round widening of the Great Rift's floor—in the Kikkar, where the Jordan Valley looks like a python that swallowed a pig.

In this land of only two short rainy seasons, people clustered around perennial springs. Unlike most surrounding small communities, though, ancient Sodom had several springs, hot and cold, and they were year-round sources of precious water if the usually dependable mountain run-offs failed to fill the rivers wrapping the site on the north and south. And, of course, the inhabitants had the reliable Jordan and its annual spring in-undations, from which they easily channeled water to their agricultural fields by digging shallow, seasonal irrigation canals.

Families and tribes looked for such stability, and in the disk area on the edge of which ancient Sodom towered, there was rich alluvial soil and the water to cultivate it. The nomadic herding and hunting groups, an-cient bedouin types such as even today live in this area, moved their tents from site to site seeking pasture. But at the same time others—Chalco-lithic farmers—settled down to harvest crops: emmer wheat and barley to grind for bread, olives that grew up in the hill country to eat and press for their oil, sugar-grained dates and chewy ziziphus fruits, tart pomegran-ates, pungent garlic and onions, nourishing lentils, and the richness of all kinds of nuts. They cooked, ate, and stored all of these in pottery made from local clays. And just across the Dead Sea, their neighbors were growing another crop, flax, and weaving linen in an emerging textile in-dustry.

In many ways, the area around ancient Sodom was like an African savanna, and human beings risked their lives daily to share this area with the wild animals that had lived there eons before humans inhabited the area. Migrating elephants trampled through the thick foliage. Lions and leopards and cheetahs terrorized the countryside's other beasts and people alike. On the banks of the Jordan, within sight of Sodom, rhi-noceroses and hippopotami and slithering crocodiles luxuriated in the rich mud of the river. Bears roamed the hills, and oryx and gazelle and nimble-footed deer and ibexes with huge horns roamed through the land.

Life was dangerous, but food was plentiful on the fertile Kikkar.

But something happened across the greater Levant that left it to the winds and animals and nomads once again, some precipitous and mysterious event long ago. Remarkably, archaeologists have found no evidence of widespread warfare or destruction. Yet the unfortified broad-house settlements of the region were abandoned—and what was left behind shows that people seemingly just walked away from their industries and houses and farms, perhaps in confusion and fear, never to return to them. This situation continued for several hundred years, through Early Bronze I.

What happened?

Archaeologists don't really know. Climate change is always a viable culprit. But they do know that when settlements and civilizations emerged again in the Levant, around 3000 BCE, they weren't just pastoral communities as before. Now powerful people began to build impressive walled cities atop strategic sites, with smaller satellites of settlements huddling all around them. Whatever had happened in that calamitous event engendered a new mind-set: "us against them."

Although this sudden cultural change has remained a mystery to many scholars, the Bible in the book of Genesis preserves a remarkable narrative that could be connected to this dramatic transition. It's the account of the Tower of Babel, specifically the confusion of languages. In fact, maybe this biblical description is just a thumbnail of a much larger concert of phenomena that succeeded in dispersing ancient people not only all over the Near East, but over the face of the globe.

But the transition from the Chalcolithic Period to the Bronze Age was much less traumatic on the Kikkar of the Jordan, and for one primary reason: abundant water resources. And the same basic population seemingly just stayed put in their breadbasket land.

Bronze Age in the Kikkar

SO A NEW ERA BEGAN, one that archaeologists call the Bronze Age. In the Early Bronze Age (specifically EB2 and EB3, 3000 to 2350 BCE), people learned to smelt copper with tin to form a harder, more versatile substance (that much later found widespread use for tools and weapons and jewelry). Larger settlements such as the kingdom centers described in Genesis 10 sprang up, places whose names would become legendary. Among them were Babylon, Akkad, and Nineveh; and down south in the Kikkar of the Jordan, Sodom and Gomorrah.

The most powerful places were the defensible ones, especially those with long vistas and steep slopes, which began to protect themselves from both distant neighbors and avarice-eyed travelers by building fortifications of mudbrick walls. In exchange for the crops and domesticated animals that flourished in the fields outside, the cities offered formal protection to the smaller communities and rural dwellers. The feudal system had begun.

With its back to the hills and its face to the Kikkar, Sodom became a constant, a sun around which the lives of surrounding towns and villages revolved, for its 360-degree views were unmatched, its fortifications impenetrable, and its water sources faithful. From Genesis 10 through hundreds of years that passed until the events of Genesis 19, this great city anchored the famous "Cities of the Plain" and the patriarchal narrative.

And though we don't yet have writings from this metropolis, we know from thousands of clay cuneiform tablets found in a similar city, Ebla in northern Syria, all about the detailed workings of an Early Bronze Age "merchant empire" such as Sodom certainly was.

Soon the Levant, the biblical land of Canaan, had products that far-away countries such as King Sargon's empire of Akkad and the pyramid builders of Egypt prized: the oil from its olive trees and the wine from its vineyards. International trade began. And Sodom sat at the intersection of international trade routes.

But unlike Sodom, its precursor in the Kikkar wasn't so stable. The fate of Tuleilat Ghassul made it the unwitting "mother" of Sodom itself. Something happened there, maybe an earthquake toward the end of the Chalcolithic Period, that caused it to lose its on-site water supply. So all its inhabitants, as many as twenty-five thousand people, moved up the road to settle the area of Tall el-Hammam—what eventually became the city of Sodom.

In and around the great city-state of the eastern Kikkar, people learned to domesticate camels and other animals to help them with travel and farming. Money and goods flowed into Sodom and out from it to far-away places. Evidence of this international trade includes the Egyptian-style scarabs and fragments of fine alabaster vessels found in the soils of Tall el-Hammam all through its Bronze Age strata.

In fact, Tall el-Hammam is a model of how large Levantine cities were built and operated. Because of its unparalleled history of long, consistent habitation (probably even by the same ethnic group from Chalcolithic times through the Middle Bronze Age, as well), we can look at Sodom and say, "This is how they did cities."

But most of those cities except Sodom and her satellites depended upon the climate that made the crops grow, fueling all the other economies. When the climate changed leading up to 2350 BCE, with a drastic drop in rainfall that destroyed the interconnected market systems and the cultures of the great fortified cities, only those like Sodom with its ever-flowing springs and rivers survived—and thrived. This climatological disaster marked the end of the Early Bronze Age, when almost everyone in the southern Levant except those in the Sodom-constellation economy moved back into the country and lived as nomads or semi-nomads, as many of their ancestors did. And so was life in the Levant from 2350 BCE until about 2000 BCE, a time period known as the Intermediate Bronze Age.

For the next three and a half centuries after 2350 BCE, Sodom was the invariant, the tether-pole of the tents of the people of the southern Levant. Drought or flood, invasion or peace, it commanded the territory and the economy it oversaw.

When in about 2000 BCE the rains returned, the surrounding population exploded, and increasingly sophisticated societies all over the region began monumental building projects whose complexity and sheer massive size made the considerable fortifications of the Early Bronze Age look almost childish by comparison. Regional cultures lubricated by regular rains made quantum leaps in two game-changing technologies: the widespread smelting of bronze for all kinds of tools, weapons, and other devices; and the development of finely wrought and varied types of ceramics made possible by a new invention, the fast potter's wheel. The Middle Bronze Age had dawned.

The long, continuous occupation of Tall el-Hammam, though, brings its own problems for those trying to date soil layers using pottery. Ancient potters didn't just stop making the old kinds of forms when a new archaeological period dawned. Nobody said, "Oh, honey, come look out the window . . . I think the Middle Bronze Age started today!"

Changes in the pottery and in the whole culture took place very slowly, almost imperceptibly, most of the time. And when the same basic culture endures on a site like Tall el-Hammam through several millennia, its people develop a natural resistance to outside influences, a cultural pride in how things were always done. Even though the residents of Tall el-Hammam embraced most of the new pottery forms, they continued to use older, tried-and-true techniques for vessels like cooking pots and vats.

The fast potter's wheel allowed artisans to fashion more refined rims, bases, and vessel bodies, and the more innovative potters pushed the new technology to the limits. Some makers of "specialty" vessels seemed to compete to see who could make the thinnest, most fragile vessels. But sometimes otherwise-magnificent vessels like chalices had slumping or wobbling rims because the thin, wet clay couldn't support its own weight. Most other vessels—like jars, jugs, bowls, plates, cups—took on more sophisticated designs made possible only by the high-speed revolutions of clay between the fingers of the potters of the time of Abraham.

In every era, travelers coming up from the Dead Sea with hair crusted by their own sweat and the wind-borne saltwater spray, or those with sand-scoured faces coming from the desert heights of the east, or those who could see the alluring green of the valley from clear across the Rift to the west—everyone must have coveted Sodom.

Its sense of invincibility seems legitimate. Tall el-Hammam's massive city walls—twelve feet thick and higher than a three-story building—sat atop a huge mudbrick rampart sloping outward 100 to 150 feet at an angle of 35 degrees. It was a sight to behold, and there wasn't anything to rival it between Syria and Egypt.

It seemed that nobody could conquer it.

Why? Imagine the plight of an army that would think to try to lay siege to Sodom. In the springtime, when troops were available to go to war, temperatures regularly reached 100 degrees Fahrenheit. In the summer, it was routinely 120 to 130 degrees, sometimes as high as 140 degrees. Soldiers from higher climes may have died of heatstroke in the daytime heat. After a week of siege, an army would just disappear, man by man, in the first moonless night.

Meanwhile, up on Sodom, behind their thick, cooling, mudbrick walls, they slept peaceful and secure.

To the north, Babylon transitioned from a city-state into an empire under the leadership of the iconic law codifier, Hammurabi. In the land now known as Canaan, its inhabitants created a revolution in every aspect of material culture: settlement patterns, urbanism, architecture, pottery, metallurgy, and burial customs.

Many Middle Bronze Age sites had city walls heavily fortified by exterior earthen ramparts of appreciable size, similar to Sodom's, with defensive, towerlike gate systems. Inside their walls, such cities had administrative centers, palaces, temples, and other types of monumental public architecture. Their dead were buried in deliberately crafted family tombs outside the city, and occasionally even underneath house or courtyard floors—primarily infant burials.

This was a sophisticated society with the most advanced technologies of the area and for its time.

The History of Sodom Reflected in Acts 7

IF ANYONE DOUBTS THE INFLUENCE that the Kikkar area had throughout the entire history represented by the Hebrew Scriptures and the New Testament, consider the central role it played in the way biblical characters thought about their ancestors. When the first-century Christian leader Stephen wanted to remind his fellow Jews of some of their history's most important people and the events defining that history, he chose those specifics that had an essential tie with the Kikkar: Abraham, Joseph, the Israelites' sin with the Canaanites, Moses, Joshua, David, and Solomon. Each of these had a connection with the area that had once cradled Sodom.

Stephen began with the account of Abraham: "The God of glory appeared to our father Abraham while he was still in Mesopotamia, before he lived in Harran. 'Leave your country and your people,' God said, 'and go to the land I will show you.' So he left the land of the Chaldeans and settled in Harran. After the death of his father, God sent him to this land where you are now living" (Acts 7:2–4).

It was into a thriving and self-aware culture that Terah, a man from a long line of idol worshipers, brought his son and his wife and a grandson from a place called Ur of the Chaldeans, a place probably somewhere in what was then southern Babylonia. The rationale of his trek formed a pattern that would be repeated for thousands of years: a mysterious God calls people to set out on circuitous journeys for which he and he alone will reveal—piecemeal and daily—an itinerary that makes no sense at all to the travelers.

Along the way, Terah died in Harran (Genesis 11:32), a place where the beehive-shaped design of mudbrick houses has existed for thousands of years, perhaps even when the Urish family camped there. Probably through the herding skills he later demonstrated, Terah's son Abram acquired both wealth and living beings, human and animal, there in Harran.

At Terah's burial the group walked away from everything that tied them to their old homes in Babylon. With a new God's promises of greatness echoing in his ears, Abram and his group must have walked with dignity in sight of the arched mudbrick gateway of Tel Dan, heads held high. They were on their way to riches. Everyone would know and fear them. They'd have the run of the land. They were starting a dynasty. God said so: "I will make you into a great nation, and I will bless you; I will make your name great, and you will be a blessing" (Genesis 12:2).

Abram's ever-mobile and multiethnic entourage expanded until he had aggregated remarkable amounts of silver and gold, hundreds of servants, immense grazing flocks, and his own small guerrilla army. But even his affluence didn't protect him from the sorrowful infertility of his aging wife, Sarai, nor from the climatological swings that cyclically affected the Levant. Once he made a detour out of the land of Canaan to go to Egypt, where the routinely flooding Nile ensured regular crops (Genesis 12:10–20). The only other place in his "promised land" that had such dependable water sources was the Kikkar of the Jordan, and though he had undoubtedly heard of the famous ever-green Sodom, he hadn't yet visited it in his travels.

Upon the group's return from Egypt when the rains came back to the Levant, Abram and his wealthy nephew Lot discovered that, as expansive as the grazing fields were, they weren't large enough for both of them at the same time. Their herdsmen continually fought with each other over territory and wells. And looking on for signs of weakness and vulnerability were the Canaanites and Perizzites who'd already staked claims in the land, living mainly in cities and towns. If Abram and his nephew couldn't come to an understanding, everything they'd worked for and accumulated stood at risk.

The two men reached a gentleman's agreement that changed their lives forever. In the vicinity of Bethel and Ai, looking out over the panorama of broad, green valley, Abram gave his nephew a choice.

So Abram said to Lot, "Let's not have any quarreling between you and me, or between your herders and mine, for we are close relatives. Is not the whole land before you? Let's part company. If you go to the left, I'll go to the right; if you go to the right, I'll go to the left."

Lot looked around and saw that the whole plain of the Jordan toward Zoar was well watered, like the garden of the LORD, like the land of Egypt. (This was before the LORD destroyed Sodom and Gomorrah.) So Lot chose for himself the whole plain of the Jordan and set out toward the east. The two men parted company: Abram lived in the land of Canaan, while Lot lived among the cities of the plain and pitched his tents near Sodom. (Genesis 13:8–12)

Many people believe that Lot, seeing the lush Kikkar, whose river annually overflowed like the Nile in Egypt, chose what was most attractive, taking advantage of his old uncle's generosity.

But Lot knew that El Elyon—*Yahweh* by name—had already given to Abram Canaan—the whole land west of the Great Rift—so the deal was for temporary grazing rights for Lot and his descendants. And, since at that time Abram had no heirs, Lot could have believed he stood to inherit it all eventually. From this point of view, Lot was conceding to the two men's shared understanding of Abram's divinely issued title to all the land. He had the right to give it to anyone he wished.

But what the biblical record doesn't reveal at this point is the deciding factor in Lot's choice, a reason we'll explore in detail, one that becomes evident later on: Abram had a contract with a neighboring king, the king of Salem, and Lot's choice of land away from that area respected Abram's contract.

Perhaps Lot and his herdsmen walked away from this deal rubbing their hands together in anticipation. But Yahweh reconfirmed to Abram all the previous promises.

The LORD said to Abram after Lot had parted from him, "Look around from where you are, to the north and south, to the east and west. All the land that you see I will give to you and your offspring forever. I will make your offspring like the dust of the earth, so that if anyone could count the dust, then your offspring could be counted. Go, walk through the length and breadth of the land, for I am giving it to you." (Genesis 13:14–17)

And walk Abram did. And walk, and walk, and walk—away from Sodom, away forever, perhaps he thought, from his nephew.

But Lot and his herdsmen had walked into a hotbed of local unrest and international hostilities, and subsequent events that would make the name Sodom synonymous with holocaustal destruction forever. That violent and disturbing epoch of history we will deal with in a coming chapter.

The Forgotten History of Sodom

THE PRESENCE AND INFLUENCE OF Abram and Lot and their families in the Kikkar irrevocably changed its politics, changed its history, and even changed the land—the very dirt—itself.

When Abraham's family left Sodom for the last time, a calamity wiped out human habitation there for centuries. Life went on around the dead city, but not within its crumbled walls.

For seven hundred years afterward, the once-mighty city of Sodom and its satellite towns and villages towered like charred funeral pyres, eerie warnings to everyone who looked upon them.

Although armies, caravans, and other travelers coursed the major intersecting highways crossing the Kikkar of the Jordan, nobody built there for hundreds of years. They saw a landscape dotted with impressive ruins, but for centuries no one dared reassemble any of those stones into a dwelling, much less a city. The rivers and springs of the Kikkar continued their inevitable flow. Yet some kind of fear, some terrible memory framed in local lore, exceeded even the allure of abundant water.

History marched on around the quiet desolation of the ruined Kikkar.

Hiding in the mountains, Lot's desperate daughters had borne him sons who became the ancestors of the Ammonites and the Moabites who would occupy the Transjordan Highlands, east of the Great Rift, for all time (Genesis 19:30–38). From that point on in human history, never again would Lot's descendants and Abram's see eye to eye on anything.

To the west, across the northern tip of where the Jordan empties into the Dead Sea, Abram, renamed Abraham or "father of many" to reflect his future, settled into domesticity and dynasty building. God gave not only this durable old man but also his long-infertile wife, Sarai (whom God renamed Sarah), a new child, Isaac. But Abraham had learned well the lesson of Sodom: he needed to keep his son and grandchildren from the idolatrous taint that intermarriage with the inhabitants of Canaan would bring, and so he sent a trusted servant many days' journey north to his old haunt at Harran to find a wife for Isaac from among some of his own people (Genesis 24).

The son of promise, Isaac produced two heirs. Esau was a hunter. Jacob was a herdsman who pursued the next green pasture and the next still waters until one night he found himself in a wrestling match with Yahweh, miles upstream from Sodom at the Jabbok River (Genesis 32:22–32).

Meanwhile, when the winter rains beat down on the thirsty, abandoned mount of Sodom, they combined with the ashes to form a crust that seemed to freeze its destruction in time. Still no one dared to build on it. (In fact, to this day, when the salt-laden, decomposed mudbrick-and-ash soils of Sodom dry out after a soaking rain, the crusty surface still crunches loudly like frozen snow as one walks upon it. It is the concrete of death.)

Jacob and his wives were a fertile crew, producing thirteen children, and the bulk of the book of Genesis focuses on their story. Ten of the sons became so jealous of the eleventh son, Joseph, that they sold this dreamy-eyed boy to traders who took him to Egypt. Unbeknownst to Jacob and the rest of the family, who had given Joseph up for dead, the young man rose from slavery and imprisonment to become Pharaoh's right-hand man. With prophetic shrewdness, Joseph acted on his divinely inspired interpretations of the king's dreams of coming economic hardship. He set up storage of excess crops during seven years of abundance, and when they were followed by seven years of unprecedented Nile drought, he—as well as Egypt—was ready (Genesis 41).

Cyclical droughts were common throughout the Near East, but this particular one was disastrous for the land of Canaan. With dwindling food supplies, old Jacob sent his remaining sons on a long journey, some 250 miles away to Egypt, to get food. A surprise family reunion ensued, and at the invitation of Pharaoh and his "once-dead" son, Jacob and his party of seventy-plus all moved to the abundance and hospitality of Egypt.

But even in the midst of a deadly drought devastating Canaan, no one there even considered going a relatively few miles away to the Land of the Kikkar, to Sodom, to get its water or to irrigate crops around it. With its seared summit visible to anyone viewing the Kikkar from the flanking Cisjordan and Transjordan heights, Sodom was a horror to all, a cursed place, a site of only death and mourning.

Even in Egypt, people had heard of the cataclysm of Sodom. In fact, the pharaohs of the dynasty that Joseph served were themselves Hyksos—Canaanites (Semitic Asiatics) forced to migrate to Egypt by the same climatological downturn that later caused famines during the times of Abraham, Isaac, and Jacob. These transplanted Asiatics who now ruled Egypt knew the tragedy that had befallen the once-great city in their ancestral homeland—Sodom. None of its palaces, temples, or residences remained intact. But the thousands of megalithic monuments all around it—table-like dolmens, rings of standing stones, menhir alignments, and ceremonial stone circles that surrounded it for miles—still stood as sentinels over its sorrow.

Sodom's encircling megalithic sacred landscape, or sacrescape, was unparalleled in the region between Mesopotamia and Egypt (the Levant). But when the Hyksos-controlled Land of the Kikkar met its fiery doom, although the human voices of its cities and towns were forever silenced, its giant, stacked, and standing stones of cultic ritual still resonated with ancient song in remembrance of the dead.

And so it was when Jacob died in Egypt, his son Joseph, who had not seen his homeland since his boyhood, could not contain his grief. As recorded in Genesis 50, he asked Pharaoh to help him keep his promise to bury his father Jacob in the tomb the old man had prepared for himself in Canaan before he went to Egypt.

Joseph must have conferred with his Egyptian counselors, who would have told him that there was only one place in that part of the world that could properly commemorate his father's death, only one site that could symbolize the immensity of his loss. And so the entire entourage that included all of Pharaoh's high officials and dignitaries of Hyksos Egypt, along with all of Jacob's descendants and extended family, took a circuitous route to unimaginably sacred ground.

The journey to Jacob's final resting place, the patriarchal tomb at Machpelah near Hebron, was a fairly direct route from Goshen in the eastern Nile Delta. Leaving Egypt on the coastal "Way of the Philistines," as it would later be called, the party could have gone right at Gaza, then eastward up the Beth Guvrin Valley road past Lachish, mounting up to the central highlands of Canaan and Hebron. This was a well-traveled and relatively easy route.

But that isn't at all what Joseph and his Egyptian entourage had in mind. The precinct of Mamre near Hebron may have been their final destination, but first they made a deliberate and challenging detour to arrive at an ancestral place of mourning. This circuitous route after leaving Egypt took them at least two and a half times the distance that the direct route would have taken, toward a place that Lower Egypt's Hyksos holy men knew well.

Joseph's group of mourners traveled eastward past the south end of the Dead Sea on a difficult route connecting with the ancient King's Highway, then northward to Nebo overlooking the Kikkar of the Jordan (the same route taken later by Moses and the Israelites). From the Nebo (Pisgah) junction, they followed a winding road that dropped precipitously onto the Kikkar northeast of the Dead Sea to another junction at the base of what remained of Sodom's southern defenses, to the foothills of the cursed city.

This landscape had once echoed with the sounds of life, of commerce, of caravans, of vendors, of farmers and craftsmen, of laughing children, of harsh voices bartering. When the city flourished, treasured seasonal rituals celebrating solstices and equinoxes and ceremonies honoring the dead sounded rhythms of cultic song and dance to its stones of remembrance scattered throughout the surrounding plains and foothills.

But now the great stone monuments stood amid silence. There were no night fires lighting the hills where clans danced in the stone circles. No song greeting the solstice sunrise. No offerings to the gods. No libations poured over standing stones. No incantations memorializing the dead. No flasks of olive oil or bowls of grain or token ancestral bones placed in dolmen chambers. But for the wind, just silence.

Bronze Age pottery in situ; chamber of Dolmen 78, Hammam Megalithic Field.

Although generations removed from the sky-fire's deafening thunder, it was still the aftermath. Silence and ash.

The Hyksos-Egyptians and the Hebrew mourners stayed there—breathing the ashes that the keening wind still raised, that made gray-black streaks down their tear-wet cheeks—respectfully surrounding a dolmen of massive stones on which Jacob's mummified body lay for seven days.

"When the Canaanites who lived there saw the mourning at the threshing floor of Atad, they said, 'The Egyptians are holding a solemn ceremony of mourning'" (Genesis 50:11).

It's interesting to consider that the Hebrew source for the phrase "the threshing floor of Atad" may be understood not just as the property of an individual named Atad, as it is commonly translated; but can also indicate a level, flattened place (Heb. *grn*) of brambles (sticker bushes, or possibly jujube trees; Heb. *'ṭd*). In Joseph's time, it was a flat, unnatural desolation that nonetheless retained its ritual significance.

Only after this time of weeping was fulfilled did they cross the Kikkar of the Jordan, moving westward up to the central highlands of Canaan, then south to Jacob's tomb-cave at Machpelah near Hebron.

Both the Egyptian Map Lists of the Eighteenth Dynasty and the ancient Hebrew documents show that the eastern Kikkar bore the name Abel (Heb. *'bl*)—Place of Mourning—after the time of Abraham. In Hebrew it has a strong sense of "mourning a calamity." Perhaps it was the sorrow of losing an entire civilization in a fiery instant that first gave this stark landscape of an incinerated city with its stone sentinels its name. In Joseph's time, it was Abel Mizraim, the Mourning Place of the Egyptians (Genesis 50:11). Then, by Moses's day, when much of it had become overgrown with acacia trees, it became locally known as Abel Shittim, "Mourning (Place) of Acacias." Merely rendering the phrase as "grove" or "meadow of acacias" ignores the historical realities of the area.

The Hebrew-Egyptian mourners of Jacob returned to Egypt. But after Joseph and the pharaoh he had so faithfully served died, over the next generations everything changed in the land of the Nile. The Hebrews went from favor to infamy, from being guests to being slaves. Jacob's descendants in Egypt sank into poverty, servitude, and despair for generation after generation.

And during all those generations, all those years, at the edge of the Kikkar, Sodom still evoked the awe and revulsion of a crematorium for criminals.

Maybe the locals surrounding the Kikkar attributed the destruction of the cities to their god or gods. The Hyksos probably saw it as the tragic loss of a vibrant commercial center. But to all it was the astonishment, the proverb, the byword of horror.

Late Bronze Age in the Kikkar

FAR AWAY, THE STORY OF Sodom was indelible in the minds of the Hebrews in Goshen. But in the land of the Nile, Yahweh was calling his people back to the land he promised Abraham, Isaac, and Jacob.

In Egypt, a disaster of colossal economic significance paralleled the departure of the descendants of Jacob as they followed Moses into the desert, first in triumph, then in despair. The faithless held funerals of their own—every day of forty years—until all but a handful of the original participants in the great Exodus were buried beneath the desert sands.

But finally a new generation of Abraham's descendants reached the banks of the Jordan in what is known as the Late Bronze Age. The entire nation of Israel arrived at a spot the same distance to the east of the Jordan as fortified Jericho was to the west of the river they faced, with the ruined terrains of Sodom to their back. Fresh from a military victory over some of the kings of the area (Numbers 21), the Israelite army camped on the "plains of Moab . . . opposite Jericho." Some remaining kings, suspecting that the untrained Israelite army must have had divine help to accomplish such crushing defeats on their neighbors, hired a local prophet, Balaam, to curse the invaders. One of the kings took the prophet up on a nearby mountain, where they could see the devastation of Sodom sprawling before them. "Then Balak said to Balaam, 'Come, let me take you to another place. Perhaps it will please God to let you curse them for me from there.' And Balak took Balaam to the top of Peor, overlooking the wasteland" (Numbers 23:27–28).

The wasteland that Sodom had become.

In Abraham's time, it was once a verdant plain; in Moses's day, a *jeshimon,* the Hebrew word for an uninhabited desolation.

From well-watered and populated *Kikkar* to abandoned Abel.

Not long after this, the Israelite men in the camp became curious about the standing stones (menhirs and dolmens) that were present everywhere on the hillsides and plains of the area—and even more curious about the exotic Moabite women who worshiped strange deities and performed mysterious rites around them. Here around Sodom, now known as Abel Shittim, were the erected stones, the high places, the kinds of alluring divinities that would compete for the hearts of the Israelites for hundreds of years.

The Tall el-Hammam sacrescape and excavations tell the rest of the story. The Moabite women were sacred prostitutes typical of the regional cults. They were using the standing stones and dolmens as cultic monuments, charting the still-accurate astronomical alignments from stones that had stood for two thousand years, promising the future, alluring with the pleasures of the present.

But Israel's God wanted no mistake about the contamination of that place:

> While Israel was staying in Shittim, the men began to indulge in sexual immorality with Moabite women, who invited them to the sacrifices to their gods. The people ate the sacrificial meal and bowed down before these gods. So Israel yoked themselves to the Baal of Peor. And the LORD's anger burned against them.
>
> The LORD said to Moses, "Take all the leaders of these people, kill them and expose them in broad daylight before the LORD, so that the LORD's fierce anger may turn away from Israel." (Numbers 25:1–4)

Knowledge of the sacred landscape of the eastern Kikkar—the former lands of Sodom and now Abel Shittim—suggests that the bodies of the Israelites who perpetrated these evils may have been stripped and laid naked on dolmen top-stones and left to the fierce heat of the sun and the appetites of scavenging birds. The convenient megaliths of pagan ritual became ready-made platforms of defiling excarnation.

The punishment for this flagrant and ungrateful disloyalty to Yahweh called for such extraordinary penalties. Over the bodies of the perpetrators—disemboweled and dismembered by vultures and ravens—Sodom stood watch, its crumbling mudbricks and choking ash a warning as ominous as a corpse in a crossroads.

Perhaps people no longer spoke the name of Sodom after a while. It was known only by its clinging atmosphere of loss—its name "Mourning (Place) of Acacias," Abel Shittim.

There was now a new biggest and best city in the fertile disk— though less than one-tenth the size of the once-great Sodom—and its name was Jericho. In fact, this whole area now had a new name as well. No longer was it merely the Kikkar of the Jordan, as Abraham had known it; it was now called "the Kikkar of the Valley of Jericho" (Joshua 4:13; see also Deuteronomy 34:3).

Not only that, but whereas the Israelites had to fight their way from the Sinai Wilderness up through the Transjordan to Nebo (Numbers 21– 33; Deuteronomy 2–3) and engage against all the inhabitants of the Transjordan from Edom to Bashan, the plains of Moab around Sodom/Abel was a resting place where they did not have to fight anyone.

That's because there were no cities on the plains of Moab to engage and conquer. The region that lay below Pisgah was the ancient, Eden-like Kikkar with powerful cities that, several centuries previously, Lot and every other visitor to the region had coveted. Now, in the days of Moses, its cities lay in ruins.

Perhaps that lesson of the cost of idolatry and excess, and perhaps the lesson of Sodom itself, could have formed a reason for Moses to take the people up to the sterile summit of Sodom. For one thing, the views from the top would have given the awestruck Israelites a strategic map of the area they would soon enter. But perhaps even more important, the sight of the twelve tribes camped in precise arrangement on its upper and lower levels, visible for miles in all directions, might have been the final factor that made the inhabitants of Jericho lose heart, as one of its inhabitants,

Rahab, described: "I know that the LORD has given you this land and that a great fear of you has fallen on us, so that all who live in this country are melting in fear because of you" (Joshua 2:9).

But Rahab's Jericho, at its greatest, could never be comparable to the size and fortifications Sodom once boasted. The great mass of rubble still towered over the valley. It was little peanut Jericho looking over at myriad Israelite cooking fires atop the hulking Sodom ruin.

Amazingly, the lure of the land around Sodom, in the Kikkar on the east side of the Jordan where the great charred city was, proved irresistible to the descendants of Reuben and Gad and the half-tribe descendants of Manasseh. The rainfall of that time must have produced grassy fields, because the level of the Dead Sea into which it drained was much higher than it was in Abraham's time—when it was like the garden of Yahweh (Genesis 13:10).

It was there for the taking, because all the fortified cities that had once guarded it lay in ruins. Once they saw it, these three tribal groups made a bargain with Moses for the rich grazing lands on the dawn side of the Kikkar, a place so appropriate for their nomadic lifestyle that they literally couldn't see past the Jordan to the Promised Land (Numbers 32:16–19).

Moses agreed, though he must have known, and history proved, that the idolatrous poison that seeped from Sodom and its sacrescape would infect those people who chose to live on that side of the Jordan, away from their brothers.

Near death, Moses turned his mind to one more monumental task to do for the nation of wanderers he'd led for forty years. One can imagine Moses sitting there in the evenings, overlooking the Kikkar beyond the Jordan that he would never enter, putting the finishing touches on the history and law books of the Bible that would bear his name. Exodus, Leviticus, Numbers, and Deuteronomy would be rolled up in tightly bound parchment scrolls.

And Genesis. The book of beginnings of all things—and the book that told the end of another story, of Moses's ancestor Abraham, and his nephew Lot, and what happened to the dreadful, deserted mount on which he now stood.

He penned Yahweh's words comparing Israel's rebellious nature to Sodom and Gomorrah in Deuteronomy 29:22–23:

> Your children who follow you in later generations and foreigners who come from distant lands will see the calamities that have fallen on the land and the diseases with which the LORD has afflicted it. The whole land will be a burning waste of salt and sulfur— nothing planted, nothing sprouting, no vegetation growing on it. It will be like the destruction of Sodom and Gomorrah, Admah and Zeboyim, which the LORD overthrew in fierce anger.

And later in Deuteronomy 32:32: "Their vine comes from the vine of Sodom and from the fields of Gomorrah. Their grapes are filled with poison, and their clusters with bitterness."

His writing near an end, the aged Moses passed leadership to his aide Joshua, no longer the young man who first went undercover on a spy mission into this very land thirty-eight years before. With perhaps a longing eye for the lush Kikkar of the Jordan, Moses made his way on a lonely, nearly straight-up climb to a rocky peak nearby:

> Then Moses climbed Mount Nebo from the plains of Moab to the top of Pisgah, across from Jericho. There the LORD showed him the whole land—from Gilead to Dan, all of Naphtali, the territory of Ephraim and Manasseh, all the land of Judah as far as the western sea, the Negev and the whole region [Kikkar] from [of] the Valley of Jericho, the City of Palms, as far as Zoar. Then the LORD said to him, "This is the land I promised on oath to Abraham, Isaac and Jacob when I said, 'I will give it to your descendants.' I have let you see it with your eyes, but you will not cross over into it."

And Moses the servant of the LORD died there in Moab, as

the LORD had said. He buried him in Moab, in the valley opposite Beth Peor, but to this day no one knows where his grave is. (Deuteronomy 34:1–6)

Perhaps the Israelites mourned for Moses where their ancestor, Joseph, mourned for his father, at the dolmens of Sodom.

In the King James Version of verse 5, Moses is said to have died "according to the word of the LORD." In Hebrew, this is literally "upon the mouth of the Lord." Based on that, the medieval Jewish rabbi Maimonides recounts that of all 903 ways to die, Moses's death was the easiest, for there on that mountain, overlooking Sodom, God took away the soul of Moses with a kiss.

In about 1350 BCE, with the dramatic march of a now-seasoned army of Israelites across the suddenly and divinely desiccated Jordan riverbed at flood stage, the taking of the Kikkar and the lands beyond began.

From that moment on, even more of the most important events of Israel's history took place within view of, or perhaps even upon, the mound of Sodom. Everyone passed by there.

No one could ignore the massive ruin; everyone knew its story.

Iron Age in the Kikkar

BUT OVER TIME, PEOPLE BEGAN to lose their fear of the looming mound with the 360-degree views and perennial springs, perhaps to forget—or to regard as only legendary—the stories of why and how it was destroyed. By the time the archaeological period known as Iron Age 2 began about 1000 BCE, people had started to build again on the upper tall, and by the time of Solomon, Israel's third king, the walled town built there on the meter-deep layer of ash was similar in size to the city he would build for himself.

Solomon's father, King David, had spent time on the Kikkar of the Jordan and southwest across the Dead Sea at En Gedi. These were some of his most treasured hideouts during his life as a fugitive from family and foe.

And he knew it well: this was the region in which he hunted lion and bear—in fact, in which such beasts hunted him. And he must have known that the God who saved him from the paw of the lion and the paw of the bear and the power of the giant Goliath (1 Samuel 17:37) was also the God who had destroyed Sodom.

But by the time David stopped running from his enemies and died an old man, he had amassed an expansive realm with his military victories, and his son Solomon, he of immeasurable wealth and wisdom, inherited territories promised to the nation by God through Abraham, but never realized until Solomon's rule. It extended to the area around Sodom, an area then known as Gilead.

Was Sodom's ancient ruin-mound the site of one of Solomon's Gilead district cities (1 Kings 4:13)? It was a strategic site—and we know a well-planned Iron Age 2 city, built on its ancient ramparts and destruction debris, was there at the time of his reign.

However, from that time on, the city built on the ruins of Lot's home never recovered the status of the great city that had been there in the Middle Bronze Age. But from its heights, many more important events could have been overseen. For instance, it was within its view that the great prophet Elijah went deathless to heaven in a whirlwind right at the banks of the Jordan River, near Tall el-Hammam (2 Kings 8:2–15).

The story of Sodom became a symbol to which Israel's prophets referred over and over again through their history. Nobody ever forgot what happened there. As the nation faced extinction and deportation, God's spokespersons told people again and again that they would face a catastrophic fate like that of the ruined cities.

Isaiah used Sodom to depict calamity: "Unless the LORD Almighty had left us some survivors, we would have become like Sodom, we would have been like Gomorrah. Hear the word of the LORD, you rulers of Sodom; listen to the law of our God, you people of Gomorrah!" (Isaiah 1:9–10).

Sodom was the picture of arrogant, flagrant sin: "The look on their faces testifies against them; they parade their sin like Sodom; they do not hide it. Woe to them! They have brought disaster upon themselves" (Isaiah 3:9).

Nor were other nations exempt from the threat of Sodom's destruction: "Babylon, the jewel of kingdoms, the glory of the Babylonians' pride, will be overthrown by God like Sodom and Gomorrah" (Isaiah 13:19).

Jeremiah, too, used Sodom and Gomorrah as pictures of adultery and lying in Jeremiah 23:14, 49:17–18, and 50:39–40. In Lamentations 4:6, the unexpected and precipitous fate of Sodom was emphasized: "The punishment of my people is greater than that of Sodom, which was overthrown in a moment without a hand turned to help her."

The prophet Ezekiel, too, used Sodom to shame Jerusalem. Even Sodom, he said, never did what Jerusalem did. He went on to identify the sins of Sodom: lewdness, arrogance, gluttony, uncaring attitude toward the poor, haughtiness, and "detestable" acts:

> Because you did not remember the days of your youth but enraged me with all these things, I will surely bring down on your head what you have done, declares the Sovereign LORD. Did you not add lewdness to all your other detestable practices?
>
> Everyone who quotes proverbs will quote this proverb about you: "Like mother, like daughter." You are a true daughter of your mother, who despised her husband and her children; and you are a true sister of your sisters, who despised their husbands and their children. Your mother was a Hittite and your father an Amorite. Your older sister was Samaria, who lived to the north of you with her daughters; and your younger sister, who lived to the south of you with her daughters, was Sodom. You not only walked in their ways and copied their detestable practices, but

in all your ways you soon became more depraved than they. As surely as I live, declares the Sovereign LORD, your sister Sodom and her daughters never did what you and your daughters have done.

Now this was the sin of your sister Sodom: She and her daughters were arrogant, overfed and unconcerned; they did not help the poor and needy. They were haughty and did detestable things before me. Therefore I did away with them as you have seen. Samaria did not commit half the sins you did. You have done more detestable things than they, and have made your sisters seem righteous by all these things you have done. Bear your disgrace, for you have furnished some justification for your sisters. Because your sins were more vile than theirs, they appear more righteous than you. So then, be ashamed and bear your disgrace, for you have made your sisters appear righteous.

However, I will restore the fortunes of Sodom and her daughters and of Samaria and her daughters, and your fortunes along with them, so that you may bear your disgrace and be ashamed of all you have done in giving them comfort. And your sisters, Sodom with her daughters and Samaria with her daughters, will return to what they were before; and you and your daughters will return to what you were before. You would not even mention your sister Sodom in the day of your pride, before your wickedness was uncovered. Even so, you are now scorned by the daughters of Edom and all her neighbors and the daughters of the Philistines—all those around you who despise you. You will bear the consequences of your lewdness and your detestable practices, declares the LORD. (Ezekiel 16:43–58)

Later, other prophets such as Amos and Zephaniah kept alive the lessons of Sodom: "'I overthrew some of you as I overthrew Sodom and Gomorrah. You were like a burning stick snatched from the fire, yet you have not returned to me,' declares the LORD" (Amos 4:11).

Zephaniah 2:9 repeated the theme—straighten up or you will end up like Sodom and Gomorrah: "'Therefore, as surely as I live,' declares the LORD Almighty, the God of Israel, 'surely Moab will become like Sodom, the Ammonites like Gomorrah—a place of weeds and salt pits, a wasteland forever. The remnant of my people will plunder them; the survivors of my nation will inherit their land.'"

The Kikkar in New Testament Times

IN NEW TESTAMENT TIMES, THE neighborhood of Tall el-Hammam witnessed more history.

It may have been along the east-west Kikkar route—connecting with the King's Highway that ran past Sodom—that Joseph and Mary furtively traveled to Egypt to escape the danger, of which God warned them, to their young son, Jesus.

In the wilderness across the Jordan is where both John the Baptist and his cousin Jesus prepared for ministry; and when Jesus came to the wild-man John to be baptized, it was only a few miles west of Tall el-Hammam.

Other indications are that Jesus walked in this area as well; but there is no hint that he ever ascended Sodom, or passed over the rubble of its once-great gates where his ancestral relative Lot once sat.

But with the passage of centuries the site had regained a reduced glimmer of its former glory. One of the rulers—Herod Antipas, who killed Jesus's cousin John the Baptizer—in fact may have used it as the site of one of his residences. A giant bath from Jesus's time, measuring forty meters from corner to corner—now under excavation at Tall el-Hammam—certainly befits a royal playground.

That Jesus knew of—and treated as historical fact—the existence of Sodom and its horrific destruction is beyond question. In Matthew 10:1–15,

Jesus took certain cities of his homeland to task, saying that the way they rejected his message was so disgraceful that even Sodom and Gomorrah earned a less severe judgment than they did. Not only Jesus's teachings, but also his miracles had been wasted on such cities:

> Then Jesus began to denounce the cities in which most of his miracles had been performed, because they did not repent.
>
> "Woe to you, Korazin! Woe to you, Bethsaida! If the miracles that were performed in you had been performed in Tyre and Sidon, they would have repented long ago in sackcloth and ashes. But I tell you, it will be more bearable for Tyre and Sidon on the day of judgment than for you. And you, Capernaum, will you be lifted up to the skies? No, you will go down to the depths. If the miracles that were performed in you had been performed in Sodom, it would have remained to this day. But I tell you that it will be more bearable for Sodom on the day of judgment than for you." (Matthew 11:20–24)

Another time Jesus emphasized the precipitous and catastrophic way that Sodom was destroyed: "It was the same in the days of Lot. People were eating and drinking, buying and selling, planting and building. But the day Lot left Sodom, fire and sulfur rained down from heaven and destroyed them all. It will be just like this on the day the Son of Man is revealed" (Luke 17:28–29).

After Jesus died and ascended, his disciples Paul, Peter, Jude, and John the Revelator continued to use Sodom as an example of terrible, deliberate evil and terrible, deliberate destruction (Romans 9:29; 2 Peter 2:6; Jude 1:7; and Revelation 11:8—an astonishing scripture that predicts the infamy of Sodom even in the future).

Sodom was real, Jesus said.

Respect the symbol of Sodom, his apostles warned.

But what happened at Sodom that caused it to be a symbol that Jesus's listeners, more than sixteen hundred years after its destruction, needed no explanation when its name was mentioned?

What caused people to stay away from it for seven hundred years, hardly daring to set foot on its crumbling, ashy soil?

One thing is certain. Seven centuries of abandonment of prime real estate didn't happen because of chicken pox.

FOUR

Warlords and Destruction:
The Bible and the Backstory

W HAT LED UP TO SODOM'S TERMINAL EVENT, THE CONFLA-gration that became a metaphor of catastrophe for the rest of history?

Reading the biblical account of Abram and Lot's amicable agreement about where to pasture their flocks, with the emphasis on relationships and geography, can draw attention away from some of the other realities of life in the ancient Levant. The Egyptian Execration Texts and the Amarna Tablets, ancient documents that illustrate some of the geopolitical situations in this region, offer great insight. These documents list not only some of the great Levantine city-states, but also the nomadic groups who coexisted there.

One group was the Shasu, a term used to delineate the migrative bedouin-types who had no particular allegiance to anyone. They had similar ethnic roots and may have even shared a common language. The Shasu tended to stay to themselves, minding their flocks and herds as they moved to and from seasonal pasturelands. Although they wouldn't shrink from a fight if necessity demanded it, they were most often mild-mannered, peaceful folk. And they provided commodities that city and town dwellers craved: meat and milk products.

The other group the ancient sources speak of were the Habiru or 'Apiru. These were multiethnic bands of disenfranchised people. Often comprising outcasts, brigands, and exiles of every imaginable background and skill, from commoners to royals, they were a motley company. To the city and town dwellers of Canaan, they were little more than thugs.

While a somewhat mysterious group seen in ancient texts that mention them, the oft-disparate 'Apiru had at least one thing in common: they joined up with a particular 'Apiru band as a matter of choice or the necessity of survival. And survive they did, doing whatever it took. Sometimes they kept flocks and herds, or ran caravans, or did a little farming if they could—but always with the drifters' option to roam when it suited them.

It was also common for an 'Apiru band—often numbering into the hundreds—to "run protection" for city-states as mercenaries, providing front lines of defense for their host kings, who in turn allowed them to graze their animals on city-state lands by contract. The leaders of 'Apiru groups were, for all practical purposes, warlords.

The consonants of 'Apiru/Habiru have the same vocal values as the word "Hebrew" (*'ibri*—as in "Abraham the Hebrew" in Genesis 14:13), but there's a lot of scholarly debate about whether the two terms are actually related or not. Certainly, the 'Apiru in general aren't equivalent to the biblical Hebrews like Abraham* and Lot or, later, Joshua and the Israelites. But it's obvious that Canaanite city dwellers would have seen the multiethnic group of Abraham and his descendants as 'Apiru. After all, what else could they call them?

Undoubtedly, the patriarchal Hebrew clans in Genesis, and their descendant nomadic Israelites, display all the elements of 'Apiru life and activity known from the ancient Near Eastern texts. For this reason it's doubtful that the linguistic similarity of the terms *'Apiru* and *Hebrew* is merely coincidental. But even if you deny the linguistic connection, a reasonable link exists on cultural grounds alone.

---

* "Abram" and "Abraham" are interchangeable and represent pre- and postcovenant names of the same person.

Take the multiethnic characteristic, for example. Over his lifetime Abram's entourage often included other ethnic groups like Hagar the Egyptian (Genesis 16:1), Eliezar of Damascus (Genesis 15:2), "the people they had acquired in Haran" (Genesis 12:5), his Amorite companions Mamre, Eschol, and Aner (Genesis 14:13, 24), and servants and slaves of diverse origin (Genesis 20:14).

Abram also made land-use, water-use, and protection contracts with a colorful array of Canaanite leaders and kings: Melchizedek king of Salem (Genesis 14:18–20), Bera king of Sodom (Genesis 14:21–24), Abimelech king of Gerar (Genesis 20:14–15; 21:22–34), and Ephron the Hittite (Genesis 23:3–20). No doubt there were many others.

We know as well, from the biblical account about Abram's nomadic travels before and after his negotiation with his nephew Lot, that the men's two herding groups had migrated to Bethel and Ai, where they pitched their tents and built an altar to Yahweh. From there the massive group of 'Apiru traveled to the Negev and Beersheba, and then back to Bethel and Ai, where they made their famous agreement.

Abram had also spent time in Shechem territory (Genesis 12:6–8), one of two city-states operating in the hill country of Canaan, the other being Salem or Jerusalem. Like Sodom, both Shechem and Salem existed not just as fortified cities on hills with kings, but also as city-states that controlled the lands around them.

Thus Abraham didn't just wander the Canaan highlands making money through sheep and goat breeding. He was far more powerful than this. In fact, he was a warlord, as the geography- and name-rich fourteenth chapter of Genesis shows.

And he was a warlord of true 'Apiru proportions, when international combat broke out with Sodom at its center. In fact, Abram and his guerrilla warriors changed history.

Warlords in the Kikkar

THOUGH IT SEEMS THE WALLS of Bronze Age Sodom were never breached by an invading enemy, Genesis 14 relates that during the lifetime of Abraham, Sodom's King Bera began paying tribute to a foreign king named Kedorlaomer from Elam (the region later known as Persia).

No ancient records tell the reason for this, but other situations from that era of which we do have records could shed some light. Sometimes tribute arrangements were the results of marriages between political entities. (For instance, after the death of King Tutankhamun, his young widow, Ankhesenamun, sent urgent communications—which still exist in the Hittite archives—to the great Hittite king Suppiluliuma, asking for one of his sons to come and marry her to protect her throne. Such an arrangement would have come with a cost to Egypt, and perhaps Bera made such a pact.) At other times they were part of international treaties. At any rate, Kedorlaomer and other eastern kings managed to wrangle some servitude from the Kikkar kingdoms for twelve years.

The cities of the Kikkar, Sodom and Gomorrah, Admah and Zeboiim, along with Zoar, simmered with discontent. And then the ruler of Sodom and his king-neighbors decided they'd had enough:

> At this time Amraphel king of Shinar, Arioch king of Ellasar, Kedorlaomer king of Elam and Tidal king of Goiim went to war against Bera king of Sodom, Birsha king of Gomorrah, Shinab king of Admah, Shemeber king of Zeboiim, and the king of Bela (that is, Zoar). All these latter kings joined forces in the Valley of Siddim (the Salt Sea). For twelve years they had been subject to Kedorlaomer, but in the thirteenth year they rebelled. (Genesis 14:1–4)

Kedorlaomer called in reinforcements. According to researcher C. E. Morgan, a Bronze Age army that would cover the territory from the north all the way to Sodom would have numbered about three thousand well-trained and disciplined soldiers. They came for several purposes, but ostensibly to quell this uprising in an attempt to make a clean sweep of all the ethnic and political groups in the area:

> In the fourteenth year, Kedorlaomer and the kings allied with him went out and defeated the Rephaites in Ashteroth Karnaim, the Zuzites in Ham, the Emites in Shaveh Kiriathaim and the Horites in the hill country of Seir, as far as El Paran near the desert. Then they turned back and went to En Mishpat (that is, Kadesh), and they conquered the whole territory of the Amalekites, as well as the Amorites who were living in Hazazon Tamar [= En Gedi—2 Chronicles 20:2]. (Genesis 14:5–7)

Why did Kedorlaomer and his troops go as far south as El Paran in the desert, where the Horites were? Perhaps it was because of the copper mining industry that existed there in antiquity, and the eastern kings loaded up with the valuable metal they needed for making bronze weapons and other implements.

> Then the king of Sodom, the king of Gomorrah, the king of Admah, the king of Zeboiim and the king of Bela (that is, Zoar) marched out and drew up their battle lines in the Valley of Siddim against Kedorlaomer king of Elam, Tidal king of Goiim, Amraphel king of Shinar and Arioch king of Ellasar—four kings against five. Now the Valley of Siddim was full of tar pits, and when the kings of Sodom and Gomorrah fled, some of the men fell into them and the rest fled to the hills. (Genesis 14:8–10)

Several times in antiquity the surface of the Dead Sea rose and fell by as much as 450 feet, reflecting climate cycles. In some periods the water's recession laid bare wide, flat spreads of land, particularly along the west and north shores. At such times—and the time of Abram was one of these—the exposed Valley of Siddim can exactly be equated with "the Salt Sea" of which Genesis speaks. Furthermore, during periods when the water level was this low, these expansive beaches had numerous dangerous and often invisible sinkholes, while at other times the Dead Sea would cover that same area with several hundred feet of water.

Kedorlaomer's forces, moving northward from En Gedi (Hazazon Tamar), collided with the army of Bera and his fellow Kikkar kings in the Valley of Siddim near the northeast corner of the Dead Sea. There the Kikkar coalition resistance suffered a catastrophic loss in battle. In full retreat, many of them became mired in the slime pits (sinkholes) that still snag anyone who doesn't walk carefully around certain areas of the Dead Sea. Others ran for the mountains.

With no resistance, Kedorlaomer's united forces amassed in front of the massive gates of Sodom. From there, either by payoff (which would avoid a long and costly siege) or by force, they plundered the great "red palace" of King Bera, from which the latter looked out over his usually secure dominion. From there and throughout the city, the invading army collected all the valuables they could find from within its 150-foot-thick stone and mudbrick defenses, and then did the same to Sodom's main satellite town, Gomorrah.

Among the valuables they took were people. And among the people they took were Lot, the nephew of Abram, and all his family, and all his possessions: "The four kings seized all the goods of Sodom and Gomorrah and all their food; then they went away. They also carried off Abram's nephew Lot and his possessions, since he was living in Sodom" (Genesis 14:11–12).

A man who escaped the armies of Kedorlaomer made his way through the Judean wilderness to an area near Hebron where massive oak trees grew. There Abram the rich man lived: "One who had escaped came and reported this to Abram the Hebrew. Now Abram was living near the great trees of Mamre the Amorite, a brother of Eshcol and Aner, all of whom were allied with Abram" (Genesis 14:13).

An 'Apiru warlord had the resources to follow up on this situation.

Abram formed his own coalition with three local brothers, already allies: Mamre, Eshcol, and Aner. The combined forces of the four were probably between six hundred and a thousand armed men, well trained in guerrilla tactics and night fighting (Genesis 14:15).

The Hebrew word for the "trained men (*yalid*) born in his [Abram's] household" refers not just to their birth circumstances but to their covenantal membership in an elite military force. Why did Abram have these men at his disposal, in his own household?

Certainly they weren't necessary merely for protecting flocks and shepherds. Instead, they were part of a security force that Abram hired out, as did other 'Apiru leaders. In exchange for grazing rights around certain city-states, Abram and his mercenaries provided a first line of defense against invaders and other enemies. (Abram's example was carried on by his descendants: his grandson Esau, hardly the pastoral type, also had a personal security force of four hundred in his household—Genesis 33:1.)

Abram's covenantal agreement with the Amorites around Hebron meant that not only his soldiers but theirs as well were bound as allies.

When Abram heard that his relative had been taken captive, he called out the 318 trained men born in his household and went in pursuit as far as Dan. During the night Abram divided his men to attack them and he routed them, pursuing them as far as Hobah, north of Damascus. He recovered all the goods and brought back his relative Lot and his possessions, together with the women and the other people. (Genesis 14:14–16)

Significantly, Abram didn't get involved in the Sodom battle against Kedorlaomer's forces. That's because he was contracted to another city-state, Salem, and its King Melchizedek just as Lot had obviously made a similar treaty with Bera of Sodom.

Perhaps it was the combined forces of Abram and his Mamre allies; perhaps it was the leadership quality of Abram's personal army of 318 warriors; certainly it must have been Abram's fury or his sense of destiny that fueled their march to Dan (Laish) in the north. They constantly gained ground on Kedorlaomer and his allies, who were loaded down not only with plunder from Sodom and salt and bitumen and copper from the southern mines, but with captives, too—perhaps several hundred of them.

At Hobah north of Damascus, some 120 miles from Sodom, Abram's agile troops struck. In a daring night raid, the Mamre group in a split offensive attacked the invaders and recovered everything and everybody that had been hauled away from Sodom. They began the long, arduous journey back.

Bera the king of Sodom, delighted that someone had recovered his city's citizens and possessions, traveled to a valley outside Jerusalem, where he and Abram apparently met for the first time. Why did Bera come to the Shaveh (likely Kidron) Valley near Salem (Jerusalem) to recover the spoils of war recovered from Kedorlaomer?

Undoubtedly it was because that's where Abram and his troops stopped to fulfill a covenantal obligation. A warlord could receive grazing rights in exchange for protecting the surroundings of a city-state. If the city-state was threatened by an enemy, the warlord's men would rise to the occasion and fight to protect it. But under such a contract a warlord was free to battle against whatever other cities or enemies he wished, so long as he fulfilled his contract with the "home" city.

A warlord's troops took the risks when engaging in a battle should it occur. For this, they were entitled to anything they took from those they defeated. However, as suggested by Abram's arrangement with Melchizedek, the king of the city-state the warlord protected had a right to part of those spoils—in this case, 10 percent, to be exact.

What happened in the Valley of Shaveh outside of Jerusalem or Salem shows that Abram had made, in fact, such a mercenary's agreement with the king of Salem, Melchizedek. And though the author of the book of Hebrews would later appropriate the symbol of one person rendering a toll to another (Abram giving tribute to someone to whom he owed allegiance and who could bless him), the Genesis event in history is about an agreement between a warlord and the king of the city-state he'd sworn to defend, to divide spoils of war according to a prearranged percentage.

The fact that Melchizedek also served as priest for the same-named God who'd called Abram out of Mesopotamia to come to this land was even more reason for Abram to give freely to Melchizedek and to feel affinity with the king who came out from his palace into the valley of royalty, who greeted him with bread and wine, praise and fellowship.

> After Abram returned from defeating Kedorlaomer and the kings allied with him, the king of Sodom came out to meet him in the Valley of Shaveh (that is, the King's Valley).
> Then Melchizedek king of Salem brought out bread and wine. He was priest of God Most High, and he blessed Abram, saying,
> "Blessed be Abram by God Most High,
> Creator of heaven and earth.
> And blessed be God Most High,
> who delivered your enemies into your hand."
> Then Abram gave him a tenth of everything. (Genesis 14:17–20)

But then King Bera of Sodom thought to strike a deal with the man with whom he, unlike Melchizedek, had no covenant. In fact, it's even possible that hapless Lot had served as Bera's warlord and not only had failed at his job but had gotten himself, his family, and all his possessions hauled off as well.

In reality, by their mutual contract Melchizedek and Abram owned the people and goods that Abram took in battle from Kerdolaomer. King Bera's magnanimous "offer" of the physical plunder wasn't his to extend. And accepting it from Bera's hand would have been a conflict of interest for Abram, who had a contractual agreement with Melchizedek. Given that Bera's Sodom (Tall el-Hammam) was at least ten times bigger than Melchizedek's Jerusalem and copiously more prosperous, it's thought-provoking to consider that perhaps Bera was trying to coax Abram away from his relatively meager covenant with Salem. But Abram refused to jeopardize his friendship with his religious soul mate, Melchizedek. Besides, the Jerusalem city-state occupied the heart of Abram's grazing territory.

Abram's first use for the plunder was to recompense the allies he enlisted, and for the physical needs of his soldiers as well. Beyond that, he refused to let Bera go back to Sodom pretending to be a benefactor who'd enhanced the warlord's wealth.

But King Bera of Sodom needed the people. The kinds of building projects in his city required major manpower that Bera couldn't do without: the defensive ramparts at Tall el-Hammam, surrounding both the upper and the lower city, were constructed with between 150 million and 200 million mudbricks with a slickly groomed 35-degree outer slope that needed constant attention. The manufacture of bricks for defensive purposes alone would have employed thousands—with slave labor hard to come by—as shown by the reluctance of the Exodus pharaoh to let such a similar workforce go. The copper, salt, bitumen, and food supplies carried off by Kedorlaomer were products Bera could easily replace—the people were not.

Abram's statement "I have raised my hand to Yahweh . . . and have taken an oath" no doubt refers to specific language used in the formulation of the Abram/Salem pact, with part of that being some kind of general stipulation against making a like covenant with a nearby competing city-state like Sodom.

> The king of Sodom said to Abram, "Give me the people and keep the goods for yourself."
>
> But Abram said to the king of Sodom, "I have raised my hand to the Lord, God Most High, Creator of heaven and earth, and have taken an oath that I will accept nothing belonging to you, not even a thread or the thong of a sandal, so that you will never be able to say, 'I made Abram rich.' I will accept nothing but what my men have eaten and the share that belongs to the men who

went with me—to Aner, Eshcol and Mamre. Let them have their share." (Genesis 14:21–24)

The Biblical Account of the Destruction of Sodom

AFTER THE BATTLES AND THE division of spoils, Lot returned to Sodom, this time no longer as a nomad living solely outside its walls but as a resident, one who even sat in its gate in a position of honor. Perhaps King Bera retained Lot in this high-profile position as a means of keeping the lesser warlord's powerful uncle "attached" to Sodom, since the services of the mightier Abram the Hebrew weren't for hire directly.

But aside from that detail, and one about the betrothals of his two daughters, the biblical record is silent about Lot's activities during the years that passed while his uncle Abram was entering into a covenant relationship with Yahweh–El Elyon, taking on a concubine, and learning of his aged wife's surprise pregnancy.

But just as Abraham was alarmed when he heard that Lot and his family had been kidnapped, he was moved to action again when he learned of the disaster that was about to befall Sodom, Lot's home. In a touching interlude between friends, Yahweh told Abraham that he couldn't conceal from his friend what was going to happen and even allowed Abraham to try to bargain for a reversal of the judgment Yahweh had announced against Sodom (Genesis 18:16–23).

When Abraham went to bed that night, did he wonder if there were ten salvageable people in Sodom? The question was answered the next day, in an unmistakable way.

On the one hand, the account describes great wickedness and great destruction. On the other hand, the city of Sodom was the "good time" capital of the crossing trade routes, making Corinth in the New Testament pale in comparison with its debaucheries, arrogance, and pride.

Through history, biblicists have typically made Sodom's perceived sexual practices the reason for its destruction. But that assessment is at best incomplete and at worst inaccurate, according to the Bible, archaeology, and anthropology. The sexual and religio-sexual practices of Sodom were no more or less evil or wicked than those of any typical Canaanite city or town. In such a caravanning center, perhaps all visitors were met with such an "obligatory invitation to party" as the angels received in Sodom.

I'm sure that much of the city's commerce circulated around serving the deviant sexual desires of dissolute caravanners and nomads from across the Fertile Crescent and beyond. (Recall Rahab the prostitute in the western Kikkar city of Jericho generations later, recorded in Joshua 2:1.) Both male and female ritual prostitution was routine in the repertoire of Canaanite worship—a practice even picked up by the sons of Eli at the Tent of Yahweh, so 1 Samuel 2:22 attests—as was ceremonial bestiality. In this regard, Sodom was no different from other large southern Levantine cities.

From what Abraham would have known about the Cities of the Kikkar, from his perspective they were probably all deserving of destruction by El Elyon (certainly one of the reasons that Yahweh wanted Joshua to eliminate the Canaanites altogether). Their moral depravity was comprehensive, multifaceted, deep-seated. Nonetheless, the specific biblical reasons for the destruction of Sodom and Gomorrah were these: "Now this was the sin of your sister Sodom: She and her daughters were arrogant, overfed and unconcerned; they did not help the poor and needy. They were haughty and did detestable things before me. Therefore I did away with them as you have seen" (Ezekiel 16:49–50).

(It's interesting that this passage says "as you have seen." Obviously those living in Judah, Jerusalem in particular, were familiar with the ruins of Sodom in the days of Ezekiel.)

The actual destruction scene of Sodom in the Bible is one of scandal and ambivalence, fear and flight. On the other hand, the account in Genesis 19 provides some important clues to help identify, almost four thousand years later, the actual place where those events took place:

The two angels arrived at Sodom in the evening, and Lot was sitting in the gateway of the city. When he saw them, he got up to meet them and bowed down with his face to the ground. "My lords," he said, "please turn aside to your servant's house. You can wash your feet and spend the night and then go on your way early in the morning."

"No," they answered, "we will spend the night in the square."

But he insisted so strongly that they did go with him and entered his house. He prepared a meal for them, baking bread without yeast, and they ate. Before they had gone to bed, all the men from every part of the city of Sodom—both young and old—surrounded the house. They called to Lot, "Where are the men who came to you tonight? Bring them out to us so that we can have sex with them."

Lot went outside to meet them and shut the door behind him and said, "No, my friends. Don't do this wicked thing. Look, I have two daughters who have never slept with a man. Let me bring them out to you, and you can do what you like with them. But don't do anything to these men, for they have come under the protection of my roof."

"Get out of our way," they replied. And they said, "This fellow came here as an alien, and now he wants to play the judge! We'll treat you worse than them." They kept bringing pressure on Lot and moved forward to break down the door.

But the men inside reached out and pulled Lot back into the house and shut the door. Then they struck the men who were at the door of the house, young and old, with blindness so that they could not find the door.

The two men said to Lot, "Do you have anyone else here—sons-in-law, sons or daughters, or anyone else in the city who belongs to you? Get them out of here, because we are going to destroy this place. The outcry to the Lord against its people is so great that he has sent us to destroy it."

So Lot went out and spoke to his sons-in-law, who were pledged to marry his daughters. He said, "Hurry and get out of this place, because the Lord is about to destroy the city!" But his sons-in-law thought he was joking.

With the coming of dawn, the angels urged Lot, saying, "Hurry! Take your wife and your two daughters who are here, or you will be swept away when the city is punished."

When he hesitated, the men grasped his hand and the hands of his wife and of his two daughters and led them safely out of the city, for the Lord was merciful to them. As soon as they had brought them out, one of them said, "Flee for your lives! Don't look back, and don't stop anywhere in the plain! Flee to the mountains or you will be swept away!"

But Lot said to them, "No, my lords, please! Your servant has found favor in your eyes, and you have shown great kindness to me in sparing my life. But I can't flee to the mountains; this disaster will overtake me, and I'll die. Look, here is a town near enough to run to, and it is small. Let me flee to it—it is very small, isn't it? Then my life will be spared."

He said to him, "Very well, I will grant this request too; I will not overthrow the town you speak of. But flee there quickly, because I cannot do anything until you reach it." (That is why the town was called Zoar.)

By the time Lot reached Zoar, the sun had risen over the land. Then the LORD rained down burning sulfur on Sodom and Gomorrah—from the LORD out of the heavens. Thus he overthrew those cities and the entire plain, including all those living in the cities—and also the vegetation in the land. But Lot's wife looked back, and she became a pillar of salt.

Early the next morning Abraham got up and returned to the place where he had stood before the LORD. He looked down toward Sodom and Gomorrah, toward all the land of the plain, and he saw dense smoke rising from the land, like smoke from a furnace.

So when God destroyed the cities of the plain, he remembered Abraham, and he brought Lot out of the catastrophe that overthrew the cities where Lot had lived.

This story is in the timeless words of the Hebrew Scriptures, now being retold in the excavation of the ash-laden soils of Sodom, at Tall el-Hammam.

If Tall el-Hammam is Sodom, it should be clearly seen in three identifying features.

It must be located where the Bible, the only ancient document that describes its geography in detail, says it is. It must be in the right place.

Second, Tall el-Hammam can be Sodom only if excavation, text, and chronology reasonably intersect. Its destruction must have happened at the right time.

Finally, it must have the right stuff: architecture and artifacts have to fit.

Right place, right time, right stuff.

PART TWO

Right Place, Right Time, Right Stuff

THE SCIENCE OF TALL EL-HAMMAM

BACKSTORY

Dr. C's Search

The years were busy that followed Dr. C's revelatory (or at least, "coming-to-Genesis") experience in 1996 in a hotel room, where he sat with just his Bible and his questions about the location of Sodom and Gomorrah and the Cities of the Kikkar. He pushed the nagging questions below the surface of a busy professional career, but they always seemed to bubble up, taunt him, torment him.

As a scholar and researcher, he stayed busy, advancing his skills as a field archaeologist and ceramic typologist with the excavations at Bethsaida, Kursi, and Khirbet el-Maqatir. Ancient pottery became his focus, and he spent thousands of hours poring over published depictions of ceramics from excavations across Israel and Jordan, studying them firsthand in the musty basement storage rooms of museums, universities, and government facilities, even examining the thousands of ancient vessels crammed into the antiquities shops of old Jerusalem, and hidden away in the secret vaults of private collectors. A passion for sure.

But meanwhile he kept probing for information about Sodom. What he'd read in the hotel room—and hundreds of times since—in Genesis about Abraham told him two things.

It told the archaeologist in his soul that the famines and other historical details from the life of that patriarch indicated that he lived sometime in the Middle Bronze Age—a fact ratified by prominent archaeologists and Near Eastern scholars from W. F. Albright to K. A. Kitchen.

And it told the biblical scholar in his soul that Abraham looked out over the Kikkar of the Jordan, on the well-watered disk that he and Lot could see in its entirety from the region of Bethel and Ai; and that along with Sodom there had been at least three other notable, flourishing cities nearby.

Four or more Middle Bronze Age cities in the Kikkar of the Jordan, east of the river.

All the time Dr. C would ask fellow scholars about what they knew of excavations of significant sites in the Kikkar of the Jordan. There were Tuleilat Ghassul (abandoned ca. 3800 BCE, about two thousand years too early) and Tall Iktanu (published as an unfortified site abandoned before 2000 BCE, also long before the time of Abraham). Thus both were much too old to make a good match. And neither was fortified as Genesis 19:1 would require.

So he kept thinking, and wondering and researching. But few in the scholarly world apparently gave the idea any credence at all, despite the fact that many of the scholar-explorers of the nineteenth century, even beyond, had said that the Cities of the Kikkar had to be northeast of the Dead Sea—astute geographers like C. R. Conder, H. Tristram, G. Grove, W. M. Thomson, S. Merrill, W. F. Birch, W. W. Moore, T. Saunders, and others (see Clark-Grove 1860s Map, Bible 1880s Map, and Smith-Grove Map).

The latest and most authoritative publications had maps of archaeological sites with gaping blank spots in the area just north and east of the Dead Sea. It was as if the area Dr. C had identified as the eastern Kikkar had become invisible to American, European, and Israeli archaeologists. Even the sources that in passing mentioned excavations didn't identify any Middle Bronze Age sites on the eastern side of the Kikkar:

- *The New Encyclopedia of Archaeological Excavations in the Holy Land* (E. Stern, ed.): Iktanu and Tuleilat Ghassul—both much too early, he already knew.

- *The Archaeology of Society in the Holy Land* (T. E. Levy, ed.): nothing.

- *Archaeology of the Land of the Bible ca. 10,000–586 B.C.E.* (A. Mazar): nothing.

- *The Land of the Bible: A Historical Geography,* revised (Y. Aharoni): only Tuleilat Ghassul.

- *The Archaeology of Ancient Israel* (A. Ben-Tor, ed.): the too-early Tuleilat Ghassul and Iktanu.

In fact, any recent atlas of the Holy Land showed only two or three sites in the area (Iktanu, Ghassul, Abel Shittim) and didn't assign an exact location. Only Iktanu and Ghassul had been rigorously, scientifically excavated anytime in the recent past, just enough to disqualify them as the destroyed Cities of the Kikkar.

When Dr. C's colleagues and the maps and professional books he consulted had no answers, he began to ask himself questions. Was his search for the Cities of the Plain just a deluded, misled illusion? What made him think that the sites many thought were Sodom and Gomorrah were cases of mistaken identity?

After all, most everyone believed W. F. Albright and G. E. Wright, whose opinions about a southern location for Sodom and Gomorrah had influenced archaeologists for generations. They suggested these ruins were underneath the waters of the Dead Sea's shallow southern basin. Even people who knew what previous explorers had said about the Kikkar and its suitability for consideration as the site of the Cities of the Plain dismissed those old observations as just nineteenth-century musings.

So Dr. C decided to look again at the two sites near the southern end of the Dead Sea, developing what his research associate Dr. Peter Briggs called a "criterial screen" to cross-check his thinking.

Are the ruins of Bab edh-Dhra and Numeira located north of the Dead Sea within the flat, circular area identified as the biblical Kikkar of the Jordan? he asked himself, and had to answer, No, they aren't—not even close.

Are they visible from the area of Bethel/Ai from which Lot viewed the "entire Kikkar of the Jordan"? Certainly not (see Map 4).

Are the ruins of those two cities located on the eastern half of the Kikkar, between the Jordan River and the foothills of the Transjordan Highlands, as Genesis suggests? No.

Is the candidate for Gomorrah adjacent to the one everyone thinks is Sodom, in the kind of "sister-city" identification we see in Genesis? No, they're about twelve miles apart.

Does any stratum from the excavation of these sites reveal that they were occupied and operational during the Middle Bronze Age? In fact, are there any remains of a typical fortified Middle Bronze city in either of these ruins? No, and no.

Was the site of Bab edh-Dhra large and sophisticated enough to be the Sodom that Genesis describes—a city prosperous enough to plunder? No. It always teetered on the edge of viability in a harsh and marginal agricultural zone.

Did the excavations at Bab edh-Dhra and Numeira unearth evidence of their fiery destruction at any time during the Middle Bronze Age? Well, yes, on the fiery destruction, but toward the end of the Early Bronze Age—Bab edh-Dhra in 2350 BCE. But Numeira was simply abandoned about 2600 BCE. On both counts, too early for Abraham and Lot. And the separate demises of the two cities, centuries apart, were hardly simultaneous.

Does the excavation data from Bab edh-Dhra or Numeira reveal a long occupational hiatus from the time of a Middle Bronze Age destruction until any significant reoccupation? No Middle Bronze destruction at either site—because both were destroyed long before that, and never resettled.

In fact, he knew that the destruction of Bab edh-Dhra was paralleled at Early Bronze Age sites across the entire Levant. It wasn't an isolated destruction but rather the result of a major climate shift that put them all out of business. That didn't fit at all with the targeted termination of the Cities of the Kikkar.

So Dr. C concluded that he knew where the Cities of the Plain *were not,* but no one could tell him where they were.

Was it just pride or stubbornness, he wondered, that he would be unable to get out of his mind the idea that Sodom and the other cities were where the Bible said they were? So why was it so hard for him to find publications or colleagues who would agree with him, or knew anything about the area northeast of the Dead Sea?

"We'll just have to go to Jordan and see what we can find," said Dr. C's wife, Danette, over coffee in the late spring of 2002. A trim and vigorous brunette companion through multiple excavations, she was always up for the next adventure. "I miss the dust of the Holy Land in my eyebrows," she said with a grin.

Soon the tickets were purchased for Dr. C, Danette, and the rest of the away team, dear friends Travis and Charity Jones, a couple in their late twenties. The itinerary: find the research, walk the turf.

Danette and Steven Collins at Tall el-Hammam.

Travis and Charity Jones.

On the airplane flight to Tel Aviv's Ben Gurion International Airport, Dr. C felt his heart sink. Was he wasting the time and money of his friends and wife, on a wild-goose chase for something no American archaeologist gave him hope of finding? Well, at least they would enjoy socializing with some old friends in Jerusalem—his years of excavating and leading tours in the Holy Land had produced some lifelong friendships and some insider information on interesting out-of-the-way places to see. A little sightseeing in Israel might soften the blow of what threatened to be some coming days of fruitless searches and frustration.

"Doing some research?" Dr. C's friend Travis, a wiry and earnest young man who once dared to skinny-dip in the Sea of Galilee, leaned across the two sleeping wives in the airline seats between them when he saw Dr. C's reading light on in the middle of the night.

"Yeah," Dr. C responded. Actually, some re-research. He was reading the Genesis account of the Cities of the Plain again. And again. And again.

After they visited friends in Israel, it was time to travel east. Though he had traveled through the Kikkar many times, on this trip into Jordan Dr. C made the decision to avoid the area at first, like the unconscious decision not to look an old friend in the face until you've gotten to the truth of a rumor you've heard about him. Crossing into Jordan on the Sheikh Hussein Bridge opposite Beth Shean, the group visited some archaeological sites in northern and southern Jordan, and for their final sightseeing stop stood where Moses stood on the peak of Mount Nebo, overlooking the Kikkar of the Jordan.

Did the ruined Cities of the Plain exist there now? Dr. C wondered. He believed the scriptural record that they once were there. Did the lack of evidence of excavations indicate the cities had been completely destroyed and thus no longer existed? He could hardly bear that thought.

Sightseeing was over. The group drove northeast to Amman to a couple of meetings with Dr. Fawwaz Al-Khreyshah, the director general of the Jordanian Department of Antiquities. He pointed them toward sources detailing survey work that had been done in the Jordan Valley north of the Dead Sea. Perhaps they could find some of the information they sought there, he said, and wished them well.

But the make-it-or-break-it research destination of the trip was to Amman's American Center of Oriental Research (ACOR). The building was without frills, square but inviting. Dr. C had been a member of American Schools of Oriental Research (ASOR) for a long time, so he had facility privileges. He'd even done research in the ACOR library a few times over the years.

Dr. C stood outside its entrance, half afraid to enter, predicting in his gut the disappointment that finding nothing would bring. At least they had the premises practically to themselves. Between excavation seasons, the nearly deserted building echoed with their footsteps as they walked to the library. Not even the librarian was on duty.

The shelves of books and unoccupied tables stretched before them. Dr. C began searching through stacks of volumes of the *Annual of the Department of Antiquities of Jordan*. His heart was sinking with each fruitless search. Travis was looking through the shelves, in search of possible sources, and Danette and Charity alternated between doing their own searches and making photocopies. Everyone was having a good time, except Dr. C.

Issue after issue of *ADAJ* told him nothing.

"Aha!" Travis's voice rang out over the large table where he had spread out some books. *"Aha!"*

The little book he held in his hand was a treasure trove. *The Antiquities of the Jordan Rift Valley* by R. G. Khouri contained detailed descriptions of every known archaeological site in the Jordan Valley between the Sea of Galilee and the Dead Sea.

And a map. Whereas every other map of the Kikkar had just blank spaces and question marks, this one showed not just one or two sites, but fourteen little black dots with names.

Fourteen talls.

Tall Nimrin, Tall Mustah, Tall Bleibel, Tall Ghannam, Tall Ghrubba, Tall Kafrayn, Khirbet Kafrayn, Tall el-Hammam, Tall Rama, Tall Iktanu, Tall Sahl es-Sarabet, Tuleilat Ghassul, Khirbet Sweimeh, and Tall el-Azeimeh (see Map 7).

All Dr. C could do for several minutes was stare at those little black dots and grin. If the picture of the Kikkar he'd derived from the biblical data was factual, then a handful of those dots could very well represent the ruins of Sodom and Gomorrah, Admah and Zeboiim.

Perhaps the lost cities weren't lost anymore.

Danette laughed aloud as she began making a list on a piece of paper for Dr. C. Charity and Travis jumped up and down and hugged each other, their nearly identical brown ponytails bobbing up and down. The four huddled over the list and giggled, then everyone but Dr. C began looking for more materials. With the names of ancient sites now in hand, the research materials fanned out before them like the very Kikkar itself, fertile and expansive.

Dr. C sat alone at the table with the handwritten list and the book. Nobody had to tell him that precious little excavation had gone on at the sites. But he already knew that two of them, Tuleilat Ghassul and Tall Iktanu, had occupation layers that were too early for Abraham. The list narrowed to twelve.

Dr. C returned to Khouri's book. In it were reports of how in the early twentieth century and then again in the 1970s people had done surveys of the talls. In addition, these investigators had done sherding—a surface examination of pottery remains—on the talls.

But what's found on the surface is by definition just a surface look, he said to himself. Only an excavation, digging carefully down through the layers of time, can tell the truth about the occupational history of a tall. However, the sherding report from one of the sites made it almost certainly a much too modern site. Down to eleven candidates.

He made a mental note of what earlier surveyors had found, and went on to Khouri's information about the comparative sizes of the remaining eleven talls.

Four were significantly larger than the others: Tall Nimrin, Khirbet Kafrayn, Tall el-Azeimeh, and Tall el-Hammam.

"Look, everybody!" Dr. C called Danette, Charity, and Travis to the table. "I knew from Genesis there had to be at least two large cities on the Kikkar, and there are four of them!" He pointed triumphantly to the paper on which he'd written the names of the four sites.

The remaining hours of the day flew by in the ACOR library. The names of the sites were like keys that opened hidden doors all over the library. Sherding reports on the eleven sites all looked promising, with wide ranges of pottery from Chalcolithic up through the Iron Age. But sherding reports weren't enough.

"We need excavation reports," Charity said, raising her expressive eyebrows as Travis rubbed her shoulders and nodded. All four rose to their feet and began to look.

Of the eight smaller sites, only two had been excavated, and there was little to learn there, except which ones to eliminate. Ghrubba was mainly Neolithic and Chalcolithic—way too early. Tall Sahl es-Sarabet had only Islamic artifacts—way too late. The list narrowed to seven when only four of the other small sites showed any sherding evidence of Bronze Age pottery.

More books, more reports, more copying. At the end of the tiring, exhilarating day, two things were clear. Only two of the remaining candidate sites were the large and imposing ruins one would expect from a site that was once a fortified Middle Bronze Age city such as Sodom. One, Tall Nimrin, had been excavated to a significant degree and looked promising. It had "monumental Middle Bronze walls," according to a 1989 excavation report. Even more intriguing, its Middle Bronze Age occupation ended suddenly, and it was evidently abandoned for at least five hundred years thereafter. The excavators could find no Late Bronze pottery because the site, like Rip Van Winkle, had slept right through that period with no one occupying it.

Dr. C could hardly contain his excitement. Could this great ruin be Sodom?

According to Khouri's book, the other large tall, Tall el-Hammam, hadn't been excavated, but a survey team in 1975–76 had found some Middle Bronze Age pottery. Not much, and on the surface, but there. Later, in 1990, while excavating nearby at Tall Iktanu, archaeologist Kay Prag did a small excavation on far western Tall el-Hammam and also confirmed the presence of Middle Bronze Age pottery at the site. But the site had remained untouched from that time on.

"Let's do this right," Dr. C said to his friends over dinner that night. "Let's go to each of the fourteen sites. Let's walk around and photograph each one and look at the pottery firsthand."

(Khouri's little book had acted as a portal to imminent discovery. What so many scholarly sources had virtually ignored, Khouri had summarized with care and skill. A few years later, Rami Khouri would visit Dr. C at the Mövenpick Dead Sea Hotel headquarters of the Tall el-Hammam Excavation Project, and the two of them would discuss theories of Sodom's location and the remarkable finds emerging from the earth on the eastern Kikkar. And Dr. C would express his appreciation to the *Beirut Star* journalist for his part in helping solve an ancient mystery.)

The next day they traveled on the Dead Sea highway, plunging into the depths of the Jordan Rift Valley. As soon as they could see the Kikkar through the morning haze, Dr. C pointed to the reason why ancient people called it a "disk," and why it was known for its fertility. Everything in its circle was green: fruit trees, rows and rows of vegetables, fields of spiky grains.

By the end of the day they'd photographed and sherded five of the candidate sites. Only one stayed on the "short list" of qualified sites: Tall el-Azeimeh had plenty of Bronze Age and Iron Age pottery.

"Not much curb appeal, though," observed Danette. The assessment of the ever-practical woman was true: the low-profile mound was not impressive. Whatever strategic heights and glory it may have had, none remained; it was more sprawling mess than menace.

"Not much to be afraid of there, I suppose," Charity added. "Can you imagine threatening someone with that?" The group stood considering this, then broke out in laughter that lasted all the way back to their hotel.

Though they'd visit the remainder of the sites the next day, none made the impression on them that Tall el-Hammam did. On Highway 40 angling northwest, the rays of the morning sun lit something that stood out in the distance. It was surrounded, here and there, by megalithic stone dolmens.

I love this place, Dr. C said to himself. *These dolmens are like old friends to me.*

But the others weren't looking at the smaller stone structures. They were looking at the enormous mound they were approaching (see Hammam Vicinity Map).

"Wow," Charity breathed.

"It looks like a massive ship, riding on a sea of fields," Dr. C said. It was one of the largest talls any of them had ever seen in the Jordan Valley, the height of a nine-story building, with steep, rock-strewn slopes that looked sculpted against the eroded mountains behind it.

"It's way bigger than Khouri described it," Danette said. "But look at the shape of it—no doubt about it, it's got Middle Bronze characteristics."

Dr. C had to keep himself from running up the steep slope. Although they were walking over a late Iron Age settlement on the brow of the mound, there were indications of Bronze Age ceramics all around—Early, Intermediate, Middle. And though no one had actually excavated here, the gaping trenches, two to three meters deep and running the entire east-west length of the tall, exposed some of its more ancient secrets.

"Where did these trenches come from?" Travis asked.

"Oh, the Ottomans and the Jordanians used this place for tank installations, I think," Dr. C said absently, picking up a promising potsherd and turning it to see a broken edge.

"Well of course they did," said Danette, shielding her eyes and looking across the Jordan Valley. "Nobody could sneak up on you. You can see all the way to Jerusalem from here."

Travis stood scratching his chin. "Isn't it ironic that everybody wanted this strategic advantage, to be on top of this place?" he said. "It'll be interesting to see when it was occupied."

Dr. C was already down the slope, picking up sherd after sherd and tossing them aside. He looked like a crazed fruit inspector who couldn't be pleased. No matter what he picked up and looked at, he tossed over his shoulder. Jumping into one of the trenches, he began picking up exposed sherds from the trench floor and examining them closely and then laying them back down. He was grinning from ear to ear.

"You know what that means," said Danette. "He's seeing here what he saw at Tall Nimrin."

"You mean he's *not* seeing what he *didn't* see at Tall Nimrim," Charity laughed. "There must be no Late Bronze pottery here, either, which means it was abandoned for centuries, too."

From that moment on, Dr. C began to suspect that what had begun with a mystery in a hotel room would be uncovered here in the open air of Tall el-Hammam.

There would be more visits to the other talls of the Kikkar. More discoveries of the doublets of cities. The chase was on. Could they be the famous Sodom and her daughter-city Gomorrah, and Admah and her nearby Zeboiim?

As their time on the Kikkar of the Jordan, the land watered like the land of Egypt and like the garden of Yahweh, came to a close, three of the members of the survey team slowly made their way back to the minivan.

Dr. C remained behind for one last look.

The summit of Tall el-Hammam was still, cool, quiet. Surrounded by heaps of stones that once were her city walls and palaces, he squatted down and picked up a handful of soil, the decomposed mudbricks of a ruined, doomed city.

The tall had already given whispers of information through her sherds of pottery. But would she ever be given the opportunity to articulate her long-buried secrets?

As he let the reddish-brown dirt slip through his fingers, Dr. C spoke aloud as if to Tall el-Hammam herself. "Maybe someday you'll tell us what you know."

He walked slowly down the eastern slope, wondering at the mysteries and histories beneath his feet.

Just before he reached the bus, he turned again. "I'll be back."

FIVE

Right Place:
Centuries of Seeking Sodom

PERHAPS THERE'S NO MORE CHILLING ACCOUNT OF THE LIFE and death of a city in all of literature than the story of the destruction of Sodom.

It has drama: a divine back-and-forth bargaining for its fate.

It has vivid description: fire from heaven, furnace-like smoke rising above lifeless ruins.

It has pathos: yearning for possessions, the wistful turning back that leads to death.

It has tragedy: abandonment and curse, with a sense of near-irredeemable loss.

The story carries weight with our souls because we perceive it isn't just a story from the past—it's the whiff of hell itself in our nostrils.

Such an unforgettable story brands people's minds. We have an understandable desire to know more, and for more than 150 years of modern time people have speculated on where these events took place.

If you look at almost any recent map of the Holy Land, two things about Sodom and Gomorrah are evident. First, if they appear on the map at all, they have a question mark after the names. Second, they're always located near the south end of the Dead Sea.

This southern location derives its support almost exclusively from the

writings of the influential early-twentieth-century scholars W. F. Albright and G. E. Wright, who advanced the idea that the two large cities
and smaller Zoar (also mentioned in the biblical account of the destruction) were located somewhere toward the southern end of the Dead Sea,
possibly along the eastern shore or even underwater. For that reason, the
cities had never been found, such thinkers speculated.

This theory had a snowball effect, and with this absence of proof,
from that point on, scholars and laypersons alike just assumed they were
correct. (In fact, based on these theories, a Russian exploration group
using submarine photographic technologies has spent considerable time
and money in recent years trying unsuccessfully to locate the cities on the
floor of the Dead Sea.)

Other people with far fewer archaeological credentials—and much
more active imaginations—went on to formulate theories about the "lost
cities," producing wacky books and videos that show perfectly natural
white marl formations near the Dead Sea in which they "see" the walls of
buildings, point out balls of brimstone, and speculate over anthropomor-
phic "salt pillars" like Lot's wife to the south and west of the great body of
water.

Even conservative and respected Bible dictionaries and atlases usually
locate Sodom and Gomorrah in the barren southern wastelands. To most,
the perceived one-to-one correspondence between the geologic formations there and the account in Genesis 19 seems a no-brainer. They see
the presence of minuscule bits of bitumen and asphalt there and think
that because in battle some of Sodom's soldiers slid into slime pits near
the Dead Sea, the city must have been located there. They see a mountain on the south side of the Dead Sea, traditionally called in Hebrew
"Mount Sodom," which is made entirely of halite or rock salt, and say it
exemplifies what happens when something is turned into salt, as was Lot's
wife.

There's a huge problem with thinking like this. Consider the irony:
most "higher critical" archaeologists and those who are agnostics or athe-
ists don't believe that the Bible's account of Sodom is history. They think

the stories of Sodom and Gomorrah were etiological, that is, either written long, long after the fact by someone who wanted to teach a moral lesson (enshrined, supposedly, in the mists of distant mythic history), or written by someone who saw the desolation and strange geographical features south of the Dead Sea and wanted to offer a colorful explanation of how they came to be.

But people who look only at geological features to ascertain the location of a site for an event, and ignore the geographical details in the only ancient document that describes the event, become etiological legend-spinners themselves.

That's right: the only ancient account of Sodom is in the Bible (others, based on the Bible, appear only hundreds of years later). So why would you want to try to find the site of Sodom if you won't take the only ancient written witness for it and its geography seriously?

Actually, there are at least five theories about the location of Sodom and the Cities of the Kikkar:

1. At or near the southern end of the Dead Sea

2. At or near the northern end of the Dead Sea

3. Underneath the waters of the Dead Sea, whether north or south

4. In the realm of myth or fiction

5. In an undiscoverable place because they were completely obliterated

Sodom and the Cities of the Plain— South of the Dead Sea

THE FIRST AND MOST POPULAR version, the *southern Sodom theory*, identifies a string of ancient sites in the vicinity of the southeast shore of the Dead Sea as the Cities of the Plain as detailed in Genesis. The two main excavated archaeological sites are named Bab edh-Dhra and Numeira, and they're located in the area east of the Lisan Peninsula (the land bridge that in modern history has come to separate the shrinking Dead Sea into two bodies of water).

Bab edh-Dhra is most often tagged as Sodom, and just to the south lies Numeira, a candidate for Gomorrah; a handful of ruins lie farther south. Because of rumored—as of yet undiscovered—asphalt and petroleum deposits in the area, some people believe this is the site of the Sodom story. But the ruins are small, unlikely candidates for the reputation of the cities described in Genesis. In addition, the pottery found in the excavations shows that they were destroyed centuries before the Abrahamic period (Middle Bronze Age). And as for the tar-bitumen-asphalt "connection," it's simply a geographical non sequitur picked up from a faulty reading of Genesis 14:10.

Practically all scholars place the patriarchal period—Abraham, Isaac, Jacob, and Joseph—between 2000 and 1500 BCE, the Middle Bronze Age. This is supported both by the biblical chronology itself and by cultural and linguistic details in the biblical text that are consistent with that time period.

For any sites proposed as the Cities of the Plain, their time of destruction must date to the Middle Bronze. However, Middle Bronze Age cities, those from the time of Abraham, do not exist in the Dead Sea valley south of the Jordan River's emptying into the Dead Sea. None.

And of course, the descriptions of what Lot and Abraham saw from Canaan's central highlands, overlooking the Kikkar of the Jordan, don't fit at all. When Lot "lifted up his eyes" to witness the "whole disk of the Jordan," he was standing in the vicinity of Bethel and Ai. Look on a map. Better, go there and stand on the edge of the plateau near Bethel and Ai, above Jericho, overlooking the southern Jordan Valley.

What can you see? Exactly what Lot saw when he looked eastward from that vantage point—the *entire* Kikkar of the Jordan north of the Dead Sea (Genesis 13:10). You *can* see the northern tip of the Dead Sea from there, but you *can't* see farther south, and certainly not the area of the Lisan land bridge or anything remotely close to it. Lot settled in the area he spied from the heights of Bethel and Ai—the eastern Jordan Disk (see Map 4).

Sodom cannot be south, because while the Jordan Disk is fully visible from the area of Bethel and Ai, the middle and southern parts of the Dead Sea aren't visible. Furthermore, the Bible provides many more geographical markers as to the location of Sodom, as we will see. But one place that the biblical Sodom can't be is south of the Dead Sea.

(Note: A few scholars entertain a combination view—Sodom and Gomorrah in the southern Dead Sea area; Admah and Zeboiim north of the Dead Sea. However, the biblical text seems to indicate that all these cities were in closer proximity to one another.)

Sodom and the Cities of the Plain— North of the Dead Sea

THE *NORTHERN SODOM THEORY* WAS actually the well-studied opinion of many important explorer-scholars of the nineteenth century, most of whom spent vast amounts of time and energy meticulously studying and mapping the geography of the Holy Land. In the case of Sodom and the Cities of the Plain, these explorer-scholars followed the abundant geographical clues in the biblical text, primarily Genesis 13:1–12. Some of them recognized that particular passage of scripture as definitive for the location of Sodom, and followed it to an area northeast of the Dead Sea, on the alluvial plain of the southern Jordan Valley, where they observed a large number of ancient ruins, one of which is Tall el-Hammam. Here are the observations of one such explorer, W. M. Thomson, in his 1882 book *The Land and the Book: Southern Palestine and Jerusalem.* Thomson concluded, after riding all over the area on horseback, that the northern location of Sodom was the only one that the geography itself would allow:

> It appears to be certain, from Genesis 13:1–13, that at the time of the separation between Abraham and Lot they were at or near Bethel, some twelve or fifteen miles north of Jerusalem, and sixty or seventy miles from the south end of the Dead Sea. Lot, therefore, without a miracle, could not have seen that region at all, however high he "lifted up his eyes." The distance is too great, there is a haze over the sea which obscures the view, and, finally, high mountains on the western shore entirely intercept the prospect. And, furthermore, it's evident that the region at the south end of the sea can't be called the "plain of the Jordan" in any admissible sense; that plain stops at the north end. Moreover, Lot, when he separated from Abraham, is said to have "journeyed east"; whereas he must have gone to the south, if Sodom was at that end of the sea.

The northern Sodom theory became less popular during the twentieth century because of Albright and Wright, but a few scholars continued to argue in its favor, based on a face-value reading of the Hebrew text of Genesis 13. Because much of the southern Jordan Valley was off-limits due to military presence from the 1960s through the late 1990s, the abundant archaeological sites in the area remained virtually unknown, as most of them were unavailable for exploration and excavation. However, since 2001, news of evidence of the existence of a thriving Bronze Age civilization in this area has once again brought the northern Sodom theory into prominence.

Sodom and the Cities of the Plain—Under the Dead Sea

THE *"UNDERWATER" THEORY HAS* A long history but is the least
scientific of the views on Sodom's location, because there is no proof to
support it. Muslims believe that Sodom and Gomorrah lie beneath the
Sea of Lut (Lot), as they call the Dead Sea. The underwater theory was
resurrected for Westerners in modern times by W. F. Albright. He acknowledged that the traditional southern sites—Bab edh-Dhra and Numeira and their neighbors—were lying in ruins hundreds of years before
the time of Abram and Lot and thus they could not possibly have been the
biblical Cities of the Plain.

However, even though Albright acknowledged that there were no
sites in the southern Dead Sea area that could possibly date to the time
of Abraham (Middle Bronze 2, ca. 1800–1550 BCE), he clung stubbornly
to the idea of a southern location and concluded that since he couldn't
find them, the ruins of Sodom and the Cities of the Plain must be under
the shallow waters of the Dead Sea's southern basin, south of the Lisan.
That area, he hypothesized, must have once been a fertile plain that,
after the destruction of its cities, sank in an earthquake and was covered
by the waters of the Salt Sea. With this theory he joined a long line
of both scholars and crackpots from medieval times to the present
who postulated a similar scenario for the deep northern basin of the
Dead Sea.

Sodom and the Cities of the Plain—Mythic Only

A NUMBER OF SCHOLARS BELIEVE that Sodom and the Cities of the
Plain *never existed at all,* but rather represent a moralistic metaphor invented by people centuries after the temporal setting for the story. For
them, identifying the physical location of Sodom and Gomorrah is an ex-

ercise in futility and any discussions about Sodom are no more than literary criticism of a legend.

However, if the Sodom narrative identifies a location for the Cities of the Kikkar that was, in fact, populated by the ruins of significant Bronze Age cities dating to the time of Abraham, you can't ignore the one-to-one correspondence between text and ground. And then if the ground reveals that a violent conflagration destroyed those cities and towns during the very time of the biblical patriarchs—this is far beyond coincidence.

Sodom and the Cities of the Plain— Destroyed Beyond Recovery

FINALLY, THE BIBLE'S DESCRIPTIONS OF the catastrophe that befell Sodom and the other Cities of the Plain allow for the possibility that they *can never be found* because all traces of them were destroyed in the conflagration or disintegrated in the Dead Sea. However, if ideal candidates do exist that fit all the biblical story's criteria, then an argument from the absence of evidence can't be sustained.

Use of the Bible in Identifying Sites

ALTHOUGH THE HOLY LAND HAS industries and charms other than tourism and archaeology (two things that bring many people to it), nonetheless most people come to it from foreign countries because of the history they read in their scriptures. But if the Bible did not exist, hardly anyone would give a mudbrick for the archaeology of either Israel or Jordan.

On the other hand, there isn't one single Levantine (Holy Land) archaeologist—even among those considered to be biblical minimalists—

who doesn't use the Bible at least periodically when doing archaeology. And in between those two extremes lies the discipline of Levantine archaeology, which, since its inception more than a hundred years ago, has consistently used the Bible as an important historical point of reference.

For example, if the Bible says that City Y lies between Cities X and Z, then that is certainly where City Y existed at one time. Proof of this: many archaeological sites in both Israel and Jordan retain their biblical names, and most were located and identified from geographical indicators found in the Bible (see maps and charts in Appendix C).

There is a proper relationship between ancient texts—the Bible being an ascendant example—and archaeology. This relationship is necessarily a two-way street: the text must be allowed to speak to the ground and the ground must be allowed to speak to the text. There must be a holistic, inclusive, interdisciplinary dialogue between the two.

Beyond this, one must be open to the possibility that a given text may supply clues toward the historical interpretation of certain archaeological findings. This is particularly true when doing geography at the level of site identification. I think there is a right way and a wrong way to do this. The wrong way includes blowing off a text because it's perceived to be inherently religious in nature.

It is no secret that many scholars have an aversion to using what they consider to be "religious" texts when doing archaeology. But this "anti-textual" position is illogical: *every* ancient Near Eastern text—whether Egyptian, Sumerian, Babylonian, Hittite, Canaanite, Assyrian, Israelite, Greek, Roman, Byzantine, or Islamic—carries within it a religious perspective and agenda foundational to that particular culture.

Thus, to disqualify a text simply because of its "religious" character is the epistemological equivalent of shooting oneself in the foot before a marathon.

Imagine turning a blind eye to the geographical details embedded in the Battle of Megiddo account of Tuthmosis III just because he converses with his god, Amun-Re, and recounts his superhuman prowess as a warrior in his defeat of the Canaanite kings arrayed against him. But this is precisely what scholars do when they reject the ancient biblical texts as a viable component of Levantine archaeology.

Does this mean that all ancient documents and their details should be accepted wholesale and without question? Of course not. Such records call on the investigator to be responsible when considering both historical and geographical information gleaned from ancient texts. But there is a legitimate way to use texts, including the Bible, when considering geographical matters. While ancient Near Eastern writers probably wrote fictions, they never invented fictitious geographies for their stories.

Indeed, in writing the history of the ancient Near East, all ancient texts must be "mined" for their historical and geographical information, with the oldest texts—those in closest chronological proximity to the historical period in question—receiving methodological priority.

In the case of the Sodom account, the Bible's version is the oldest, best, and only ancient text. And even if you take out everything that could possibly be supernatural, you still have a rock-solid account with multiple geographical markers in it.

It is illogical to presume that our twenty-first-century viewpoint and ability to construct "histories" from the mute artifacts of ancient Canaan is superior to utilizing the narrative literature of the Bible—some of whose writers identify themselves as eyewitnesses—to obtain our historical bearings. As we'll see when the evidence is presented, the relatively brief Genesis account provides numerous geographical indicators, clear chronological indicators, several architectural indicators, and multiple destruction indicators that point to Tall el-Hammam as biblical Sodom.

Could such historical specificity possibly be attributed to a cadre of late Iron Age Judahite fiction writers who lived more than a millennium after the described destruction of the Cities of the Kikkar? Could their very narrow Jewish cultural framework have provided the geography and other details if this were only a later etiological myth?

We must also question the controverted logic of suggesting that the depiction of Sodom and Gomorrah that runs throughout the Hebrew Scriptures beyond Genesis—in Deuteronomy, Isaiah, Jeremiah, Lamentations, Ezekiel, Amos, and Zephaniah—was created about the same time as, or perhaps before, its appearance among the Genesis narratives. Of course, that's ridiculous. Only the prior existence of a powerful historical memory with its searing image of debauchery and destruction could have developed over time into such a powerful representational phenomenon.

So, regardless of the critics' opinions about the historical accuracy of the biblical narratives, the Bible remains the best and most comprehensive source for the history and geography of what we call the "Bible lands." It is the biblical geography that provides the framework by which such site identifications become possible and, in some cases, even simple.

Thus, if the Bible provides enough data about the location of Sodom and Gomorrah, we may be able to "triangulate" their geographical whereabouts. There's a surprising abundance of specific geographical/topographical information embedded in the stories about Sodom and Gomorrah that allows us to identify their general location within a defined target area.

We can answer the question: is there dirt that corresponds with the document?

Right Place: Using the Bible's Geographic Markers to Identify Sodom

THE FOLLOWING GEOGRAPHICAL DATA POINTS (words and phrases) are drawn from biblical passages dealing with Sodom and Gomorrah and the Cities of the Plain, in their textual order. Most citations are from the book of Genesis; those from other books are specified. Genesis provides the primary geography, deliberately guiding readers to the infamous cities step by step—chapter 13 in particular. For maximum understanding, read the relevant passages in context before going on to this list.

"Sodom and Gomorrah" (10:19ff)

THOUGH SODOM ALONE IS OFTEN described, when these two cities are paired Sodom is always listed first. From this, we can make some assumptions. Listing Sodom first probably indicates it was the larger of the two. In addition, the Sodom-Gomorrah pair is always listed first in the descriptions of the Cities of the Plain, so these two were probably the most prominent of them. We don't know from the text their exact geographical alignment but can assume they were neighbors.

In the ancient Levant, particularly in this area, large cities generally did not exist in proximity to each other because a single city needed all the arable land and water resources around it to support its sizable population. However, it was not uncommon for larger cities to have one or more "daughter" communities in the immediate vicinity.

Note, however, that the Bible does not identify Sodom and Gomorrah (by these names) as occupied sites or geographical markers after their destruction in Genesis 19.

"Admah and Zeboiim" (10:19ff)

LIKE SODOM AND GOMORRAH, ADMAH and Zeboiim are always listed together. Admah probably was the larger of the two with Zeboiim as a daughter community. Since *Zeboiim* is a plural word (an *im* ending in Hebrew is almost always plural, like an *s* at the end of an English word), it could even refer to two or more towns or villages.

Like Sodom and Gomorrah, Admah and Zeboiim are never mentioned again by these names as occupied sites or geographical markers beyond their implied destruction in Genesis 19.

"Bethel and Ai" (13:3)

BETHEL WAS LOCATED IN THE central highlands of Canaan, approximately sixteen to twenty kilometers north of Jerusalem. Possible locations include the modern sites of Beitin, or El Bira.

Ai (Genesis 12:8) was a large ruin (Hebrew *ha'ay* means "the ruin"), about four kilometers east of Bethel, the site of et-Tell in modern Deir Dibwan.

The story of the separation of Abram and Lot recorded in Genesis 13, which took place in the vicinity of Bethel and Ai, is quite clear about what Lot could see from his vantage point somewhere in that area:

> Lot looked up and saw that the whole plain of the Jordan was well watered, like the garden of the LORD, like the land of Egypt, toward Zoar. (This was before the LORD destroyed Sodom and Gomorrah.) So Lot chose for himself the whole plain of the Jordan and set out toward the east. The two men parted company: Abram lived in the land of Canaan, while Lot lived among the cities of the plain and pitched his tents near Sodom. (Genesis 13:10–12)

I will discuss the relevant words and phrases of this passage subsequently, but at this point I should note that I excavated in the area of Bethel and Ai for six seasons, and several of my colleagues and I have hiked all over the territory in question. I am intimately familiar with what can and can't be seen from practically every vantage point between Ai and the edge of the Jordan Valley to the east. The southern Jordan Valley north of the Dead Sea and the foothills on the eastern edge of the Jordan Valley are easily visible from that area. On a clear day, you can even see a portion of the northern end of the Dead Sea itself (see Map 4).

But under no circumstances can you see with the naked eye beyond that point to the middle (Lisan) regions or the southern end of the Dead

Sea. The vantage point of the area of Bethel and Ai is a bit of evidence that should not be passed over lightly.

"Altar" (13:4)

GENESIS 12:8 SAYS ABRAM "PITCHED his tent with Bethel on the west and Ai on the east. There he built an altar to Yahweh and called on the name of Yahweh" when he first arrived in Canaan. This confirms that Abram and Lot's location, from which the "well watered" "plain of the Jordan" was visible, was indeed the area of Bethel and Ai.

"Whole Plain of the Jordan" (13:10)

THE HEBREW WORD FOR "WHOLE" or "all" is *kol,* used here to indicate the totality of what Abram and Lot saw. If the plain of the Jordan referred to the entire rift valley from the Sea of Galilee to the Dead Sea, as some have suggested, then it must be explained how Lot could have seen enough of the "plain" to warrant the use of *kol.* Thus it only makes sense that the "plain" referred to is mostly, if not entirely, visible from the foothills east of Ai.

"Plain" (13:10)

EVERY TIME THE WORD *plain* is associated with Sodom and Gomorrah, it's translated from the Hebrew word *kikkar.* However, *kikkar's* basic meaning has nothing at all to do with geography but rather shape. In fact, of the sixty-eight times that the term is used in the Hebrew Scriptures, it's applied within a geographical context in only thirteen instances. Of those thirteen, seven of them are found in Genesis in relationship to Sodom and Gomorrah, where it's translated "plain."

Word usages tend to change over time, and we can see that *kikkar* seems to pick up geographic attributes from the Bronze Age through the Iron Age. Of the seven instances of *kikkar* that appear in a Bronze Age context (Genesis 13:10–12, 19:17, 25, 28–29), all of them refer specifically to the circular plain at the south end of the Jordan Valley and associated with Sodom and Gomorrah. The single occurrence of *kikkar* within the time frame of the Late Bronze Age (Deuteronomy 34:3) refers to "the plain (*kikkar*) of the valley of Jericho," which is simply the Cisjordan extension of the same circular plain found in the Genesis passages just cited.

The three uses of the word *kikkar* in an Iron Age setting (2 Samuel 18:23; 1 Kings 7:46; 2 Chronicles 4:17) all refer to a section of the Jordan Valley near the Jabbok confluence immediately north of, and contiguous with, the circular plain of the earlier (Bronze Age) passages (see Map 6).

From the Persian Period, there are two instances of *kikkar* (Nehemiah 3:22, 12:28) with reference to the place of origin of men involved in rebuilding Jerusalem's city walls. While in each case the meaning could be construed as "surrounding region," the meaning of *kikkar* as the larger area encircling a locale (in this case, Jerusalem) still preserves the idea of a circular geographical referent. However, Nehemiah's use of *kikkar* could still be taken as a reference to men whose home villages were located in the vicinity of Jericho in the southern Jordan Valley to the east of Jerusalem.

These are all of the geographical uses of *kikkar* in the Old Testament. And it's abundantly clear that every time it's used in a Bronze Age context the meaning is specific to the circular plain of the southern Jordan Valley at the north end of the Dead Sea, upon which were built the cities of Jericho in the western Kikkar and those targeted for destruction in the eastern Kikkar: Sodom and Gomorrah, Admah, and Zeboiim (see Map 3).

In fact, trying to consider the Kikkar without Sodom and the other cities mentioned is like trying to study France without Paris.

The remaining usages of *kikkar* reveal the real sense of the term: at least forty-five times it's used to designate a "talent" of silver, gold, iron, or lead; seven times it's translated "loaf" as in "loaf of bread." The root meaning of *kikkar* is "disk" or a "circular, flat disk." A talent of silver or any other metal was a flat disk or ring of metal used as a medium of exchange. Likewise, loaves of bread in antiquity were usually flat and disk-shaped. The modern Arabic cognate of this word carries the idea of a circle. Even the modern Hebrew term for a traffic "roundabout" in Jerusalem is *kikkar*.

Therefore, when the Hebrew Bible uses the phrases "plain of the Jordan" and "the cities of the plain," there is no doubt that the very use of the word *kikkar* denotes a (relatively) flat, circular, disk-shaped region.

If the nature of the area being described were something other than a "circular plain," another word would have been selected. There are several other common Hebrew words for valley, vale, or region. Scholars who translate *kikkar* as "valley" or merely "region" have completely missed the point of the word. It's quite clear that when we search for a geographical area upon which the Cities of the Plain existed, we're looking for a region that's visibly circular and disklike.

A topographical map of the southern Jordan Valley north of the Dead Sea reveals the circular nature of the area, but the real sense of the disklike, circular plain is very impressive when you actually descend from the foothills onto the plain (*kikkar*) from the east. The kikkar sweeps around to the south and west toward the Dead Sea and around toward the north and west toward Jericho across the Jordan River.

Bear in mind that the writers of Old Testament books probably didn't have maps and would have described geographical features as they appeared when viewed from a mountain, for instance, with the element of foreshortening and the obstruction of view that things such as other mountains would have created.

"Jordan" (13:10)

THE "PLAIN" (*kikkar*) WE'VE BEEN discussing is the Kikkar of the Jordan (Heb. *hayarden*). The term *hayarden* itself means "the descent."

That this descent of fresh, living water terminates at the mouth of *ha-yarden* at the north end of the Dead Sea is clearly spelled out in passages laying out its geographical limits—Numbers 34:12; Deuteronomy 3:17, 27, 4:47–49; Joshua 15:5, 18:19 (see Map 5). At that point *hayarden* dies. Thus the plain or kikkar of the Jordan could never have included the Dead Sea valley. Furthermore, the writer of Genesis has a distinct term for the Dead Sea area itself: "the Valley of Siddim (the Salt Sea)" (Genesis 14:3). The Hebrew word for "valley" (*'emeq*) in "Valley of Siddim" is a different idea altogether, the root of which means "deep." Observably, the Dead Sea lies at the bottom of a deep valley, so the term is a perfect description of the fact.

But the term *kikkar* has nothing at all to do with elevation or valleyness and, in its relationship to Sodom and Gomorrah, refers only to an area specifically associated with the Jordan River that ends at the northern end of the Dead Sea.

"Well Watered" (13:10)

THE HEBREW WORD FOR "WELL watered" is *mashqeh*. We see its sense in its other usages as "cupbearer" and "drink." The Kikkar of the Jordan was watered by the flooding of the Jordan River, by the runoff from major wadis that brought water from both the Cisjordan and Transjordan highlands, and by numerous perennial springs.

"Like the Garden of the LORD" (literally, "the garden of the Yahweh") (13:10)

THE GARDEN OF EDEN, TO which this refers, was well watered (see Genesis 2:10ff) by a river—seemingly spring-fed—that subsequently separated into multiple channels. There are numerous springs in the Kikkar area flowing down from the surrounding hills and wadis. Then there are the abundant waters of the Jordan itself, plus several perennial streams coming from the east. All this makes the comparison to Eden natural and unmistakable.

"Like the Land of Egypt" (13:10)

HERE THE WELL-WATERED KIKKAR IS compared to (lower) Egypt and the Nile River, which flows northward, dividing into a series of channels in the Nile Delta as it empties into the Mediterranean Sea.

The parallels are striking. Both the Nile and the Jordan empty into saline waters. And—on a much smaller scale—the Jordan, like the Nile, also has an alluvial "delta" through which it empties into the northern end of the Dead Sea. Additionally, in antiquity both rivers underwent an annual inundation due to rainfall and snowmelt far upstream. It seems that the writer of Genesis was familiar with the lower Nile area and viewed the Jordan as a "Nile in miniature."

"Toward Zoar" (13:10)

THE HEBREW WORD *zo'ar* MEANS "small." Thus Zoar was probably a rather nondescript place, perhaps even just a caravan center on one of the routes to and from Egypt. Although sometimes people list Zoar (also known as Bela) as one of the five Cities of the Plain, the biblical record at no point tells us that there were five such cities unless the tabulation of Zeboiim (a plural noun) counts it as two cities.

Again, after their destruction these four cities are never mentioned again in the Bible as living cities or even as geographical markers. But unlike Sodom and Gomorrah, Admah and Zeboiim, Zoar is found beyond the book of Genesis at least as a geographical marker (Deuteronomy 34:3; Isaiah 15:5; Jeremiah 48:34).

The only thing we know about Zoar is that though it once had a king it was small, it was on the route from Egypt and Sodom, and it was where Lot ran to escape the destruction of Sodom. That isn't enough information to pin down a location, so Zoar can't be used to specifically locate the Kikkar or the cities associated with it other than to say they were north of Zoar.

Some scholars read Deuteronomy 34:1–14 and speculate that Zoar was just north of the Arnon River border in the Transjordan Israelite territory of Reuben. That would mean the (former) Cities of the Plain would have to have been north of the Arnon. This of course would eliminate any thought that Sodom and Gomorrah were south of the Dead Sea, within the borders of Moab and Edom, kingdoms that were off-limits to the Israelites and thus couldn't have been Reuben's inheritance.

"(. . . Before the LORD Destroyed Sodom and Gomorrah)" Literally, "(. . . Before Yahweh Destroyed Sodom and Gomorrah)" (13:10)

WHEREAS THE KIKKAR WAS WELL watered, like the garden of Yahweh, until the time of its destruction, it looked very different afterward and apparently underwent considerable damage that changed its physical character, at least for a significant period of time.

"Whole Plain of the Jordan" (13:11)

OBVIOUSLY, LOT DID NOT CHOOSE the whole Jordan Valley, just the Kikkar section of it just north of the Dead Sea as just described.

"Set Out Toward the East" (13:11)

SINCE ABRAM AND LOT VIEWED the Kikkar while they were near Bethel and Ai—about twelve miles north of Jerusalem, west-northwest of Jericho—when Lot separated from his uncle and traveled "toward the east," he was headed directly into the circular plain of the southern Jordan River—the Kikkar.

"East" (13:11)

FROM BETHEL AND AI, LOT went due east, precisely where the Kikkar of the Jordan is located. Had he gone toward a Sodom and a Gomorrah at the southern end of the Dead Sea, or even in the area of the Lisan Peninsula, Lot's eastward trek would have lasted only until he had crossed the Jordan, when he would have run into the mountains. From that point he would have had to go southeast and then due south. In fact, at least three-fourths of his journey would have been south if he'd headed toward the southern end of the Dead Sea.

The only biblical reference that may use the term "south" in association with Sodom is Ezekiel 16:46; but the passage, which speaks judgment against Jerusalem, uses both "Samaria" and "Sodom" metaphorically and not in a geographic sense. However, the Hebrew words translated "north" and "south" in this Ezekiel passage are rendered "left" and "right" in Genesis 13:9 and need not refer to the cardinal directions at all. The imagery is simply that Jerusalem was, in her evil, buoyed by Samaria and Sodom, her partners in wickedness.

"Abram Lived in the Land of Canaan" (13:12)

HISTORICALLY THE DEFINITION OF "CANAAN" normally didn't include the land east of the Jordan, although Genesis 10:19 says that "the borders of Canaan reached . . . toward Sodom." Abram lived in the highlands of Canaan west of the river. Thus, the distinction between where Abram lived, in Canaan proper, and where Lot chose to live, in Sodom beyond the Jordan, shows that the two men lived on opposite sides of the river.

"Lot Lived Among the Cities of the Plain" (13:12)

EVEN THOUGH THE CIRCLE OF the Kikkar extended to both sides of the Jordan, Lot chose not to live on the Canaan side with Abram, but on the Transjordan side, where the cities of his interest—particularly Sodom and Gomorrah, Admah and Zeboiim—were located. Since Lot was a chieftain among nomadic herdsmen and caravanning itinerants, it was a strategic location.

"Cities of the Plain" (13:12)

THE FOUR CITIES OF SODOM and Gomorrah, Admah and Zeboiim were located on the Kikkar. The location of an ancient city was dependent on three primary factors: water resources, arable land, and proximity to trade routes. The Kikkar area met all of these criteria, along with the strategic advantages that at least the larger cities would have coveted: height and defensive structures.

Again, such large cities dominated local resources. The plain that is clearly the Kikkar of the Jordan River was capable of supporting only a very limited number of medium-to-large walled towns (cities, Heb. *'irim*; sing., *'ir*). There is only one city of this size on the Cisjordan side of the Kikkar: Jericho.

The comparatively larger and agriculturally friendly Transjordan side of the Kikkar could accommodate two such sites with a few daughter communities, but no more. The fact that the Bible lists only four *'irim* on the plain—with only two, Sodom and Admah, as the likely larger, principal cities—is a good indication of the organic, historical link between the actual Kikkar region and the story of Sodom and Gomorrah. Two prominent cities, each with one main daughter town in tow, perfectly match the resource capabilities of the Kikkar area east of the Jordan in the time of Abraham.

"Pitched His Tents Near Sodom" (or "Pitched His Tents as Far as Sodom") (13:12)

BECAUSE OF THE FREQUENT FLOODING of the Jordan River, there were no towns along its banks. But nomadic shepherds and others camped in tents nearby when the soil was dry, after the spring flooding. Lot's tents would have been among these.

Sodom, a relatively large city on a main trade thoroughfare, with abundant water resources and plenty of arable land, probably had a considerable history prior to the time of Abram and Lot. Genesis 10:19 speaks of the existence of Sodom and Gomorrah, Admah and Zeboiim at an extremely early date.

The phrase "near Sodom" is probably better translated "as far as Sodom," suggesting that Sodom may have been on the extreme eastern edge of the Kikkar, or possibly the easternmost location of the two large Kikkar cities, the other being Admah.

"Mamre Near Hebron" (13:18)

AFTER ABRAM AND LOT PARTED ways, Abram went to the region of Hebron, on the spine of the central highlands south of Jerusalem. From this vantage point, Genesis 19 tells us, he would later view the rising smoke from the destruction of Sodom and the Cities of the Kikkar. (Since Hebron sits west of the midpoint of the Dead Sea, there's no visual advantage for either a northern or a southern location of Sodom.)

"Looked Down Toward Sodom" (18:16)

LATER, AFTER THE DESTRUCTION OF Sodom, Abraham would again have been near Hebron and able to look down toward Sodom in the Kikkar.

"A Town Near Enough to Run To" (19:20)

THE LOCATION OF ZOAR IS uncertain, especially since its size might have indicated a settlement or a caravan village, and south of the Kikkar near the Arnon River (Deuteronomy 34:1–4).

"Small" (Zoar) (19:20)

SEE ABOVE WHERE THIS APPEARS in Genesis 13:10.

"The Entire Plain" (19:25)

IT IS REASONABLE TO THINK that only the part of the plain associated with the targeted cities was destroyed, that is, the portion of the Kikkar lying to the east of the Jordan.

Likely there was collateral damage in areas surrounding the primary destruction targets. For example, Jericho was the prominent city on the Kikkar west of the Jordan, and archaeological evidence shows it was certainly occupied throughout this patriarchal period. Therefore, it may have suffered from the peripheral effects of the calamity.

"The Vegetation in the Land" (19:25)

THIS UNDERSCORES THE FACT THAT the Kikkar was full of vegetation before its destruction, and devoid of vegetation immediately afterward. This isn't to say that over time, the effects of this localized ecological disaster did not lessen or even reverse, though it must have taken decades or perhaps even centuries to recover enough to support cities and towns.

"The Land of the Kikkar" (19:28)

THIS IS, NO DOUBT, A reference to the ethnocultural identity of the civilization on the Kikkar, similar to "land of Egypt," "land of the Philistines," "land of Canaan," and "land of Israel."

A Summary of Geographical Indicators from the Text

IN A NUTSHELL, THESE ARE the geographical facts derived from the relevant biblical passages (see maps and charts in Appendix C):

1. There were probably two prominent cities on the plain (*kikkar*), Sodom and Admah. Each of these cities controlled a nearby smaller city or town—Gomorrah and Zeboiim, respectively—that was still significant enough always to be linguistically coupled with its larger neighbor. Thus the text speaks of Sodom and Gomorrah, Admah and Zeboiim. However, the presence of other such smaller daughter villages can't be ruled out.

2. After their decision, Abram remained in the highlands of Canaan on the west side of the Jordan. Lot chose to live on that portion of the Kikkar lying on the east side of the Jordan. Thus, the Cities of the Plain where Lot lived were not in Canaan (Cisjordan), but in the Transjordan area.

3. When someone stood in the vicinity of Bethel and Ai (to the east of Ai), the line of sight to the east primarily included the southern end of the Jordan Valley just north of the Dead Sea. Locations farther north and south were not visible.

4. From the area east of Bethel and Ai, the "whole Kikkar of the Jordan" was visible, not just a small portion of it. This meant that the plain was mostly, if not entirely, visible from the foothills east of Ai overlooking the southern Jordan Valley.

5. In order to reach the Kikkar and its cities, one traveled eastward from Bethel and Ai, not southeastward or southward.

6. The plain upon which the cities were located was a flattish, circular region that visually gave the impression of a large disk, hence the use of the specialized term *kikkar*. The word's

primary meaning was that of a talent (a circular, flat disk of gold, silver, or other metal used as a medium of exchange) or a loaf (a circular, flat, disk-shaped bread commonly baked in antiquity).

7. The circular plain was associated with the Jordan River, not with the Dead Sea. The Kikkar held the mouth of the Jordan, marking the end of "the descent."

8. The Kikkar was well watered, not only by the Jordan, which cut through it and provided an annual inundation (similar to that of the Nile River), but also by subterranean sources (as was Eden, Genesis 2:6).

9. The limited size of the Kikkar and the arable land and water resources of its Transjordan portion made it capable of supporting two large cities and several smaller daughter towns or villages. Sodom and Gomorrah, Admah and Zeboiim held the bulk of the circular plain's population.

10. The Cities of the Kikkar existed on a main trade thoroughfare (probably both north-south and east-west). This strategic crossroads position fostered the cities' early development, strength, and longevity—until, of course, they were destroyed.

11. Because the entire "Land of the Kikkar" was destroyed, other cities on or around the Kikkar may have suffered collateral damage or even destruction, but perhaps not to the degree that the four primary targets did.

12. With the destruction of the Kikkar and its cities, the vegetation was also obliterated in an ecological disaster that could have required a considerable period of time (decades or centuries) for recovery.

On the one hand, the geographical data from the biblical text associate the plain (Kikkar) with Sodom and Gomorrah, Admah and Zeboiim.

Therefore, they could not be anywhere south of the circular plain of the southern Jordan Valley just above the Dead Sea. On the other hand, the lowest section of the rift valley, which holds the Dead Sea, is a different and distinct geographical area (the Valley of Siddim), which is never confused in the Hebrew Scriptures with the Kikkar.

When the biblical geography of Sodom and Gomorrah is superimposed upon the physical geography of the actual land itself, it's a perfect match (see Map 8). The Cities of the Kikkar are nowhere near the Lisan Peninsula or the southern end of the Dead Sea.

And, since there are candidates that fit all the biblical criteria for Sodom's geography, including Tall el-Hammam, there isn't any reason to look for them beneath the Dead Sea or anywhere else other than in the Kikkar of the Jordan.

Exactly where the historical record says they should be.

SIX

Right Time:
Finding the Ballpark

THE BIBLE REPEATEDLY PRESENTS ITSELF AS A HISTORICAL record. To that end, it mentions specifics of geography, biography, events, genealogies, and even ties such things to a sense of chronology, the passage of time in recorded history. Unfortunately, though we may in retrospect refer to modern dating and say, for instance, that Jesus was born in the "first century," Bible writers had no such "master calendar." Biblical events are fixed in time by their relationships to other events.

Old Testament prophets such as Isaiah and Ezekiel were concerned enough about chronologies to mention them:

In the year that King Uzziah died, I saw the LORD seated on a throne, high and exalted, and the train of his robe filled the temple. (Isaiah 6:1)

In my thirtieth year, in the fourth month on the fifth day, while I was among the exiles by the Kebar River, the heavens were opened and I saw visions of God. On the fifth of the month—it was the fifth year of the exile of King Jehoiachin—the word of the LORD came to Ezekiel the priest. (Ezekiel 1:1–3)

In the New Testament, Luke tells us of the birth of Jesus by giving the specifics of political rulers at the time: "In those days Caesar Augustus issued a decree that a census should be taken of the entire Roman world. (This was the first census that took place while Quirinius was governor of Syria.)" (Luke 2:1–2).

Assigning our CE and BCE (formerly AD and BC) calendar dates to ancient events is important to some people, particularly historians and archaeologists. To others, they're irrelevant or, at best, annoying. But unraveling all the factors that determine the dates to assign to biblical events as they relate to Tall el-Hammam is a difficult task that exasperates experts. This is the most technical and knotty aspect of trying to ascertain whether Tall el-Hammam is biblical Sodom, and if you aren't into numbers and chronology controversies, it's tempting to want to ignore the issue.

Make no mistake about the importance of chronologies, however: the Bible fixes the events of the life of Abraham and his descendants in time, and expects us to do so as well. But without a master calendar, we must do what the biblical writers do, and use any fixed elements of history, geography, or archaeology at hand to extrapolate chronologies.

Furthermore, if the identification of any archaeological site from a biblical narrative is going to be reasonable, all elements of its chronology—that is, the reality of events in the space-time of the past—must be examined. The whole picture—the components of geography, chronology, archaeology, cultural context, and historical milieu—must be satisfied.

So far we've begun with the biblical narrative of the destruction of a large city-state named Sodom, and followed its insistent geography to the eastern Kikkar, dominated by Tall el-Hammam. At that site, the soil also speaks, and the pottery evidence—remember, pottery style is the primary and sometimes only way to ascertain the dating of an archaeological site in the southern Levant—says that the astonishing terminal stratum at that site has all the markings of a Middle Bronze Age city that underwent a fiery catastrophe.

Looking at Archaeological Age Designations

ARCHAEOLOGICAL AGES AREN'T JUST ARBITRARY names put on time periods. Just as the Chalcolithic Period ended and the Bronze Age began with accompanying unique characteristics, so all archaeological ages identify and categorize the characteristics of cultures, preserved in what they left behind. For instance, among those characteristics, Chalcolithic peoples left behind stone and copper implements, while their descendants in the Bronze Age showed preference for, and left behind, distinctive stone, copper, and bronze artifacts, and showed significant changes in architecture and settlement planning.

As archaeologists have been able to see refinements in their understandings of history through excavations, they've also tweaked the names of archaeological periods. Within the Bronze Age, there's an Early stage, an Intermediate stage, a Middle stage, and a Late stage (each of which refinements can affect theories about when Abraham lived). And within each age (or stage) are further, specific, numbered periods, such as Early Bronze 1, 2, and 3—again, based on artifacts and cultural styles. Each of these can be further divided into phases, such as EB1a, b, or c.

How are dates assigned by archaeologists to the time periods or "ages" they've named? For instance, how would scholars fix the year or century in which the Bronze Age began or ended in the Kikkar? For one thing, archaeologists look for consistencies in cultural artifacts, especially pottery, comparing site with site. In the same way that fashions or styles sweep across the world today, in ancient times "new" technologies—such

Pottery "reading" is an intense process in which each excavated sherd is examined by experts in order to determine the archaeological period to which it belongs. Tall el-Hammam ceramics undergo "triple-blind" analysis with three different "sets of eyes." The first and second reads occur in Jordan during each field season. A third and final read is performed in the United States.

as metal smelting that gave a community military security, and useful and pleasing styles of pottery fabrication—took hold across the Near East as artisans and craftsmen shared their ideas and methods.

In addition, some events or eras can be dated accurately through cross-checking other cultures, through such resources as records of natural events like droughts, floods, comets, and solar eclipses. Other documentary evidence useful for dating can also be found on monuments that commemorate military victories, on king lists, and in correspondence. For instance, the Amarna letters (fourteenth century BCE), which were written between Egypt and rulers throughout the Near East, link the chronologies of several civilizations.

Is Being in the Right Place Enough?

AT THIS POINT IN THE consideration of Tall el-Hammam, non-archaeologists might look at the geographical evidence and be willing to acknowledge the possibility—perhaps even the probability—that it's the site of biblical Sodom.

Right place.

But some archaeologists and Bible students may dispute this identification, not because of geography, but because of what they see as a problem matching the archaeological time period of Tall el-Hammam's destruction with an assumed time period for Abraham.

On the one hand, almost everyone would agree on when Tall el-Hammam's great catastrophe occurred. Regardless of nationality or religious belief (or lack thereof), archaeologists agree that Tall el-Hammam has a major destruction layer dating to the second half of the Middle Bronze Age (MB2), because of the site's pottery, architecture, and other artifacts that are characteristic of that period.

On the other hand, there are those for whom biblical Sodom's chronology isn't an issue. Those who consider the story of Abraham,

Lot, and Sodom to be an etiological legend wouldn't need to quibble over dates. Whether the Bible's timetables—as measured by life spans and other numbers in the text—match up with MB2 or not doesn't matter to them, because they don't believe the story is real history in the first place.

But for people who consider the Bible to be accurate in its portrayal of historical events, it matters very much.

Here's an assertion that may be controversial, but I'm committed to it—and for what I think are very good reasons: *Geography trumps chronology when you're dealing with the ancient Near East and the Bible.* That's because there are a lot of variations in Near Eastern chronologies—with high, middle, and low versions that can vary thirty to fifty years at given points. It's far looser with the high, middle, and low biblical chronologies that swing to the tune of at least two hundred years for periods preceding the reign of King Solomon—and centuries more than that, if you consider the views of renowned biblical geographer A. F. Rainey and others who view Abraham and the patriarchs as Aramean clan-heads of the twelfth and eleventh centuries BCE. Needless to say, that's a lot of chronological uncertainty and disagreement among scholars!

By comparison, geography is quite static. With few exceptions, it doesn't move around. Mount Hermon has been in the same place through all antiquity, Jerusalem is fixed, the Jordan and the Dead Sea are fixed. So if there's a tenable geographical case for the location of a biblical site, such as there is for Sodom, then you can nail down the geography so long as the stratigraphy—the archaeological artifacts, especially ceramics that anchor chronology in a certain stratum or excavation level—is in the ballpark.

Again, we begin with the text, and that's how, using all of the geographical markers in the story of Abraham, you invariably find Sodom located in the Kikkar of the Jordan, because that's what Abraham and Lot saw when they were dividing the land between them. The text specifies where Sodom was, and after a decade of intensive exploration in that area, excavating there, and even closely examining maps and satellite pictures of the topography, we've concluded that if the ruins of Sodom and Gomorrah still exist, they would have to be at Tall el-Hammam, at nearby Tall Nimrin, or at other Bronze Age sites on the eastern Kikkar. It is what it is, and it is where it is.

Furthermore, we've found within the excavated ruins of Tall el-Hammam the verification of multiple points of the Genesis Sodom account. (Right stuff: more about that in a coming chapter.) The Bible, the geography, and the site all agree.

So, what to do with disagreements regarding chronologies?

Right Time: Synchronisms

THE MAJORITY OF BIBLICAL SCHOLARS and archaeologists—among them, W. F. Albright and K. A. Kitchen—agree that Abraham lived during the Middle Bronze Age. However, they don't build their patriarchal chronologies on any literal understanding of biblical numbers, but rather on placing characters like Abraham and Joseph within the most reasonable cultural contexts. In the main they base their chronological understanding on evidence of historical synchronisms, the markers in the narratives of the Bible that allow us to know when an event happened. A modern example: if you read that a woman was wearing a ponytail and a poodle skirt and saddle oxfords and got tangled up in her telephone cord, you'd use such historical synchronisms to guess she probably lived in the 1950s.

Historical synchronisms in the biblical account place the Abrahamic narrative in the Middle Bronze Age, during the famine days that drove Semitic Asiatics (Canaanites) into Egypt, where they eventually came to rule Lower Egypt as the Hyksos (Egypt's Fifteenth Dynasty). This climatological synchronism best reflects the period we call MB2 (1800–1550 BCE), marking a period of environmental deterioration in Canaan and in Egypt.

Specifically, the biblical account of Abraham records a food shortage so severe that he, like generations of Asiatics before him, fled to Egypt along with many of his fellow Canaanites: "Now there was a famine in the land, and Abram went down to Egypt to live there for a while because the famine was severe" (Genesis 12:10).

By comparison, the first half of the Middle Bronze Age, MB1 (2000–1800 BCE), enjoyed a much wetter climate, during which Canaanite towns grew into cities and cities into city-states bolstered by high levels of agricultural production. Thus the famine-driven patriarchs belong to MB2, not MB1.

Renowned ancient Near Eastern scholar K. A. Kitchen has identified numerous instances where historical synchronisms in the text of Genesis demand that the accounts of Abraham through Joseph be put solidly in the MB2—at the very earliest, late MB1—and no earlier. I list merely seven of them here (see Appendix B):

1. The wide scope of Abraham's travels mirrors ancient Near Eastern "itinerary" documents from the first half of the second millennium BCE.

2. Long-distance marriages, like those contracted by Abraham and Isaac for their sons, parallel similar arrangements by Shamsi-Adad I of Assyria and other ancient rulers of the early second millennium.

3. Travel to Lower Egypt from Canaan, as undertaken by Abraham and Jacob, is well documented in Egyptian texts from the 1900s through the 1600s BCE, but is unknown before and after that time.

4. Far-flung political alliances like that of Kedorlaomer and his allies in Genesis 14 occur from 2000 to 1750 BCE (1650 at the extreme), and this is the *only* time frame when such far-reaching alliances were commonplace in Mesopotamia and surrounding regions.

5. Nighttime attacks such as those conducted by Abram and his Mamre coalition, and religious ceremonies celebrating the conclusion of war, are entirely at home in the second millennium BCE.

6. Covenants negotiated by Abraham match only the unique treaty/covenant structure of the first half of the second millennium, *not* those before or after.

7. The price of slaves during the 1700s and 1600s BCE averaged twenty shekels—as in the Code of Hammurabi. Slaves were cheaper before that and more expensive after that, proving that the price of Joseph sold as a slave (twenty shekels, Genesis 37:28) is authentic to that period *alone*.

We can use details like these to *exclude* possible time frames and sites in identifying Lot's Sodom—particularly the Early Bronze Age (3600–2350 BCE) and the Intermediate Bronze Age (2350–2000 BCE), and perhaps even the first half of MB1 (2000–1900 BCE).

For instance, the famines described in Genesis 12 were not a characteristic of the Early Bronze Age until the end of that period, after about 2400 BCE. So if the details of the biblical narratives of the life of Abraham—Isaac and Jacob also—are accurate, then he couldn't have lived in Canaan during the Early Bronze Age until the end of the period around 2350 BCE. But that's centuries before even the earliest biblical chronologies can be stretched. Which leads to the inevitable conclusion that Bab ed-Dhra and Numeira—the sites in the southern Dead Sea area that many believe to be Sodom and Gomorrah and which have EB3 destruction levels—don't synch. They're just too early in time—two hundred to four hundred years before the time of even the most ridiculously early date that Abram could have entered Canaan—and Numeira was, in fact, destroyed some 250 years before Bab edh-Dhra. Such a connection just won't fly.

Chronologies and the Date of the Exodus

BUT CAN WE USE DETAILS such as those found in Genesis 12–14 to *include* Tall el-Hammam as a candidate site for biblical Sodom? If biblical scholars and archaeologists can reasonably agree that Abraham lived during the Middle Bronze Age, and that Tall el-Hammam is a city that was destroyed during the Middle Bronze Age, then the two could indeed "synch."

However, the more literalistic scholars might balk at that. The problem goes back to the nature of biblical chronologies. There are two basic points of disagreement among people who believe and use the Bible's chronologies.

The first point of contention has to do with the date of the Exodus. Some believe it happened in the 1200s BCE. But others believe it happened much earlier, in the mid-1400s BCE. Each chronology camp has its reasons for the dates it assigns, but they nonetheless disagree.

The two biblical passages on which the disputes center are Exodus 12:40 and 1 Kings 6:1.

Many believe that knowing the date of the Exodus is crucial, because it anchors a biblical timetable of the number of years the Israelites were in Egypt between the time of Joseph and the Exodus, set out in the following passage, here translated in the New International Version: "Now the length of time the Israelite people lived in Egypt was 430 years" (Exodus 12:40).

This passage helps set a time frame for the Exodus by ballparking the chronological "space" between the careers of Jacob and Moses. It also influences the date range of Abraham and Isaac, who preceded Jacob.

Let me summarize briefly.

First, the only piece of evidence supporting a 430-year Israelite sojourn *in Egypt* is the Masoretic Text (ca. tenth century CE) of Exodus 12:40.

All other lines of evidence—the Septuagint (LXX) versions, the

Masoretic Text (MT) patriarchal chronologies, the Samaritan Penta-teuch (SP), the apostle Paul, and Josephus—all affirm unequivocally that the Israelites sojourned "in Canaan and in Egypt" (or "Egypt and Ca-naan") 430 years. Such was the understanding of the first-century Jewish historian Josephus—that is, there were 215, not 430, years between Jacob's entrance into Egypt and the giving of the Law at Sinai.

Because of all of these corroborating translations and witnesses, some Bible versions of Exodus 12:40 (such as the King James 2000 version, which says, "Now the sojourning of the children of Israel, who dwelt in Egypt, was four hundred and thirty years") reflect the fact that the *430 years* refers to a total time in Canaan and Egypt, including the Israelite forebears Abraham and Isaac (see Appendix A).

However, it's Paul in the New Testament who settles the issue: "The promises were spoken to Abraham and to his seed. The Scripture does not say 'and to seeds,' meaning many people, but 'and to your seed,' meaning one person, who is Christ. What I mean is this: The law, introduced 430 years later, does not set aside the covenant previ-ously established by God and thus do away with the promise" (Gala-tians 3:16–17).

Paul here confirms the LXX chronology of the sojourn: it was 430 years from the giving of the promises to Abram (Genesis 12, 15) until the coming of the Law under Moses. That includes the time in Egypt, but isn't the Egyptian captivity alone. The total elapsed time was 430 years—again, 215 years in Canaan (Abraham to Jacob) and 215 years in Egypt (Jacob to Moses).

The only conceivable objection to a 215-year sojourn in Egypt is the statement in Genesis 15:13 that "your descendants will be strangers in a country not their own, and they will be enslaved and mistreated four hun-dred years." At first glance this may seem to suggest that the Israelites would be enslaved and mistreated for a period approximating four hun-dred years, possibly supporting a long sojourn in Egypt. However, the ar-gument quickly breaks down when the text is analyzed more closely. There's actually a twofold division in the sentence: (a) "your descendants will be strangers in a country not their own," and (b) "they will be enslaved and mistreated," all in a period of four hundred years.

Thus Genesis 15:13 fits the formula of Exodus 12:40 (LXX and SP) very nicely: "Now the length of time the Israelite people lived in Egypt and Canaan was 430 years." They were "strangers in a country not their own" (Canaan) for approximately two hundred years, and they were "enslaved and mistreated" in Egypt for an additional two hundred years. Abraham, Isaac, and Jacob were only nomadic sojourners in Canaan. The land did not belong to them; it was only promised. The land became theirs only when God brought the descendants of Abraham into it forty years after the Exodus (Genesis 12:7; Exodus 6:8).

Late-Date Exodus Advocates and a Look at Biblical Numbers

THE WAY THAT PEOPLE IN the ancient world thought, reasoned, and talked is different from the way most of us do in modern times. It's true, many of us would like to bring our thinking processes up to speed to match some of our spiritual forebears—but often a reader of the Bible is perplexed by certain passages in the absence of some background investigation.

For example, the phrase "give glory to God" (Joshua 7:19; John 9:24) seems very straightforward. But in Old Testament times, this could be a rote phrase, a way to insist that a person not tell a lie. (Similarly, in English, we often ask that people swear an oath, "So help me God"—though this isn't an appeal for direct and immediate aid from God, as the phrase literally says.)

The point? Sometimes reading the Bible *only literally* won't give you the full understanding (though undoubtedly the gist of any Bible passage is accessible).

In such instances, it's essential to read the Bible *authentically,* that is, in the context of the culture its writers lived in. In some cases that means the words are certainly true but may have been used with additional, or expanded, or even symbolic significance. Who would try to assert that God has wings, based on Psalm 91:4, or that he is literally a fortified city, a rock, or a lion?—though Bible passages say so.

The same principle is often true when dealing with numbers. Perhaps millions of pages have been written about the symbolic significance of numbers in the Bible—think 666, for instance—and yet sometimes people refuse to see that the life spans of people listed in the Bible can also be symbolic: often they're what we call *honorific* or *formulaic* numbers— such as forty years for a generation. This is especially important in dealing with genealogies.

For those who believe the Exodus happened in the 1200s BCE (so-called late-date advocates), biblical numbers relating to chronology are mostly symbolic (what I call *honorific formulas*).

This is an important issue with the second anchor passage that helps determine the date of the Exodus, 1 Kings 6:1: "In the four hundred and eightieth year after the Israelites had come out of Egypt, in the fourth year of Solomon's reign over Israel, in the month of Ziv, the second month, he began to build the temple of the LORD."

In this, the second foundation passage for computing the time of Abraham and Lot (by counting backward from the established start date for Solomon's temple in 966 BCE), people who advocate the so-called late-date Exodus—and others—regard the 480 years as simply a numerical symbol meaning "twelve generations" (based on a forty-year generation, also symbolic): 12 × 40 = 480. Therefore, since an actual, physical generation is more on the order of twenty-five years, they would say that the likely span of time between the Exodus and the "fourth year of Solomon's reign" (966 BCE) is three hundred years, placing the Exodus around 1250 BCE.

Is this a valid way of looking at an ancient number? An insistence on a mathematical exactness of numbers can be problematic when dealing with any ancient history. Ancient people didn't have any concept of absolute dating like what we use. They just didn't. They used several varieties of what we call *event* or *regnal dating,* such as "in the fourth year of King Solomon" or something similar. Even that can be problematic when you have a king succeeding another in a single year. The Bible can speak of the fifth year of King A, for instance and it can be the first year of King B, all in the same twelve months.

Literal is not just the wrong word, I contend; it's also the wrong approach. If I say, "I take the Bible literally," then I'm also claiming some kind of omniscience for myself. I'm saying that I know everything there is to know about everything when it comes to the Bible and the ancient world, and I always know exactly what the Bible means in every way and on every point.

We've got to learn that *literal* carries with it a lot of cultural baggage—mostly our own baggage from the modern world. The Bible was written in ancient oriental contexts. Even those cultural contexts could change dramatically in ancient times from one period to the next.

On the chronology issue, we know the ancient Mesopotamians used numerical formulas with components like forty—which is also a common biblical formulaic or symbolic number—and much of their numbering was base six instead of base ten. If the patriarchal numbers in the Bible are like many of the ancient Mesopotamian numbers, they carry more of a symbolic meaning, like a king's reign lasting for "hundreds" or "thousands" of years in some of their king lists.

When dealing with this subject, I've learned to respect the biblical text by taking it *authentically,* not literally. By *authentically* I mean understanding it in terms of its original cultural context—understanding the intent of the writer within his own world and worldview. *Authentic* may equate to *literal* if that's what the writer intended. But words or numbers may also carry other meanings from what we might think of in our scientific, modern way of reasoning. The goal in our understanding of the Bible is what's authentic to the ancient world, not what's dictated by my own way of thinking.

Late Dates and Early Dates for the Exodus

AS WE'VE SEEN, LATE-DATERS BELIEVE that the patriarchal life spans and other chronological numbers in Genesis and Exodus are symbolic/formulaic and generally not to be taken in a literal sense.

But even if you start with a late date for the Exodus, *and* take the genealogical tallies in Genesis literally with 215 years from Abram's entry into Canaan to Jacob before Pharaoh, *and* have the Israelites in Egypt a full 430 years, you still wind up in the Middle Bronze Age ballpark, all after 1900 BCE. The occupation of Tall el-Hammam ends during MB2—same ballpark. Factor in the late-date scholars' comfort with formulaic patriarchal numbers, and you're there. Perfect synch.

There are others who believe that the Exodus from Egypt happened not in the 1200s BCE, but instead much earlier, in the 1400s. When taking an extremely literal approach to the biblical numbers, if you add the 430 years of Exodus 12:40 to their proposed date for the Exodus (1446 BCE), then add the 215 years for the Abraham-to-Jacob stretch, that puts Abraham in Canaan about 2091 BCE—too early to fit into the Middle Bronze Age culture we see in the artifacts of the destruction layer of Tall el-Hammam (see also Appendix B).

Significantly, neither can such an Intermediate Bronze Age date for Abraham possibly coincide with the abundant historical synchronisms and cultural features linking his story, and the stories of Isaac and Jacob as well, to a time well into the Middle Bronze Age, as Professor Kitchen so clearly demonstrates.

Middle Date for the Exodus

I DON'T TAKE THE EARLIEST or a late date for the Exodus, but what I call a *middle* date. Based on solid historical synchronisms, I'm convinced that the Exodus happened between 1416 and 1386 BCE—the range of dates for the death of the Eighteenth Dynasty pharaoh, Tuthmosis IV. I think I can prove this connection by identifying an overt historical synchronism: the precipitous decline and demise of the Egyptian empire during the Eighteenth Dynasty beginning with the death of Tuthmosis IV. (By the way, this matches nicely an Exodus date figured from the Septuagint, or LXX, version of 1 Kings 6:1, which is forty years shorter than the 480 years of the much-later Hebrew Masoretic version.)

The Israelite Exodus and the devastating effects of associated events upon Egypt—tenfold plagues, plundering, loss of a large labor force, heavy military losses, and the loss of its reigning pharaoh—resulted in severe aftershocks, a well-documented and measurable economic depression that overwhelmed Nilotic civilization and precipitated the eventual collapse of its once-great-and-golden Eighteenth Dynasty. In other words, you can accurately pin down the Exodus date by seeing its trickle-down effects on the Egyptian economy, society, politics, and religion. (For more information, see my book *Let My People Go: Using Historical Synchronisms to Identify the Pharaoh of the Exodus,* TSU Press.)

So I generally agree with earlier-date Exodus theories, but more in line with the fourteenth rather than the fifteenth century BCE. And I hold to that because I accept both the historical authenticity of the biblical narratives and the reasonable clarity of the history of Egypt during the Eighteenth Dynasty. They synch. They explain each other.

But as with the earliest Exodus view, there is a sticky problem for middle Exodus advocates like me who would try to grapple with the dating of the artifacts in the terminal burn layer of Tall el-Hammam, which belongs to MB2, 1800–1550 BCE. If you add the literal patriarchal numbers—430 (in Egypt) + 215 (in Canaan) = 645 years—to the Exodus date in order to get back to Abraham, you still wind up in the twenty-first century BCE, which, as we we've already seen, is too early to coordinate with cultural elements in the text (see Appendix B).

No synch.

To make it synch you've got to either opt for a much shorter Israelite sojourn in Egypt or adopt the view that the patriarchal numbers in general are formulaic in some sort of symbolic way, as late-daters do.

Looking for Reconciliations of Dirt and Documents

I'VE CONCLUDED THAT ARCHAEOLOGY AND the Bible must always remain in dialogue with one another. For biblical archaeology to be a valid avenue of scientific inquiry, it's necessary that the contributing disciplines be allowed to influence each other in substantive ways.

The subject of patriarchal dating is an excellent case in point. If Tall el-Hammam and the eastern Kikkar sites meet all the geographical criteria for the Cities of the Plain set forth in the relevant historical narratives of Genesis (*which they do*)—

If Tall el-Hammam and its satellites have occupations corresponding within a ballpark of chronological possibilities consistent with the biblical text (*they do*)—

Then it's logical to propose a Cities of the Kikkar identification. Further, if the Kikkar sites northeast of the Dead Sea were occupied during the time frame for Abraham accepted by a majority of scholars, the Middle Bronze Age (*again, they were*)—

Then a positive identification as the Cities of the Plain approaches certainty.

Additionally, if the collective civilization represented by these sites came to a simultaneous, catastrophic termination during the Middle Bronze Age, whereupon the area remained unoccupied for several centuries (*it did, with an ensuing occupational hiatus of about seven hundred years*)—

Then their identification as the biblical Cities of the Plain is confirmed beyond any reasonable doubt. To be sure, such serial logic would confirm to most reasonable minds that Tall el-Hammam and its Kikkar neighbors are, in fact, the ruins of the biblical Cities of the Plain.

However, a few scholars have resisted this obvious identification for only one reason: the date of Tall el-Hammam's destruction (and that of associated sites as well) seems too late for the patriarchal chronology to which they adhere. Recently, one such scholar said to me, "I think the geography is spot-on, and the archaeological evidence is compelling, but the biblical date for Abraham's entrance into Canaan is around 1876 BC, so how can the destruction of Sodom be around 1650 BC? It just doesn't work for me."

Now, believe me, I faced the same problem and asked the same and many other questions about this issue. I also worked through a horde of options trying to solve the problem. But before I could come to what I think is a successful resolution, I had to decide that the geographical data and its certainties must outweigh the chronological uncertainties.

Therefore, I concluded that, as long as we were in the ballpark chronologically (the Middle Bronze Age), the identification of Tall el-Hammam and its satellites as the Cities of the Plain was logically indisputable. This was the proper, scientific way to proceed because the geography was right, and the archaeology was right—the text and the ground agreed precisely—and the chronology was in an acceptable range, albeit late for some tastes.

On this basis, it was as good an identification as one could possibly make, short of unearthing a monument sign saying "Welcome to Sodom!" (And I should mention that, so far, only one identified biblical site— Ekron—has such an identifying, in situ, in-period, unquestioned inscription naming the city.)

From this point, a *wrong* procedure would be to reject the identification of the Cities of the Plain on the eastern Kikkar northeast of the Dead Sea because the MB2 date of their destruction is too late for some versions of the biblical chronology. For me, it seems illogical (and unnecessary) to throw away a host of geographical and archaeological evidence simply because a particular date for the Abrahamic narrative, in some minds, appears to be a century or two out of synch. Thus, I think the Sodom identification for the largest Bronze Age site in the region,

Tall el-Hammam, holds, as does the identification of the entire cluster as the Cities of the Plain. The dialogue between the biblical text and the archaeology confirms it.

But what can we do about the chronology for those who have problems putting Tall el-Hammam's MB2 date of destruction within the career of Abraham? Here are some options:

1. Insist that archaeological dating procedures (pottery typology, carbon 14 dating, etc.) lack precision, and that the date of Tall el-Hammam's destruction can be moved back one or two hundred years, or more, while retaining the literalness of the patriarchal numbers, and using a short Egyptian sojourn.

2. Adopt a late (thirteenth century BCE) date for the Exodus and use formulaic numbers to stay in the MB2 ballpark.

3. Identify an earlier stratum of Tall el-Hammam—say, Intermediate Bronze or Middle Bronze 1—as biblical Sodom and speculate that the site was rebuilt after its destruction in the time of Abraham. This is at least possible according to the Bible's predictions about Sodom (that it would eventually be rebuilt), and could retain literal patriarchal numbers.

4. Claim that Tall el-Hammam and associated Kikkar ruins were the etiological seedbed from which the biblical stories about the Cities of the Plain and their destruction arose late in the Iron Age, as Israelite and/or Judahite priests wove their formulaic geography into the Genesis text, perhaps embellished by vestiges of local Canaanite lore.

5. Maintain the archaeological date of Tall el-Hammam's destruction (seventeenth century BCE) as the date of Sodom's obliteration, while adopting the view that the patriarchal life span numbers don't represent literal, base-ten arithmetic values, but are either symbolic, formulaic, honorific, or a combination of two or more of these.

I don't think Solution 1 is workable, because it silences the input of archaeological science. There may be some give-and-take to the tune of fifty years or so, but swings of hundreds of years simply fly in the face of the archaeological evidence.

Solution 2 is reasonable, and is undeniably the majority view among scholars who believe that the Exodus, at least in some form, actually occurred. A mid-to-late-thirteenth-century date for the Exodus can even accommodate a version of the literal patriarchal numbers if a short Israelite sojourn in Egypt is adopted (I'll review this shortly).

Solution 3 must be considered as a possibility, although most unlikely. It's hermeneutically feasible because, in point of fact, there is no biblical reason why the Cities of the Plain couldn't have been rebuilt and reoccupied by a new population after their Genesis 19 destruction. (Insistence that the Kikkar was forever off-limits to resettlement after Genesis 19 is based on later poetic/prophetic passages and is hermeneutically weak. After all, in Ezekiel 16:53, Yahweh did declare, "I will restore the fortunes of Sodom.") However, if someone did build on top of the destruction layer immediately, we're still left with the question of what caused it to be abandoned subsequently, as the complete lack of Late Bronze Age artifacts shows, and why everyone in the area avoided and did not build in that location for seven hundred years.

Solution 4 (or a variant of it) is what my higher critical and biblical minimalist colleagues believe. This denies or minimizes the historicity of the patriarchal texts, asserting that late Iron Age writers concocted the Sodom stories in order to explain the existence of the many piles of city and town ruins on the Kikkar opposite Jericho. However, those who take this approach can still make valuable contributions to the geographical discussion, since that subject is separate from issues of textual date and authorship.

For me, Solution 5 is the best approach. Given the imprecision of both the ancient Near Eastern and the biblical chronologies, the use of historical synchronisms to establish connections between text and ground is the sensible way to advance the topic.

Tall el-Hammam Is Sodom: A Basis for Chronologies

IT'S A SIMPLE LOGIC: IF Tall el-Hammam is biblical Sodom (based on geographical and archaeological evidence), then the date of Sodom's terminal Bronze Age destruction actually fixes the date of the Genesis 19 event—done! This is the dialogical approach to the Bible and archaeology at its best. Both the biblical text and archaeology (and all relevant disciplines) are allowed to influence each other when the evidence warrants it.

In this instance, the textual geography points to the area northeast of the Dead Sea for the Bronze Age Cities of the Plain; exploration and excavation confirm the existence of numerous Bronze Age cities and towns in that location; the biblical text assigns names to the area and its main cities/towns. All is fine up to this point, and the dialogue between text and ground is fruitful and mutually corroborating.

But then we have a nagging controversy, not over the dating of the terminal destruction of sites in the area, but over the biblical chronology of the patriarchs.

This is the hurdle I faced by our third year of excavation at Tall el-Hammam, when our Middle Bronze 2 ceramic "reads" made the date of destruction clear. How much easier it would have been if the demise of the Kikkar sites had occurred around 1800 BCE! But that isn't what the archaeological evidence reveals—the date is actually about a century and a half later.

So I decided to trump the chronology with geography and allow archaeology to provide a solid hermeneutical reason to actually reassess the patriarchal dates. We now had a relatively solid date for the destruction of Sodom and the Cities of the Plain. On my part, it was time to go where the evidence was leading, and that's where I am today. Since I'm convinced that historical synchronisms support a fourteenth century BCE date for the Exodus, I had to take a good, hard look at the numerical data in Genesis in order to place Sodom's destruction not four hundred or more years earlier, but about 250 years earlier.

Is it possible to solve this 150-year discrepancy? Yes. But I admit that it's probably not possible to come up with a solution that will satisfy everyone. So be it. I suppose some people will just have to settle for solution 1, 2, 3, or 4—or come up with their own alternative conclusion.

However, if there's a reasonable possibility that the patriarchal numbers are symbolic or honorific, a chronological adjustment of only 150 years—even more—is easy to accommodate. What Albright, Kitchen, and the late-daters have done in the way of symbolic/honorific numbers for their chronology works just as well for the early or middle Exodus chronology in allowing a date for Abraham's entrance into Canaan around 1700 BCE and a Sodom destruction date matching that of Tall el-Hammam and the other Kikkar sites.

Final Words

IN THE END, THERE CAN and should be harmony in synching all the chronological factors and issues regarding the Exodus, the life and dates for Abraham and the patriarchs, and Sodom (Tall el-Hammam) and the Cities of the Kikkar.

First of all, most reputable archaeologists who accept the historical authenticity of characters like Abraham, Isaac, and Jacob place their stories in the Middle Bronze Age. The ballpark dates that K. A. Kitchen assigns for the lives of Abram through Joseph are 1900–1540 BCE, which is Middle Bronze 1–2 (see Appendix B). W. F. Albright's ballpark for Abram through Joseph is 2000–1550 BCE (also MB1–2).

My ballpark date for Abram through Joseph, using honorific numbers and genealogies, is 1750–1540 BCE (MB2), which is firmly within Albright's and Kitchen's time frame, and which corresponds to the destruction date of Tall el-Hammam's MB2 city—Lot's Sodom. Indeed, the terminal destruction date of the Bronze Age Kikkar civilization, with imposing Tall el-Hammam at its core, provides a solid archaeological anchor for the patriarchal chronology.

Second, within reason, *geography trumps chronology,* acknowledging the way academic chronologies of the Near East "float" from thirty to fifty years, and similarly the way Bronze Age biblical chronologies can "swing" as much as two hundred years or more, as the variable Exodus dates suggest.

In contrast, there's little to no "float" room with geography because mountains, rivers, cities, and kingdoms generally tend to stay put during the course of human history. The observable, common ground of geography shared by a biblical author and present-day readers is much firmer than the often malleable interpretations of ancient numbering systems. Put simply, if in a biblical identification the geography of the text and a given site match, then as long as the relevant dates land "in the ballpark," such an identification is reasonable, if not conclusive. From that point, one can continue to work with the dating of the site and the textual chronology in order to better understand the relationship between them.

Establish the geography first, then let the chronology be worked out based on the archaeological evidence and historical synchronisms. And as we've seen, Abram fits comfortably in the later part of the Middle Bronze Age for a host of reasons.

You've got to let the text and the ground talk to each other. And when they do, in the case of the chronology of Sodom's destruction, they tell a remarkable story and provide new clarity for the issue of dating the patriarchal narratives.

This is a remarkable contribution of Tall el-Hammam to biblical archaeology. Since the biblical geography points to Tall el-Hammam as the right location, then it's scientifically correct to use the chronology of Tall el-Hammam to help determine the best time frame for the history of Abram and Lot.

SEVEN

Right Stuff:
Agitations, Architecture, and Artifacts

THE STORY OF SODOM AND GOMORRAH HAS INSPIRED BOOKS and movies. It has spawned theories and theologies. And quite against the original intent of the Bible as a historical document, it has been dragged into all kinds of crackpot schemes. For instance, for anyone who doesn't take the Bible's geography and chronology seriously, it makes perfect sense to sit in a cramped mini-submarine peering through the murk of the Dead Sea looking for sunken cities.

Perhaps most infamous at spinning tales was the late Ron Wyatt. This nonarchaeologist day-tripper led tours through the wastelands south of the Dead Sea, showing people "proof" of the two lost cities. He would point to geological formations—towering marl spires, statue-like salt formations—and say they were evidence of what happened to Sodom and Gomorrah.

There are many Wyattesque arguments still used today, but they aren't confined to him alone. Here's a list of the types of things people have claimed as "evidence" for the location of the two cities. Not all are Wyattisms, but all are equally without empirical confirmation and sound reasoning.

So-Called Evidence

Sulfur Balls

THERE ARE THOSE WHO SUGGEST that the existence of these perfectly natural little sulfur nodules found among the marl layers in areas near the Dead Sea, such as the geological formations just east of Masada, prove the Bible's description of "burning sulfur from heaven." However, these bits of sulfur are embedded in, and thus sometimes wash out of, more ancient geological formations where they resided millennia before recorded history, not as a result of the destruction of the Cities of the Plain. And as we've seen, there were never any Bronze Age cities next to the Dead Sea in that area in the first place.

White "Walls" of Cliffs and Curious Marl Formations

SOME HAVE CLAIMED TO SEE architectural features—temples, palaces, even ziggurats—in the geological formations of the southern Dead Sea area. Although they may be eerie, interesting, and even beautiful, they're just natural sediments deposited by the Dead Sea, carved by erosion when lake levels are low. (Imagine the kind of "cities" these people might conjure up from Bryce Canyon National Park in Utah or Garden of the Gods in Colorado!)

Sites That Have Been Called "Sodom" for Centuries

IT IS TRUE THAT THERE'S a "Mount Sodom" near the southern end of the Dead Sea on the Israel side. However, if the Bible's geography is reliable, there are two good reasons why it can't be connected to the Sodom of Genesis. First of all, though Mount Sodom is a geological formation made mostly of salt (which reminds people of Lot's wife, as do other geological formations in the area), there is no evidence that any large civilization ever lived atop it or around it. Second, the Islamic lore surrounding the story of Lot says the city was covered over by the Dead Sea. And, as that area has been inhabited by Muslims since the beginning of that religion, they assigned such names to geographical formations readily, but with no proper understanding of the most ancient geography found in Genesis 13.

Tar Pits

SOME PEOPLE INSIST THAT SODOM must be on the south or west side of the Dead Sea, because the king of Sodom and his armies fell into tar pits—intimating that quicksand-like pools full of black goo existed in the area. However, battles were typically fought at a distance from home cities. So we wouldn't expect these particular "pits" to be close to Sodom. Further, the "pits" that fleeing or maneuvering soldiers fell into couldn't have been filled with gooey tar (asphalt, bitumen), because such substances have never existed around the Dead Sea. (That's just an unfortunate translation bolstered by overactive imaginations.)

The Hebrew term (the basic meaning of which is "clay") probably refers to the ubiquitous black, muddy slime that collects by the millions of tons at various locations around the Dead Sea. When the lake level drops to where it is today—which is where it was in the time of Abraham—thousands of potentially dangerous sinkholes form all along the much-widened western shore. Obviously, this is what the Sodom troops encountered. While it's true that you see the blackish mud more along the west and north shores of the lake, what does that necessarily have to do with the location of Sodom? Absolutely nothing.

Oil or Gas Deposits

SOME PEOPLE THEORIZE THAT THE destruction of Sodom and Gomorrah as described in the Bible was the result of cracks in the earth's crust that released a plume of natural gas that somehow ignited, immolating the cities. They theorize about oil and gas deposits in the area around the Dead Sea. Fact is, they simply don't exist. (With petroleum and natural gas prices high, if such surface-available riches were available around or under the Dead Sea, someone would be pumping them, or at least trying to get at them. No one is.) But even if such deposits did exist, an example of the ignition of a *natural* source that might destroy even a small geographical area, much less one the size of the Kikkar of the Jordan, has never been documented. Settling the issue is the Genesis 19 language that specifies that the source of the conflagration was cosmic, not terrestrial.

Volcanic Eruption

SAME REASONING AS THE OIL and gas ideas—people try to explain the Bible's history with speculation, while ignoring the language of the text and the geology of the Dead Sea region. It's true that there is a very small volcanic flow of ancient lava in the hills on the northeast side of the Dead Sea. But there hasn't been any volcanic activity in the Jordan Rift Valley since long before the first villages and towns were built, and certainly long before the Genesis events regarding Abraham. Therefore, Sodom couldn't have been destroyed by a volcano.

Burned Areas at Bab edh-Dhra and Numeira

THESE TWO SITES IN THE foothills overlooking the southeast quadrant of the Dead Sea, which some have thought were Sodom and Gomorrah, did have fire associated with their final destruction. In fact, catastrophic fires after invasions, or even after natural events like earthquakes, were common throughout the Near East. Almost all Near Eastern cities fell at one time or another to enemies who burned them (the biblical Joshua did this). But what about the charnel houses at the Bab edh-Dhra cemetery that were burned from the top down, something that people cite as "proof" of fire from above? There are possible explanations for how evidence of burning could exist on the top of such a burial monument. Maybe a large funeral bier was burned on top of it. Perhaps an invading army desecrated the local dead by burning tombs as well as the city.

But again, it's all in the wrong place at the wrong time, so it doesn't matter. And again, Numeira was destroyed about 250 years before the walled town-site at Bab edh-Dhra.

Nothing Left at All

WE MUST ADDRESS THE OBVIOUS question: What if the divine act of the destruction of the Cities of the Kikkar completely obliterated all evidence of their existence? (Wouldn't a modern-day homeowner's insurance policy interpret such a thing as an "act of God"?) Anyone who takes the Bible seriously as a historical document must admit that the biblical description allows this scenario. If the destruction of the Cities of the Kikkar was caused by something like a divinely initiated blowtorch of a firestorm with a blast of fast-moving (say, 50,000 to 80,000 mph—comet velocity), superheated (say, multiple thousands of degrees Fahrenheit) air in a concentrated, fiery downdraft, then it's entirely possible that portions of stone and mudbrick structures were not only burned, but perhaps disintegrated at the molecular level and blown away. In such a scenario, there would be little left for archaeologists to discover. Even if the geographical data preserved in Genesis led one to the very spot where Sodom once stood, the present ground may hold nothing that would suggest the existence of the former city.

However.

Although such a scenario is possible, the biblical data certainly allow for the survival of at least some remains of the Cities of the Plain, and, therefore, we should investigate that possibility. Ezekiel 16:49–50 even suggests that the ruins of Sodom may still have been standing as a silent witness to the wrath of God hundreds of years later: "Sodom . . . and her daughters were arrogant, overfed and unconcerned; they did not help the poor and needy. They were haughty and did detestable things before me. Therefore I did away with them *as you have seen*" (emphasis added).

Indeed, if Tall el-Hammam is Sodom, it's in proximity to the inhabitants of Jerusalem to whom Ezekiel's words are addressed.

Identifying Characteristics

IF WE KNOW THE RIGHT place and the right time, what should we be looking for in a site that purports to be the biblical Sodom? And what does the biblical text say that would allow for the site to be destroyed, and perhaps rebuilt?

First, the Bible *does say* the cities were destroyed by a powerful conflagration that descended upon them from above. The biblical record *does not say* all evidence of their existence was wiped from the face of the earth so that the same locale would never be inhabited again.

Second, the biblical text *does say* the pervasive fire was so comprehensive over the target area that no human being in the Land of the Kikkar survived the blast. The Bible *does not say* the fire was so hot—or perhaps enduring—that it entirely consumed bodies, buildings, and personal belongings.

Third, the Bible *does say* the new growth (such as sprouts, shoots, and buds) of the vegetation in the region was burned. The biblical account *does not say* all flora of the area was obliterated so that it could not at least recover somewhat through the course of time.

Fourth, the biblical story *does say* that all the inhabitants of the Cities of the Plain were killed. The Bible *does not say* the area became permanently uninhabitable. From the biblical story, we can conclude that the Land of the Kikkar and the cities that prospered upon it were violently destroyed in an instant of time by an awe-inspiring, fiery event.

Some would argue against the point I'm making here by citing the five biblical passages that, on the surface, seem to suggest that the Land of the Kikkar (*eretz hakikkar*), destroyed by the wrath of God, became a locale where virtually nothing would grow and was eliminated for all time as a place of habitation.

1. The first passage is Deuteronomy 29:23:

> "The whole land will be a burning waste of salt and sulfur—nothing planted, nothing sprouting, no vegetation growing on it. It will be like the destruction of Sodom and Gomorrah, Admah and Zeboiim, which the Lord overthrew in fierce anger." All this text says is that God's judgment against a disobedient Israel will be like the destruction of Sodom and Gomorrah on the day they were destroyed.

2. The second passage is Isaiah 13:20:

> "Babylon . . . will be overthrown by God like Sodom and Gomorrah. She will never be inhabited or lived in through all generations." The simile here necessarily applies only to the overthrow of Babylon.

3. The third passage is Jeremiah 49:17–18:

> "As Sodom and Gomorrah were overthrown . . . so no one will live there; no man will dwell in [Edom]." The comparison is to what Sodom and Gomorrah were like at the time they were destroyed, not to the condition of the land in the long term.

4. The fourth passage is Jeremiah 50:40:

> "As God overthrew Sodom and Gomorrah . . . so no one will live there; no man will dwell in [Babylon]." Again, the same simile is here applied to Babylon, still as a symbol of destruction, not necessarily in every aspect.

5. The final passage is Zephaniah 2:9:

> "Surely Moab will become like Sodom, the Ammonites like Gomorrah—a place of weeds and salt pits, a wasteland forever." When dealing with similes, metaphors, and other figures of speech, you must be very careful to ascertain their character, which is often hyperbolic. In this passage it states that the lands of Moab and Ammon will become "a wasteland forever," yet in the very next sentence it states that "the survivors of my nation will inherit their land." But if the land is "a wasteland forever," how can it be reoccupied and lived in by God's people, Israel? The literary reality is that when the symbolic analogy of the destruction of Sodom and Gomorrah is used to depict the wrath of God against other nations, the meaning is clearly confined to the fact of destruction and does not extend to the manner of destruction or to the duration of the resultant damage.

Undoubtedly the event constituted an ecological disaster of significant proportions. As a result, the region may have been practically uninhabitable for a considerable period of time, possibly decades or centuries, at least in terms of a concentrated urban population. However, the biblical evidence also allows the possibility that the Land of the Kikkar may have recovered eventually to the point where it could once again sustain a substantial population.

Stratigraphy Does Not Lie

THE EARTH IS A VERY careful record keeper. In the case of the layers of occupation of an archaeological site, the earth itself tells the history of the people who built on it. With few exceptions, the farther down one digs, the further into the past one goes.

Imagine a stack of high school yearbooks, with the earliest year's volume on the bottom. Each book higher on the stack would tell a newer story, and cultural changes could be tracked by observing hair and clothing styles, for instance. But suppose that in a stack of fifty yearbooks, carefully maintained, for a venerable school, there are seven years of contiguous yearbooks missing: the yearbook for 1968 is followed by the book for 1976.

For some reason, no yearbooks were published in those years. A normally curious person would want to know why.

And normally curious people want to know why a civilization—built upon one of antiquity's best-watered agriscapes at the crossroads of the region's main north-south and east-west thoroughfares—collapsed suddenly and literally disappeared from history for seven hundred years. It's a phenomenon that begs for an explanation.

The ash and destruction debris from Tall el-Hammam's terminal Middle Bronze 2 occupational level ranges from half a meter to two meters thick over both the upper and lower talls. Embedded in those layers are broken and tumbled mudbricks, smashed and charred pottery vessels and other day-to-day objects, and human bones—all violently churned into a telltale, ashy matrix.

Obviously, Tall el-Hammam suffered a violent end. Could it have been an earthquake? Perhaps; but what appears in the excavation seems out of character for an earthquake, far beyond the simple lurching and collapse of structures that buried objects and inhabitants. If an earthquake was the culprit, then why was the city not rebuilt as it had been after previous quakes? Cities on crossing trade routes with abundant water and arable land were almost always rebuilt after earthquakes or military destruction. But this was the utter annihilation of an entire civilization and what had been one of the mightiest city-states in the southern Levant for more than two thousand years.

Furthermore, it wasn't just Tall el-Hammam that had the mysterious gap of human occupation for seven centuries. The vibrant, prosperous lifestyle, unchallenged for two thousand years from the Chalcolithic Period through the Middle Bronze Age and then conspicuously absent, is an occupational profile also seen collectively in the Kikkar sites surrounding Tall el-Hammam—talls Iktanu, Azeimeh, Mwais, Rama, Kafrayn, Tahouneh, Barakat, Nimrin, Bleibel, Mustah, and many smaller sites. Archaeologists familiar with this Kikkar phenomenon call it "the Late Bronze gap."

Confirmed Stratigraphy

THERE IS A CONFIRMED STRATIGRAPHY that reveals the occupational history of Tall el-Hammam. After seven seasons of excavating in a joint scientific project with the Jordan Department of Antiquities, we can now speak specifically and authoritatively about those levels. We've excavated far enough to see that Chalcolithic builders left their iconic architecture there. Later, the Early Bronze 2 occupants built the first extensive fortifications surrounding both the upper and lower talls, strengthened significantly during the Early Bronze 3.

The Intermediate Bronze Age occupants seem to utilize most or all of the EBA footprint, including the fortifications, even blocking some of the gate passages.

Excavations on the lower tall reveal a continuous occupation from the Chalcolithic Period through MB2.

The Middle Bronze Age—which includes the time of Abraham—is strongly attested architecturally at Tall el-Hammam, particularly in its fortification ramparts and walls on both the upper and lower talls, in monumental buildings, and in numerous domestic contexts.

No structures belonging to the Late Bronze Age or Iron Age 1 are presently known. (There's that Late Bronze gap again.) Perhaps one structure can be dated to the waning years of Iron Age 1, whereas the Iron

Age 2 city is extensively attested by both monumental and defensive architecture, and in domestic contexts, mostly on the upper tall. Iron 3 (Persian Period) seems present, but yet unconfirmed by anything more than reuse of older buildings. The presence of artifacts from later archaeological periods is minimal.

All this shows the bizarre evidence that Tall el-Hammam's entire civilization ended abruptly toward the end of MB2, and the abandoned sites present for consideration a chronological and geographical hole punched in the Bronze Age. Smaller town sites sprang up only some seven centuries later. However, the Bronze Age continued uninterrupted in regions surrounding the Kikkar of the Jordan—along the Mediterranean coast, up and down the Shephelah, throughout Canaan's central highlands north to south, in the northern four-fifths of the Jordan Valley, in the Transjordan Highlands—with abundant Late Bronze Age sites. But not in the Kikkar.

While the Bronze Age continued to play out through the next four centuries in lands to the east, west, and north of the Kikkar, the cities and towns on the Kikkar itself were frozen in time by what can only be described as a fiery catastrophe—an ecological disaster of biblical proportions.

And Sodom, the jewel of the Kikkar, became as repulsive as human dung for a reason.

Architectural Indicators in the Biblical Text

WHILE THE BIBLE GIVES SO many clues to the geographical location of Sodom that it seems almost to be drawing a map, there are far fewer identifying details about the features of the city itself. But there are tidbits of data indicating that at least the city of Sodom had particular features potentially identifiable in the archaeological record of the appropriate period. And if a candidate site should present itself, enough of these features may be present to aid in its identification as Sodom.

The following data points from Genesis provide several architectural indicators about the city of Sodom:

"Lot Was Sitting in the Gateway of the City [Sodom]" (19:1)

A GATEWAY MEANT SODOM WAS a fortified city. And it was sizable enough to warrant a city administration replete with a king and a system of judges. And it was cosmopolitan enough to integrate a nomadic (or seminomadic) Hebrew herder or caravanner like Lot into its society—to the extent that he became a judge or city official (elder), that is, one who "sat in the gate" (see Deuteronomy 22:15, 25:7; Joshua 20:4; 1 Samuel 9:18; 2 Samuel 19:8; Ruth 1:1, 4:11). Perhaps such a one arbitrated disputes between local nomadic peoples and the city administration.

Sodom was, no doubt, an active commercial hub that welcomed large numbers of foreign traders from points throughout the Near East. A rough estimate of the minimum size of such a principal city in the ancient southern Levant would be fifteen or more acres within the fortification perimeter, with an upper limit of fifty acres or more. (Some Canaanite cities, such as Hazor, were even larger.) A smaller associate town, such as Gomorrah or Zeboiim, might have been three to ten acres within the city wall, if there was a fortification system.

Consider Sodom's relative size in comparison with the other Kikkar cities in the Genesis text. Sodom was the largest Bronze Age city on the Kikkar of the Jordan: (a) it's always mentioned first when listed with its neighbors; (b) it's the only one ever mentioned by itself alone, while the others appear in a list only after Sodom; (c) the king of Sodom, Bera, is the only ruler of a Kikkar city who speaks in any of the narratives; and (d) Kedorlaomer seems to have plundered only Sodom and its satellite Gomorrah, indicating its greater wealth as compared with Admah and Zeboiim.

"The Gateway" (19:1)

THE DEFENSIVE SYSTEMS OF MIDDLE Bronze Age (2000–1550 BCE) cities were quite distinct from those of earlier periods. Walls were generally built with an exterior, abutting glacis or sloping rampart that made direct, level access to the city walls and gates impossible. Thus Sodom's resulting mound, or tall, would likely have the "sculpted" slopes typical of most sites with significant MB occupation.

"Gatehouses" were generally multichambered, and many MB gateways had arched passageways, such as those of Dan and Ashkelon. The foundations of such gatehouses usually consisted of several courses of stone topped with a superstructure of mudbrick. Since Sodom was a relatively large MB city, its fortifications would have been typical for "upper limit" cities of that period.

While large MB cities may have had many smaller pedestrian (postern) gates around the perimeter, they're known to have only one *main* gateway, of monumental proportions. Where Lot sat was "the" main gateway of the city.

"City" (19:1)

THE HEBREW WORD FOR CITY is *'ir* and usually refers to a fortified city or town. In many cases it's the word for a city-state controlling a surrounding territory that included smaller daughter villages and associated agricultural lands. Sodom, like other large fortified cities, had at least one acropolis area as well as monumental buildings (temples, palaces, and administrative buildings), markets or plaza areas, and domestic housing. All of these buildings were accessed by a system of streets and walkways. A significant percentage of the population probably lived outside the city walls, in villages and hamlets servicing agricultural fields.

"In the [City] Square" (19:2)

SODOM WAS LARGE ENOUGH TO have public architecture with at least one plaza or square (Hebrew, *rekhov*). These kinds of open areas served as markets and meeting places and were accessed by streets and alleyways. Public squares were often found just inside the city gate, and sometimes contained open-air worship centers with standing stones. There may also have been an outer plaza formed by blocking and guiding walls constructed around the immediate approach to the city gate (this also served to limit straight access to the gateway itself). The phrase "in the gateway" probably refers to a plaza just inside or outside the gate where the elders and officials of the city held meetings and made judgments among the people.

"His House" (19:2–4)

LOT HAD ACCUMULATED ENOUGH WEALTH to occupy a residential property within the city wall. Thus Sodom had a residential section with permanent housing.

"[Lot] Prepared a Meal for Them, Baking Bread" (19:3)

HOUSES OFTEN HAD OPEN-AIR COURTYARDS with cooking areas and ovens. Because Lot's family prepared a meal for their visitors, including the baking of bread, their house probably included such a courtyard. The courtyard would have been enclosed as an integral part of the house or domestic compound.

"Surrounded the House" (19:4)

THIS INDICATES THAT LOT'S HOUSE (or domestic compound) had streets or alleyways around its perimeter. If his house simply fronted a street, the men of the city could have only come "to the house" or stood "against the house." But they literally "surrounded around the house" (Hebrew, *nasabu 'el-habayith*). In such a case, the most likely meaning of the word *sabab* is to completely encircle a location. If this is what happened, then Lot's house was a relatively large, freestanding structure bordered all around by streets or alleyways. Remember that Tall el-Hammam has a large but finite surface area. To have a freestanding house in a densely populated, bustling urban center would, perhaps, be extraordinary.

"The Door" (19:6, 9–11)

TYPICALLY, HOUSES HAD A SINGLE entrance. Doors swung in top and bottom sockets that were usually made of stone.

"My Roof" (19:8)

ROOFS WERE USUALLY FLAT, AND sometimes multistoried. Rooftops were probably used as a workspace for drying various foods and brush and animal dung for fires.

"Led Them Safely Out of the City" (19:16)

IT'S POSSIBLE THAT LOT'S FAMILY hadn't lived in Sodom for very long and therefore weren't entirely familiar with its street patterns for ingress and egress. As a result, they needed to be escorted through the narrow maze of streets in order to get quickly and safely out of the city. This could indicate that Sodom was a relatively large city with complex streets and pathways, and that Lot's house was located some distance from the city gate. The language of the passage also could accommodate an escape through one of the city's small pedestrian gates.

A Summary of Architectural Indicators
from the Biblical Text

THESE INDICATORS FROM THE BIBLICAL text provide a considerable amount of data regarding some of Sodom's Middle Bronze Age
architectural features. Before we started excavating Tall el-Hammam,
we outlined the following architectural facts, explicit and implicit, from
the biblical text:

- Sodom was a typical Middle Bronze Age fortified city of
  substantial size, surrounded by thick, protective walls abutted
  by a sculpted glacis or earthen ramparts, or both.

- The main gateway of Sodom, in typical MB fashion, probably
  consisted of a large gatehouse with multiple chambers,
  probably with an arched passageway.

- An acropolis area with at least one monumental temple and a
  palace with associated administrative buildings.

- One or more public squares. If there was only one such
  public gathering area, it was probably just inside the city gate.
  Depending on its size, the city may have had other public
  plazas.

- An upper-city acropolis crowded with buildings representing
  the city's religious and political institutions, and a lower city
  containing residential housing, workshops, businesses, and
  small cult shrines.

- Some freestanding houses of wealthier inhabitants,
  surrounded by walkways and/or streets, with enclosed
  courtyards for cooking and baking.

- A fairly complex system of streets and alleyways, so that

a relatively new resident under duress might not easily remember the fastest exit route out of the city, especially through the main city gate.

The Witnesses: Absence of Late Bronze Age

As we've previously discussed, aside from the equivalent of a Sodom City Limits sign, no identification of Tall el-Hammam as Sodom can be ironclad. However, given the biblical parameters, we can look at some characteristics of the tall and see how they attest to such an identification.

The first is the absence of Late Bronze Age artifacts. In fact, there's no evidence of Late Bronze habitation at Tall el-Hammam. At all. This is true of all the other sites on the eastern Kikkar as well. However, even if some artifacts from that period do emerge, the Bible says that Moses and Joshua brought the Israelites to camp out in this area for quite a while before they crossed over to Gilgal and Jericho. It's easy to imagine, even if they didn't camp on top of the ruins of Sodom, that they would have wandered around on the huge mound, marveling at the sheer size of the ruins and wondering about the fate of its inhabitants. Besides, the top of the upper tall is absolutely the best lookout point on the eastern Kikkar. They could have left some debris, dropping a water jug or other "new" item, although we haven't seen anything from that period yet in the excavation. We did discover some Late Bronze Age pottery in a tomb about two hundred yards east of Tall el-Hammam proper. One of our staff humorously dubbed it "the tomb of the last wilderness wanderer" to die before Joshua crossed over the Jordan.

The Witnesses: Bricks Blown Away

THE ARCHAEOLOGISTS J. W. FLANAGAN, D. W. McCreery, and K. N. Yassine, who in the 1980s and 1990s excavated Tall Nimrin, six kilometers to the north, noted something very peculiar in their excavation reports. They found Middle Bronze wall foundations—deep-sunk, large bases intended to anchor the superstructures of large buildings—inside the city perimeter. But they found no MB residences, none of the typical eighteen-inch-thick walls of domestic dwellings. They said this was "highly unusual."

Either the foundations and mudbrick walls of the domestic dwellings are mysteriously missing from inside what may be a city wall, the report says, or whatever was built on top of the "platform" retained by the large walls is, likewise, absent. I've examined Tall Nimrin, excavation reports in hand, on several occasions and this description is entirely in line with what's there.

Without actually stating it, the report implies that at least some of the city may have been swept from its foundations—stripped from its platform, except the largest and heaviest and deepest foundations; the lighter, more ephemeral structures just wiped away.

We're seeing a similar phenomenon as we excavate more and more of Tall el-Hammam. We saw it first on the lower tall, where the terminal destruction layer is lying right on the surface. There's a lot of ash, but very little mudbrick remains. Preserved there from the Middle Bronze Age are the stone foundations of its twelve-foot-thick city wall and defensive towers, and its 100–150-foot-thick defensive rampart: the big stuff. Inside the city wall—which itself is missing from the foundation up—only one to three courses of MB domestic foundation stones remain. The mudbrick superstructures are entirely gone.

Now, it's normal when a city is abandoned for those sun-dried bricks to gradually erode away into the mud they came from. Usually an excavator has to dig through several feet, representing two to four stories, of decomposed mudbrick debris, but we aren't finding much of it at Tall el-Hammam. However, we've found broken pieces of mudbrick strewn throughout the ash matrix.

Someone might contend that local farmers take that mudbrick layer to spread it on their fields, which is possible, but why go all the way to the top of the tall to get it? The entire lower rampart is huge and built entirely of mudbricks, and it's still amazingly preserved. It's easy to get to, but practically untouched in places.

It's interesting that at Tall el-Hammam nobody ever built on top of the lower tall's exposed foundations. However, in the Iron Age, people requisitioned those stones to build their walled town atop the upper tall, and a small cultic area outside their city wall on the lower tall.

The Witnesses:
Architecture, Fortifications, and Gateway

A Sprawling City

THE FOOTPRINT OF THE WALLED Middle Bronze Age city at Tall el-Hammam is nearly sixty-five acres. With these dimensions, it ranks in the top 1 percent of the southern Levant's largest Bronze Age urban centers. MB Jerusalem and Jericho are diminutive by comparison.

It's the largest Bronze Age city on the Kikkar by several orders of magnitude. If, as the Bible clearly indicates, Sodom was the largest city in the Land of the Kikkar during the Bronze Age, then Tall el-Hammam is it, hands down.

A Fortified City

TO SAY THAT TALL EL-HAMMAM was fortified is like saying that New York is a pretty big town.

During the time of Genesis 10 (EB2–3), Sodom's city walls were eighteen feet thick and as much as forty feet high, with imposing defensive towers spaced approximately every fifty yards around its 1.5-mile circumference.

TeHEP director Steven Collins, with assistant director Gary Byers, standing atop the stone foundation of the eighteen-foot-thick Early Bronze Age city wall.

Later, the MB builders took those immense EB fortifications and buried them under a new, even more massive defensive complex ringing the city to a width of up to 150 feet. The MB city wall (mudbrick on stone foundation) was twelve feet thick, probably up to thirty-five feet high, with intermittent towers, and a mind-boggling mudbrick, smooth-faced rampart sloping 35 degrees away from the outer face of the city wall for up to 150 feet. As if that weren't enough, inside the outer defensive perimeter they also built a freestanding, mudbrick rampart around the upper city, soaring 90 feet above the lower city rooftops. Collectively, this is one of the largest and most complex Middle Bronze Age defensive systems in the southern Levant.

A Monumental Gateway

DURING THE EXCAVATIONS OF 2012, one of the most exciting discoveries in seven field seasons at Tall el-Hammam came to light: the main Middle Bronze Age monumental gateway complex.

Several distinct features make this one of the most impressive gate systems ever unearthed in the southern Levant. First, the central gatehouse has two outside-corner towers with entrances into each through the city wall. We don't know yet whether there are two, four, or six chambers (side rooms) inside it, but that will become clear as excavations continue. What we do have thus far is the first pair of gate piers creating the main passageway (six and a half feet in width) and both side tower entrances. The width of the gatehouse is approximately seventy feet.

Second, we've unearthed the stone foundation and up to a dozen mudbrick courses of a large, external flanking tower measuring thirty-one by forty-six feet, not including the twelve-foot-thick section of Middle Bronze city wall to which it attaches. The top of this left (as one faces the city wall from outside) tower originally stood as much as forty-five feet above the plaza surface below. Based on the rule of symmetry for such gate complexes, we anticipate that a matching right tower will be found equidistant on the opposite side of the gatehouse.

Third, we've identified a large exterior gate plaza that is cordoned off by guide-walls, several feet thick, channeling foot and cart traffic into a restricted-access area. This was a center of commercial activity in peacetime; a death zone for attackers in times of war. It was a gateway befitting a great and influential city.

A Powerful City-State

GENESIS 19:28 CALLS THE AREA occupied by Sodom and Gomorrah, Admah and Zeboiim, the "Land of the Kikkar." This geographical formula with "land" (Hebrew, *'eretz*), used frequently in the Hebrew Scriptures, often carries an ethnocultural, even ethnolinguistic, connotation—as in land of Egypt, land of the Canaanites, land of Moab, land of Israel, land of the Philistines. And it's likely that such a meaning is intended in Genesis 19:28. In fact, civilization flourished continually in the Land of the Kikkar—the Kikkar of the Jordan—for at least seven thousand years before it all came to an abrupt and violent conclusion toward the end of the Middle Bronze Age.

Archaeological sites like Jericho, Tuleilat Ghassul, Tall el-Hammam, and a host of other settlements large and small testify to the ability of the well-watered Kikkar of the Jordan to support large populations of people in what was truly an agricultural paradise. It's no wonder that the Cities of the Kikkar are mentioned in Genesis 10 along with great Mesopotamian urban centers like Babylon and Akkad. The area had one city-state, perhaps two, during the Early Bronze Age, Intermediate Bronze Age, and Middle Bronze Age. If there were two, the larger—which likely also controlled the other—was the one centered at Tall el-Hammam. Throughout its 2,500-year occupation, Tall el-Hammam dominated the Kikkar. It makes perfect sense that "Land of the Kikkar" refers to the long-enduring civilization anchored by Tall el-Hammam.

City Squares, Monumental Buildings

MIDDLE BRONZE AGE TALL EL-HAMMAM had at least two city squares, or plazas, associated with its main gateway. Through our excavations we've also documented a major palace structure with red-plastered walls up to 6 feet thick (perhaps the palace of King Bera?), a sacred precinct with a large temple sporting walls as much as 10 feet thick, and a substantial administrative complex measuring at least 67 by 200 feet. The stone foundations of Bronze Age buildings and houses are present everywhere across Tall el-Hammam, with many of them protruding from the ground.

Residential Compounds

ON THE WESTERN SIDE OF our big Trench LA.28, a sizable domestic compound is located just inside and to the left of the main city gate.

Excavating Bronze Age domestic structures in Trench LA.28, Season Five.

While we've excavated portions of several houses on Tall el-Hammam's lower tall (even one on the upper tall), this one, being excavated by Gary Byers, TeHEP assistant director, is special for at least three reasons. First, it has a very long history. We've been able to trace the evolution of its walls from a Middle Bronze (surface) phase back through Intermediate and Early Bronze phases, beginning (at least) in EB3. Each successive rebuilding and remodeling is slavishly attached directly to earlier construction, and all are on precisely the same footprint. Obviously, this house served its family for many, many generations.

Second, it has many rooms connected by doorways, and probably had at least a second story accessed by ladders. There are several in situ door socket stones throughout the house.

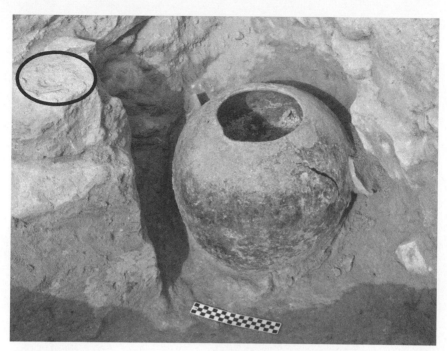

Middle Bronze Age door socket stone (circled, left) in situ, with Intermediate Bronze Age hole-mouth storage jar installed beneath an earlier floor level.

Third, it has a sizable court-yard kitchen with stone work-ing surfaces, hearths, grinding tools, and numerous smashed pottery vessels from cooking pots to jugs and juglets to large storage jars. A "rouletting wheel"—a 1 × 2.5-inch ceramic cylinder with repeating spiral designs—was found amid kitchen vessels, conceivably used for impressing its design on flatbreads for ceremonial meals.

Fourth, the compound seems to be surrounded on all

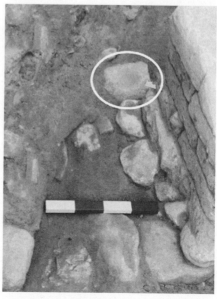

Early Bronze Age doorway with stone threshold and door socket stone in situ.

sides by streets and alleyways—in essence, a freestanding house, like Lot's house. Only further excavations will reveal if other domestic dwellings at Tall el-Hammam are similar to this one, but there are probably others like it.

Many Streets and Alleys

TALL EL-HAMMAM IS A HUGE place. At a normal, unhurried pace, it takes a good ten minutes to walk the north-south diameter of the lower tall. But that's as the crow flies, without obstructing houses and buildings. But since the site is packed with these structures, there were certainly streets and alleyways connecting all parts of the city. We have direct confirmation of a "ring road" running along the inside of the city wall. We also have streets and alleys leading through the domestic areas we've excavated.

Dr. C (standing, center) inspects excavations in Trench LA. 28, Season Six.

The axis of the main gateway leads directly to the sacred precinct at the geographical center of the lower city. As big as Tall el-Hammam is, getting through it in a hurry may have been difficult for newcomers and visitors.

Each of the previous points links precisely with biblical descriptions about Sodom's size, wealth, prestige, fortifications, architecture, and complexity. It's a match in every possible way.

But there's more.

The Witnesses: The Piriform Juglet

MONUMENTAL WALLS AND PALACES AND gate structures certainly confirm the suitability of Tall el-Hammam as a high-priority candidate for biblical Sodom. But not all the artifacts we've found there are massive.

Excavation of an MB2 domestic structure in the upper city, Season Two (2007).

A significant find we encountered early on was a gray-ware juglet about the size of a baseball. It's piriform, that is, teardrop-shaped. That vessel style has a long history, beginning in the EB3 period. At Tall el-Hammam we can trace the entire history of this juglet form from its inception, through each successive period, down to near the end of MB2. The earlier ones are handmade, but often exquisitely formed. The bodies of Middle Bronze Age piriform juglets were turned on a fast potter's wheel, then finished off by hand. The MB2 "button" base version is distinctive, while others of the same period have a simple pointed base. The first button-base piriform juglet we excavated was found alongside two MB-style storage jars and a clay-lined storage bin—all common to the Middle Bronze Age. All of these were found in a house in the upper city, covered with about a meter of ash and destruction debris.

The "Late Bronze Age Gap" at Tall el-Hammam is dramatically demonstrated in this trench on the upper tall. Here you can see the Iron Age 2 city wall (A) built directly on top of the Middle Bronze Age mudbrick defensive rampart (B) that surrounds the upper city. There is a seven-century time gap between the two structures. The same gap is evident over the entire site, indeed over the entire eastern Kikkar of the Jordan.

Right on top of that debris was an equally distinctive Iron Age building. There, in a kind of snapshot, was the history of the destruction of Tall el-Hammam: an unmistakable Middle Bronze Age stratum buried by the ashes of a catastrophe, and then nothing.

Nothing.

Nothing for at least six hundred years, until the Iron Age 2, about 1000 BCE.

The Witnesses: Human Remains in the Destruction Layer

IN THE FIRST FIVE SEASONS of the excavation, we found interesting artifacts: bronze weapons and jewelry, stone grinders of all shapes and sizes, vessels of alabaster and gypsum, Egyptian-style scarab seals, decorative stone and ceramic cylinder seals, loom weights, spindle whorls, hammer stones, sling stones, gaming stones, figurines, and huge amounts

Artifacts from Tall el-Hammam: (1) piriform juglet, (2) arrow point, (3) battle-ax head, (4) Hyksos scarab, (5) metal objects, (6) scale weights, (7) melted bronze, (8) ceramic rouletting wheel, (9) trumpet vase fragment, (10) piriform juglet.

of pottery. All of these were buried in layers of ash and destruction debris.

Artifacts from Tall el-Hammam: (1) bowl bases, (2) piriform juglet, (3) alabaster bowl fragment, (4) ceramic Asherah figurine, (5) olive press stone, (6) cosmetic palette, (7) piriform juglet, (8) gaming stone, (9) loom weights.

The question might arise: Why have we found at Tall el-Hammam so few precious metals and other "treasures"? One possible explanation is that grave-robbing is an ancient profession. While people may have been unwilling for seven hundred years to build atop the ashes, that certainly wouldn't have deterred the activities of those who would have seen the ruined mound as a giant, accessible tomb and would have dug through the ashes and carried off anything valuable. It's also possible that the nature of the destruction so severely disrupted the city and its contents that few artifacts survived in situ. Indeed, many of Tall el-

Hammam's artifacts are found fragmented and "floating" in the ash/debris matrix and not in contact with surfaces like floors or streets.

Artifacts from Tall el-Hammam: (1) ceramic cart wheel, probably for cultic use, (2) ceramic animal figurine, (3) ivory inlay, (4) stone incense altar, (5) alabaster vase, (6) ceramic rouletting wheel, (7) ceramic counting token, (8) mudbrick fired pottery-sherd in a conflagration, (9) chalice, (10) slow potter's wheel or tournette, (11) pilgrim flask.

However, until 2011, we hadn't found any human remains associated with the Middle Bronze 2 destruction layer.

For an archaeologist, finding human remains is part thrill and part terror. Even though we'd been meticulous in every phase of the excavation, we exercised painstaking care with the human remains. The field archaeologist and supervisor for the excavation square where the first nonburial remains were found was Carroll Kobs. I asked her at least a dozen times to walk me through the excavation process—to take me centimeter by centimeter down across that area to confirm the orientation of everything. We looked at the mudbrick fragments, the pottery, the ash matrix, the bones and bone fragments. Then we went through the process again with other field archaeologists, both American and Jordanian.

There are several reasons for this extra caution. First of all, we're excavating in a mainly Muslim country, and that religion is quite specific about how the remains of Muslims should be treated. So we had to assure ourselves and them that these were too early to be Muslims. (Over the years we've encountered countless burials from virtually every archaeological period, and also numerous Muslim interments. We have lots of experience with skeletal orientations and the burial customs of the different cultures.)

Second, we had to ascertain if these were bodies in a burial situation—postmortem interments. We were reasonably sure that wasn't true in this case. First of all, this was apparently a residence. Second, any kind of postmortem burial would be cut through the layers in the ground, and that kind of thing sticks out like a sore thumb—unless, of course, the material was washed in by water; but there isn't any sign of waterborne sediment in this area.

All the archaeologists on site agreed that the skeletal remains were intrinsic to the ash layer, which dates to the Middle Bronze 2 according to the ceramics. The material is within a half meter of the surface, at the level of the Middle Bronze 2 houses, streets, and alleyways. The human remains are mixed in with fallen mudbricks, pottery, other artifacts, and lots of ash.

It was a dire way to die: their world disintegrated around them and then engulfed them.

Third, finding human remains changes the character of a dig. Aside from finding gold or jewels or controversial documents, nothing inflames public interest more than the discovery of bodies. (And to be honest, I was very nervous about that.)

We're just beginning to find near-complete skeletal remains, but there are human bone fragments—a rib here, a vertebra there, skull fragments—that are visible all through the MB2 stratum in this particular area, even in the balks (the unexcavated vertical sections that separate trenches or squares of archaeological digs.)

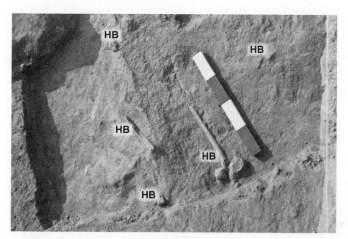

Human bone (HB) scatter in the ashy matrix of Hammam's MB2 destruction.

So far, we've identified the remains of two adults and one child, and innumerable bits and pieces of many others. What we see are bodies wrenched around in a facedown position, as if they were thrown down in the process of turning away from something—in an unconscious reaction, as if protecting themselves.

Some of their joints are hyperextended or twisted apart unnaturally, not in any normal or burial position. One is charred off at mid-femur. Their condition at death attests to "extreme trauma." This is terminology from our osteologists as they observed and documented the condition of the bones in situ. On site for the examination of these bones were Dr. John Moore and Dr. John Leslie. (Dr. Moore was a maxillofacial surgeon before retiring, while Dr. Leslie is a practicing physician; in addition, both have master's and doctoral degrees in archaeology and biblical history, and Dr. Leslie also holds a Ph.D. in experimental pathology.) We also enlisted the expertise of the volunteer who excavated the child, Victor Bauer, who taught human anatomy and physiology for over thirty years. Moore and Leslie made extensive field notes and took numerous photographs during this phase of the excavation, all under Carroll's supervision and the critical eyes of the senior staff.

(left to right by row) TeHEP assistant director, Gary Byers, 2007; Dr. Kay Prag flew in from the University of Manchester to confer with Dr. C, 2009; osteologist Dr. John Leslie, 2007; Dr. William Fulco examines pottery from Tall el-Hammam, 2007; Dr. Bob Mullins during a pottery reading, 2011; Dr. Carl Morgan supervising on site, 2008; TeHEP photographer Mike Luddeni, 2008; videographic documentarian Daniel Galassini, 2007.

(left to right by row) Dr. Ziad Al-Saad, Director General of the Department of Antiquities, Jordan, and Dr. C, 2011; Carroll and Jeff Kobs using Munsell Soil Color Chart, 2012; field archaeologist Dr. Steve McAllister, 2008; osteologist and geographer Dr. John Moore, 2007; Dr. C and Abu-Ahmed, 2010; TeHEP artist and field archaeologist Ginny Kay Massara, 2006.

Staff consultations are a daily routine. Dr. C wore this kofia only one day in seven seasons. That same day, local landowner Abu-Ahmed wore Dr. C's hat.

This was essential. We had to take a cautious approach.

The destruction matrix lay undisturbed since the event that caused it. This is the terminal destruction layer—the big, bad one that ended the life of the city and the entire surrounding area for the next six or seven centuries.

All the materials in the matrix were laid down together with the humans in the mix, an unspeakable concrete. It was violent, probably instantaneous.

And these human remains, these skeletons, aren't from just any layer in the dig. They're from MB2, the time of Abraham. They're surrounded by a thick layer of architectural debris—parts of buildings—and voluminous, bitter ash.

This is a grisly scene. It is destruction, literally, of biblical proportions.

And the meaning of this find can't be casually brushed aside: this is quite possibly but one death scene, with bodies and body parts still examinable, for an event described in Scripture.

Perhaps we've touched the very people Abraham bargained about.

Dr. C's Dream

Even as a boy, Steven Collins knew that bones tell stories, that things once living could speak like Abel from the ground.

"I loved reading about evolution. I wanted to know about ancient things," he says, "about stone tools and who used them, about what ancient people left behind them." A child of the 1950s and 1960s growing up in California and New Mexico, Steven accepted without question his teachers' version of a human race rising in bone-fragment re-creations that unfurled themselves over millions of years, from crouching simians to standing tool-bearers. He read *National Geographic* and science the way his classmates read comic books.

A history teacher directed his readings to ancient Egypt, Greece, and Rome.

"The rest of ancient history was of little interest to me," he admits. "I never even thought about the Near East much." Instead, he lived in ancient worlds in his mind, peopled with *Australopithecus* and Cro-Magnon, and by the time he finished high school, he decided to major in anthropology in college.

And yet, standing alongside the mental world that Steven inhabited was another one that never seemed to intersect—much less, conflict with—his studies. From his childhood he attended a church where his father was a deacon and Sunday school teacher, and the whole family knew Bible stories by heart.

While he loved the Bible, he rarely approached it devotionally or doctrinally; nor, he admits, did he make the kind of emotional connection with the Bible that many others around him did and expected him to.

"Reasoning, thinking, solving problems: that's how I saw myself," Collins says. "I saw the Bible as a historical document to be studied and was always more drawn to apologetics and history. I wanted to solve mysteries—that was my connection with the biblical text."

What he called "the Sunday School Bible," the stories he was told in classes when he was young, turned him off. "They seemed like fairy tales," he says. "But the real Bible, when I read it firsthand, was hardcore, human stuff—gritty, violent, compelling, even pretty nasty at times."

The Bible depicted a separate history from what he studied in school, almost like a parallel reality. His balancing act of the apparent disparity between the two didn't emerge as rebellion or bad behavior; to the contrary, he was a model teenager. "The Bible was one world," he remembers, "and many of my interests, like all the reading I was doing in anthropology, made me live in another."

Still, in his junior year of college, what he was studying in his anthropology classes veered onto an unavoidable collision course with his homegrown cultural faith. "I was majoring in evolution," he says, "and that flew in the face of the accounts of the creation, Noah's flood, early men.

"I came to the point where I had to decide what to do with the text. Could I trust what it said—as history—or was it merely what my education was telling me, mythical stories, products of ancient imaginations that had nothing substantive to say about the real world?"

He pursued becoming what he characterizes as an "evidential factualist." Such mental distance, he hoped, would allow him to assess whether the Bible correctly represented reality, and whether his professors' opinions and conclusions were valid. He single-mindedly pursued his questions about the Bible's truthfulness and how it fit with the archaeology of the ancient Near East.

He saw his pursuit—the defense of "the much-maligned Bible"—as a battleground, one for which he must deliberately arm himself. In graduate school, he discovered his facility with ancient languages, first Hebrew, then Greek, and then Ugaritic, Aramaic, Akkadian, and other lost languages. Through his bachelor's, master's, and doctoral programs he devoured anthropology, geography, linguistics, archaeology, and biblical studies.

His love of ceramics from the ancient Levant (the area between Egypt and Mesopotamia)—the "time and date stamps" of archaeological excavations—advanced him to expert status, making him a sought-after consultant. Beginning in the late 1980s, he worked as a field archaeologist whom colleagues and students knew as "Dr. C," and helped supervise several excavations in Israel and led study tours in Israel, Jordan, and Egypt. With his father, who became a minister late in life, Steven founded a biblically based school and museum, and became a popular teacher and speaker.

The night in the hotel when he read the biblical account of Sodom and knew that it could not match up with the modern maps he held in his hand, his life changed forever. As he pursued possible sites in the Kikkar of the Jordan for the one location that might be Sodom, he began to create a "wish list" for things he hoped to find at such a site, and at the top of that list was a gate.

Not just any gate. What Dr. C wanted to find was the monumental gate of Sodom. Whenever he returned to the Genesis 19 passage that told of Lot sitting in such a gate, he could see in his mind's eye this resident alien's robes flowing in the breezes of the Kikkar; could imagine the passage-house and massive gate towers behind him.

Any site that could properly be identified as Sodom would have to include the Middle Bronze Age, the time of Abraham. And it would have to be large, as befitting the supremacy, the dominating character, that the writer of Genesis gave to it. And if such an important Bronze Age city existed, it would certainly have the kind of gateway that other large Middle Bronze Age fortress cities had. Dr. C had seen, measured, and studied most of them firsthand: Dan, Ashkelon, Gezer, Megiddo, Hazor, Shechem, Beth Shemesh.

Such gateway structures stood on foundations of stone with superstructures made almost entirely of mudbricks, plastered over with mud clay. They had rounded or corbeled arches forming their passageways. Inside a gatehouse there were usually from four to six chambers (two or three on each side). Sometimes there was one set of thick, wooden doors. Often there were two sets. Doors were hung on bronze-tipped wooden posts that turned in lower and upper socket stones.

The outside of the gatehouse toward the entry side generally consisted of two corner towers from which the gate entrance was defended. The towers had multiple stories accessed by ladders. The tops of the towers—likewise the entire city wall—had strategically placed crenellations and firing notches for archers and slingers. The towers likely had vertical window notches for use by archers.

Outside the city wall in front of the gatehouse, there was usually a wide area often surrounded by thick walls that directed people into this outer gate plaza through narrow entryways fed by several roads coming to the city gate from different directions. On an average day, these were bustling, noisy marketplaces. In wartime, the outer plaza was a killing zone specifically designed to thwart frontal attacks against the heavy-but-vulnerable wooden doors. The outside faces of the doors were probably sheathed in thin plates of bronze to protect against fire.

Once you passed through the main gateway into the city—through one or two sets of gates—you entered the main city square, a large plaza also serving as a commercial district. There were places for visitors to make offerings to the city's patron deity, no doubt attended by priests, priestesses, and sacred prostitutes promoting a more hands-on kind of worship at a nearby temple. Sitting on benches inside the gatehouse or in the interior plaza were city officials transacting business. Also "sitting in the gate" were elders adjudicating disputes and witnessing contracts.

The gateway was the heart of city life.

Small town, small gateway. Large city, large gateway. The greatest cities were no doubt recognized by the distinctive look of their monumental gate complexes. It was their unique identity. It was their "face" to the world.

From the moment he set foot on Tall el-Hammam and saw ruins from nearly four thousand years earlier so near the surface, Dr. C dared to hope that the immense mound would yield a gate. Beginning at the first excavation season in 2005 and up until the late winter of 2012, the team found ramparts and walls and towers from the Middle Bronze Age, from the Intermediate Bronze Age, from the Early Bronze Age.

The excavation team worked exclusively on the upper tall during the first three seasons. Then, during Season Four, Dr. C instructed his surveyor, Qutaiba, to lay out a series of squares (a trench) that he'd marked off on the lower tall the previous season. It looked like a relatively well-preserved area—technically defined as Area L, Field A—along the "28" (north-south) gridline, across the southern defenses to about twenty yards inside the city wall.

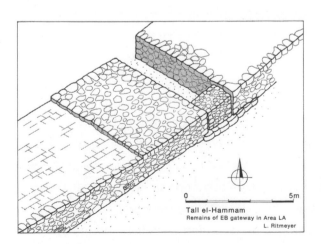

Tall el-Hammam
Remains of EB gateway in Area LA
L. Ritmeyer

What became known as the "big LA.28 Trench" delivered time and time again: a huge swath of the southern defensive rampart and city wall; sections of the roads ringing the city inside and out; an EBA gateway, blocked during the IBA; Chalcolithic and EB1 houses; EB2–3, IB1–2, MB1–2 houses; all or pieces of more than four thousand different ceramic vessels; evidence of earthquakes and

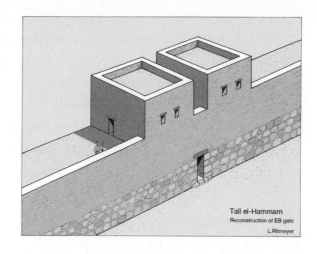

rebuilding; clear indications of unbroken occupation for over 2,500 years.

Work proceeding in Trench LA.28, Season Six (2011).

And not least: dramatic, unmistakable signs of the fiery, catastrophic destruction.

On January 30, 2012, the winter excavation season was well under way when supervisor Carroll Kobs ordered the clearing of what appeared to be a three-foot-wide postern gate through the MB2 city wall—the first MB2 entryway of any kind discovered at the site up to this point. The news spread through the crew, igniting excitement.

Dr. C considered the nature of this find. The MB2 builders put their new city wall just inside the old EB/IB wall.

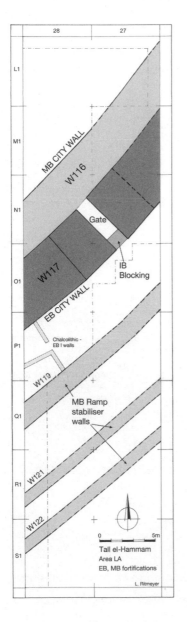

Then they used the old, eighteen-foot-thick, five-course-high stone foundation—with about three to four feet of the original mudbrick super-structure left intact—as a footing for the thickest part of their defensive rampart abutting the outer face of the MB2 city wall. The mudbrick top of that stable EB3 city wall also made a solid footing for other MB2 defensive construction.

But what would more excavation reveal? Dr. C tried to modulate his hope. The site was immense, the excavation crew limited in size and time.

On February 6, Carroll pushed her blond hair back from her forehead as she spoke with Dr. C, her expression a mixture of fatigue and anticipation. "That MB2 postern passageway is cutting through the mudbricks of the EB city wall, like it's leading down into something outside the wall," she said. "But where is it going?"

Dr. C stood looking down at the passageway. Since much of the tall's Bronze Age architecture is at or within a few inches of the surface, the solution was straightforward. He looked at three twenty-by-twenty-foot squares.

"Let's clear it off, these three squares," he said. "Down to the yellowish mudbrick—but don't go through it!"

The fact that the yellowish mudbrick topping the old EB wall was crusty and stubbornly hard made the excavators' progress slow as they began troweling and brushing away the looser soil. Carroll's face was

Clearing a section of the Early Bronze Age city wall (mudbricks, center right), the Middle Bronze Age city wall (stones, upper right), and other structures associated with Tall el-Hammam's defenses.

covered with the ashy dust that rose above the scene. She rushed from place to place, recording details, making notes. The stress on her face showed how important it was to her, and Dr. C felt a twang of fellowship with her as he walked briskly the three hundred yards across the huge mound to inspect another area of activity. He had scarcely arrived when his cell phone rang.

Carroll's voice was terse. "You'd better come see this."

Dr. C walked the ten minutes across the rocky mound back to the big trench. All the crew and local workers were on break, watching. The area had been cleared and swept. Carroll stood on the yellow mudbrick at the outer face of the EB city wall.

"You're gonna love this," she said, grinning through the grime on her face. With her trowel she pointed to the old yellow EB wall and what was abutting it. A large expanse of tightly laid reddish-brown mudbricks was a flourish of distinct, contrasting color.

"Wow. This couldn't be more obvious if they were black and white," muttered Dr. C as he bent down for a closer look. "But I have no idea what this means."

What was beneath the rest of the ashy soil? Which direction should he go next? He realized that the crew was silent, watching him for a reaction.

"Good job, gang!" He smiled and waved over his shoulder as he walked away. "Carry on."

Dr. C turned his attention to other active excavation areas. The meticulous Dr. Carl Morgan was uncovering a segment of the sacred precinct some two hundred yards to the north. And on the southwest corner of the lower tall, evidence of an important tower was emerging under the direction of the excavation's Season Seven Jordanian codirector, Yazeed Eylayyan. Nicknamed "the Bulldozer," Yazeed had an energy and tenacity that were matched only by his professionalism and attention to detail. His intelligence and movie-star good looks belied the fact that he was a highly experienced archaeologist with a near-legendary reputation as an excavator.

The sacred precinct and the tower and other areas kept everyone busy for the coming week. But as he oversaw the work, Dr. C kept thinking about the contrasting bricks. *Dr. Ritmeyer will know. When he comes, he'll know.*

Dutch-born Leen Ritmeyer is the world's leading expert on ancient architecture. He has studied every gateway, indeed drawn every type of ancient building, for nearly every important archaeological excavation in the southern Levant over the past thirty years. A good friend of Dr. C, he had participated eagerly in the documentation of this site with an agreeable professional opinion that Tall el-Hammam *might* be Sodom, but he never committed to more.

In the early morning sunshine of February 14, Leen Ritmeyer stood looking intently at the newly discovered reddish-brown mudbricks. "Keep brushing away along the face of the wall," he said to one of the volunteers cleaning the yellowish mudbricks at their glaring junction with the reddish ones.

Within less than two minutes, a corner appeared, and sighs of anticipation rose from the other volunteers who were gathering around. Everyone knew Ritmeyer's reputation for an almost preternatural ability to anticipate the layout of buried ancient buildings—a skill honed by decades of excavation drawings of sites all over the Levant.

He started running out his tape measure. "The opposite wall face should be about here, in line with the passageway coming through the MB2 city wall. Clear this little area, here," he said in his distinctive Dutch accent.

Within a few minutes the full width of the reddish-brown wall was exposed—more than ten feet thick.

Dr. C points to the seam where MB2 tower bricks (foreground) abut the mudbricks of the EB3 city wall.

"Seven cubits—monumental," he said, smiling and nodding.

The face of the opposing wall in line with the passageway was already exposed. It, too, abutted the yellowish mudbricks of the EB wall. Leen pulled his tape measure across the space between what could be clearly seen as two reddish-brown walls, and marked off ten feet. "Clear this off—the other corner is here."

And it was.

There was complete silence on lower Tall el-Hammam.

"It's a massive tower," Leen said confidently. "And that is *not* a postern gate," pointing to the newly cleared entryway through the MB2 city wall. "It's the entrance to this tower from inside the city."

By the end of the third day, the team had clarified the entire footprint and foundation of the recently discovered large tower. Indeed, it was massive.

Dr. C stands on the remains of the mudbrick superstructure of the MB2 gateway complex's left tower. Note the ten-foot-thick walls surrounding the inner chamber.

Dr. C could hardly believe his eyes. But there it was. An enormous MB2 tower built against and over the old EB city wall, entered by a three-foot-wide passageway through the MB city wall, cutting through eighteen feet of preserved yellowish EB mudbricks. It opened into a ten-by-fifteen-foot chamber, surrounded by tower walls more than ten feet thick.

Features visible in Trench LA.28 toward the end of Season Seven (2012): EB3 city wall (A); EB3 gateway blocked during the IBA (B); MBA city wall (C); exterior left tower of the MBA gateway complex (D); entryway through the MBA city wall into the left tower (E); domestic area (F).

The footprint of the tower, not counting the thickness of the city wall, was an immense thirty-one by forty-six feet. And, according to Ritmeyer, such towers would typically rise higher than the city wall, in this case to as much as forty-five feet above the plaza below.

"This isn't a regular defensive tower along the wall—too big," Ritmeyer said. "And it's external, extending outward from the city wall. This must be a monumental tower flanking the main city gate."

He rubbed his bearded chin, speaking almost as if to himself. "Logic, simply logic."

"But we already know there aren't any openings in the MB2 city wall foundation for at least two hundred feet left of where we were standing," Dr. C said, thinking of where he'd been, outside and facing it.

"It's all about symmetry," Ritmeyer replied mildly. "Since there isn't another tower or penetration through the city wall to the left, then the main gateway and the opposing tower to this one should be to the right."

He stepped off about twenty-five yards down the MB city wall to the right of the tower's base, which for the first time in nearly four thousand years stood exposed to sunlight. "That should do it," he said. "Clarify the wall from there to here. The main gate should be along this stretch."

Carroll mobilized volunteers and workers to begin clearing away the shallow soil covering that section of the city wall. "How wide should a main gateway be?" she asked.

Dr. C observed the scene with awe as he watched his friend. He gave expert answers without a hint of any kind of arrogance that could have accompanied his world-class status. "Two meters—four and a half cubits." Ritmeyer swept his arms out.

Dr. C figured in his head: a little over six and a half feet. And Ritmeyer began to grin, an infectious and excited grin that energized the whole excavation group—an energy that remained even after he and his wife, Kathleen, returned home to Wales a few days later.

On February 21, Carroll's husband, Jeff Kobs, discovered the left side of another opening through the city wall emerging about seventeen feet to the right of the monumental tower.

Could this be it, the great gateway of Genesis 19? Dr. C wondered. Through the crew ran a jolt of suppressed excitement. The last discovery of a main MB gateway in Israel or Jordan had taken place more than twenty years earlier.

The excavators worked briskly, and within an hour, the right side of the passageway saw daylight. Dr. C leaned in to look. "How wide is the opening?"

"Ninety centimeters." Three feet. Carroll's voice was flat. "Too small to be the main gate." She measured and remeasured. "It doesn't make sense."

The mood at the excavation deflated. Time was running out. There were only a few days left in the excavation, and all the leads to the great gate, if there was one, had not produced results.

That night back at the hotel, people washed the pottery and submitted it for reading, holding pieces up to colored charts and measuring and recording. There was a somberness there, a feeling of incompletion. For many of the excavators, this was their once-in-a-lifetime dig, and it was almost over.

Early the next morning, Yazeed's crew wrapped up work on their tower. With a grace and willingness uncommon in the testosterone-riddled, male-dominated world of Jordanian archaeology, the tall man reported for duty under Carroll's supervision to complete her area's work. The sense of fleeing time made dirt literally fly as the excavators continued exposing the city wall, much of it near the topsoil level. Another six yards appeared.

Carroll ran from place to place, keeping up with the measurements and paperwork. Too little time. So much would have to be put off until the next season.

A few hours later, Dr. C, who was helping with the sacred precinct excavation, heard his phone ring. Carroll's voice was nearly breathless.

"You're not going to believe this—we've got another opening through the MB city wall."

(left to right) Drs. Ritmeyer, Kobs, and Collins review plans for architectural reconstruction drawings of the monumental gateway.

Dr. C walked as quickly as he could to Trench LA.28. The outer left corner of the passageway was clear. Square. Solid. "How far is this from the right corner of the opening we found yesterday?" Dr. C asked.

"Five point four meters," said Jeff, a seven-season veteran volunteer.

About eighteen feet, thought Dr. C. Interesting, but nothing definitive.

"Put away all the larger picks and teriahs," Carroll told the workers the next morning, January 23. "Use only the Marshalltowns and brushes. Go only a foot deep—that's all we'll need. Let's find that other corner."

Three feet cleared—no corner.

Six feet cleared—no corner.

"I've got to go finish with Carl," Dr. C said. "Keep me posted."

His phone rang again forty-five minutes later.

"Shall I tell you now or wait till you get here?"

Dr. C just wanted the measurement.

"Two point nine zero meters." Carroll's north Texas drawl elongated the words. Just over nine feet. Substantially wider than Leen had suggested. Dr. C's eyebrows rose. He walked briskly back to the LA.28 Trench.

"It does seem a bit wide. But maybe it's just bigger than most," Carroll offered as he approached.

He shook his head, studying the situation intently. "Clear the whole passage."

About a foot and a half in from the outside left corner the stones made a sharp right turn. An inside corner.

Three more feet to the right, a left turn, parallel with the direction of the passageway: an outside corner. It cornered again, left, at the inside face of the city wall.

Dr. C laughed out loud. "It's a gate pier." With that identification, the opening shrank from 2.9 meters (over nine feet) to 2 (six and a half feet).

"That's it! That's your two-meter gate passage," Carroll said, turning her beaming face to Dr. C and Jeff. "But where's the pier on the other side?"

The workers moved carefully, metal and bristles painstakingly exposing the stones.

Suddenly, the top outside right "corner stone" wobbled and tipped outward. Jeff bent over for a closer look. He held out an open hand. "Let me see your trowel." He jammed the trowel down into the soil where the eighteen-inch boulder had been perched. It easily penetrated to the handle. Nothing but dirt.

"Just 'tumble.'" Dr. C felt uncertain, but at once Jeff stood up, grinning widely. "That isn't the corner," he chuckled. Then he pointed with the trowel three feet to the right.

"*That's* the corner." The two-meter passage had just rewidened to 2.9.

But before the crew's eyes, mirror-image turns and dimensions revealed the symmetrical twin of the left pier. At last it was certain: the width of the gateway was two meters (six and a half feet). Just what Dr. Ritmeyer said it should be.

This was the main passageway of *the* city gate.

A week later the excavation equipment was all packed up, and Dr. C stood a few feet away from the first trench he'd laid out with his own compass back at the end of Season Three, just in case he decided to focus a future excavation on the lower city. He had been so close for years.

Tears came so quickly, so suddenly, that they splattered onto the lenses of his sunglasses.

For ten years Dr. C had studied the topography of the impressive mound. For seven seasons he'd directed its excavation—digging, cataloging, recording, anticipating.

Literally under his feet, where he'd excavated for the last four seasons, had been the thing he'd most wanted to find all along. The fulfillment of a long-buried dream was now all but blinking in the bright sunlight.

Beside him, the accented voice of Leen Ritmeyer spoke in measured rhythms in the morning air, freely and eloquently describing the looming height, the grandeur, the indomitability of the ancient gate. Upon his return to Jordan, he'd come immediately to the excavation to see what had been uncovered.

He and Dr. C and videographer Daniel Galassini walked through the exposed foundations that told the story of the might of the proud ancient city. Through the previous night, Ritmeyer had worked feverishly on top drawings that he now held under one arm.

In the distance, the tamarisk trees bordering the Jordan River made their own curving green line through the Kikkar.

"Here," Ritmeyer said, pointing in one direction on Tall el-Hammam, "you can expect to find more features of the gateway in future excavations. But what we can already see is amazing."

Most important of all, the site now had a great gate.

Dr. Ritmeyer stood in the passageway. "Four cubits and a span—two meters!" he shouted into the clear air as he raised both fists in the

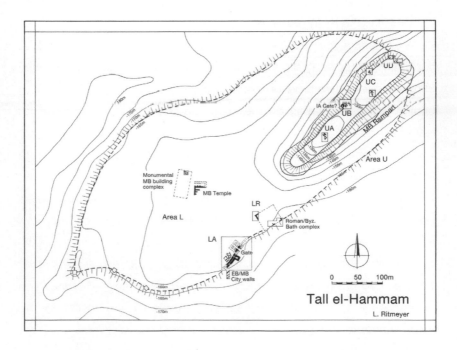

air and shook them joyously. "This is *the* monumental gateway of the city—the gateway of Sodom."

With a start, Dr. C realized what the world's foremost expert on ancient architecture had just said. And as modern men do, they high-fived each other, then began to walk toward the outer gate plaza.

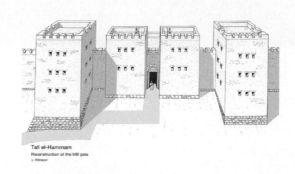

Tall el-Hammam
Reconstruction of the MB gate
L. Ritmeyer

Dr. C shows the flour-like consistency of the gray-black ash that covers the entire MB2 gateway plaza to a depth of twenty inches.

There, in the last hours of the excavation, Dr. C had ordered several small probes.

The entire area, he found, was covered by twenty inches of heavy, dark gray ash, lying directly on the plaza surface.

Just outside the monumental gateway was the truth about Sodom, a mute witness of what was left when the entire city burned to ashes— on the last day of the Bronze Age in the Land of the Kikkar.

Tale of the Trinitite

What does a necklace pendant found in the tomb of King Tutankhamun have to do with the story of how Sodom was destroyed?

The piece of jewelry is a brightly colored pectoral or chest ornament. At the top are depictions of cobras, a human eye, and tiny human figures. At the bottom are papyrus and lotus flowers. But the centerpiece is a scarab whose body is made out of a translucent pale green substance, obviously the focal point of the piece, obviously precious.

Though made three centuries after the destruction of Sodom, this pectoral reflects the great value put on the small, green, glass-like image. And glass it indeed is, high-grade desert glass, produced not by human glassmakers, who at that time in history were not yet technologically capable of this art, but rather by a heat also not intentionally attainable in the Bronze Age. A superheat that was the result of a cosmic-originated event: the collision of an explosive phenomenon with silica sand in the western Egyptian desert.

Just how this literally out-of-this-world phenomenon became connected with Tall el-Hammam is one of the most intriguing stories coming out of the ancient mound.

During the first three seasons of excavation, the Tall el-Hammam

Project was an exercise in patience. As in any dig, the archaeologist must go down through more recent strata before arriving at the more ancient. On this tall's upper mount was a city from the second half of the Iron Age, a stratum about nine feet thick. Dr. C, as a responsible archaeologist, treated all artifacts with care and provided documentation for the sake of later generations of scientists. Once a site has been excavated, there are no do-overs.

However, previous "excavators" at the site had no such noble aims. During the twentieth century the commanding views from the top of Tall el-Hammam provided a strategic advantage for tanks and large guns, which were hauled up the side of the mount, dredging pits and trenches across its surface. It was at the bottom of one of these trenches, through the saddle-shaped swale at the lowest point of the upper tall's ground, that Dr. C knew he would have the most immediate access to Bronze Age material with the least amount of excavating through overlying layers.

He couldn't undo the military damage. But he could use it.

There was a problem with this deepest area, though: within a week or two, the seasonal rains might arrive and drown the swale for the rest of the season, making excavation impossible. Working quickly but carefully, Dr. C and the team made a sounding, or exploratory shaft, going back through centuries of history in almost nine feet.

Each worker excavated for an hour at a time, inches at a time, squaring the balks (side walls) of the ever-deepening pit, photographing, drawing, cataloging, discussing. Finally the probe reached a layer of distinct, ash-laden, hard-packed soil. Dr. C and square supervisor Ginny Kay "G.K." Massara fingered through the pottery pail containing the first sherds from this new layer. It clearly dated to the Middle Bronze Age.

Dr. C descended the ladder to have a look. At the bottom of the probe, archaeology grad student Carroll Kobs was busy troweling meticulously through the hard-packed soil of Locus 7.

"Everything okay down there?" asked G.K.

"How about some water?" Dr. C replied. No sooner had he said it than he felt a little splash of water landing on his hat.

"Thanks a lot, G.K.!" he shot back, shaking his fist with a smile.

"Didn't say how you wanted it." G.K. grinned.

"I think this is the MB destruction layer—still stinks," Carroll Kobs said as she braced herself against the balk in order to stand up. At shin level all around in the cramped shaft was a layer of ash and rubble, dark and sullen, still bearing the scent of burning.

"Definitely a sealed locus," she stated confidently. This layer had remained undisturbed from the time it was deposited in antiquity.

The stratum right on top of it was from Iron Age 2, about the tenth century BCE. The new locus underneath jumped back six or seven centuries—a gap in time that would soon take on great significance.

Dr. C could hardly contain his excitement. Except for the massive mudbrick ramparts surrounding the upper city already under excavation, this was the first time at the site that his hands had touched the Middle Bronze Age destruction from the time of Abraham and Lot. A stickler for keeping balks straight and clean, he tweaked a surface here and there with his Marshalltown trowel while Carroll cleaned up the loose soil with a dustpan and sent it back up in the bucket that was attached to a rope.

The Marshalltown makes a distinctive, bell-clear sound when it strikes anything harder than soil, and suddenly he heard the ringing of Carroll's trowel filling Square UB.21W.

G.K. heard it, too. "Found something?" she called down from above.

"The surface of something, probably pottery," Carroll responded. With the edge of her trowel she eased the ashy soil away, then gently whisked it clean with a small brush. The object was about the size of the palm of her hand. She ran the point of her trowel along one edge of it and lifted it from the dark brown matrix. She held it up toward Dr. C.

His heart sank, and she could see it in his almost-blank stare. Glinting back at him was a greenish, glass-like surface.

"What's a sherd of glazed Islamic pottery doing all the way down here in a Middle Bronze Age context?" he wondered aloud. Glazing like this didn't exist in the Near East until after the seventh century CE, no less than 2,300 years later.

He took it from her hand, balancing it, glaze up, on his left palm. Then he picked it up with the thumb and forefinger of his trowel hand and turned it over. Ordinary Bronze Age pottery on that side. The striations left by fast wheeling, the composition of the clay, color, texture—everything Bronze Age. In fact, his trained eye and expertise in ancient Levantine ceramics told him that the curvature of the piece meant it came from the shoulder of a Middle Bronze 2 storage jar, one that could store forty or more gallons of olive oil, wine, or water. He'd examined such fragments and intact jars, called *pithoi*, hundreds of times. They were as common in and as characteristic of the second half of the Middle Bronze Age as eight-track tapes in the 1970s.

"Middle Bronze Age?" Carroll offered with a wide, forced grin.

"Yeah. Whew." He sighed aloud. She could see the life returning to his eyes.

But never, never such a storage jar with glaze. Never with something like glass on the outside.

His jaw began to relax. He'd seen clinkers before. In the ancient world, kilns would fire between 900 and 1,200 degrees Fahrenheit, and smelting furnaces could intentionally be coaxed to a temperature of only around 1,600 to 1,800 degrees, what was necessary to melt copper. But when gateway chambers—hollow stone-and-mudbrick rooms that often were used to store grains and olive oil—of ancient cities were besieged and burned, the flammable grains and oil would catch fire and, under the right conditions, the towering mudbrick structures could form a chimney so efficient that not only would the combustibles burn, but even mudbricks of the gatehouse could melt.

"Well, if Sodom burned as the Bible said it did," Dr. C said quietly to Carroll, "then we should expect to see evidence of things melting and burning, right?"

"Ya think?" she laughed back.

Feeling lighter now than just a few moments before, he carefully noted the location of the sherd in situ, then passed it up top to be put into the pottery pail for that locus. Carroll had already begun troweling again, looking for more artifacts, when he heard a shout from above.

"Looks like trinitite, Dr. C!" The voice belonged to Gene Hall, a volunteer excavator who, when in the military back in the 1940s, had spent time at a place called Trinity Site in southern New Mexico.

"Looks like what?" Dr. C called up.

"Trinitite. It's what happened there in the first atomic explosion when the silica sand at ground zero melted from the heat of the blast." Gene's voice sounded giddy. "I've been there. There are pieces of this stuff all over the ground at Trinity Site. I've still got some. They had to come up with a name for it, so they called it trinitite."

Dr. C scrambled up the ladder. He'd never heard of trinitite, much less seen any.

"Okay, in the sand. At Trinity Site, in southern New Mexico, I get that. But what melted the surface of this MB2 sherd?" Dr. C examined it closely in the better light. "This thing's been buried here for almost four thousand years."

By that time other workers had heard the discussion at UB.21W. A small group gathered and passed the mysterious sherd from hand to hand.

"What's remarkable about this sherd is that the other side isn't melted," Dr. C observed, turning it over and over in his hand. "So why is the outside melted and the inside isn't? And look. The surface melt on the outside face is really thin. Only a couple of millimeters. And see how the glass laps over the edge of the break just barely, maybe one millimeter? Seems like the heat that melted the surface didn't last very long. The melted surface clay was viscous only long enough to flow slightly over the edge of the break, then it stopped. So the surface got really hot, then cooled quickly. That's pretty obvious."

The implication of what Dr. C had just said wasn't lost on anyone standing in the circle. They'd heard or read his theory about Tall el-Hammam being biblical Sodom.

"But why just this one piece? Why wouldn't this stuff be all over the place?" asked Carroll.

"Well, we just cracked into the Middle Bronze Age to the tune of about two square meters, about a foot deep," Dr. C said. "Who knows what else is down there across the upper tall? Right now it's an anomaly. But it is what it is. We'll have to get it analyzed back in the States."

G.K., the pottery and object registrar for the project, carefully stored the "clinker" after she'd properly logged it. Excavation photographer Mike Luddeni took a series of photos of it.

But Dr. C had to know what it was. He had to have independent verification of what they'd unearthed.

Upon his return to the United States a few weeks later, Dr. C had just completed a lecture about the progress of the excavation in Socorro, New Mexico, when a man strode up to him.

"I'm Dr. David Burleigh," the dark-haired man said, "and I'm a materials scientist at New Mexico Technical University. Have you done any scientific testing on that piece of glazed pottery you have?"

Dr. C standing on the Middle Bronze Age destruction level of Tall el-Hammam (upper city) which yielded an MB2 pottery sherd with the outer surface melted into glass.

Dr. C breathed a prayer for divine providence. "Not glazed—melted. But no, not yet. Don't really know where to start."

"Well, I do. If I can have your permission to section off part of the sherd, we can put it through some rigorous testing with the machines we have."

Dr. C hardly dared to breathe. "I need to have someone independent of the dig examine it and tell me three things," he said. "First, is the glassy material something that came from somewhere else and dripped onto the piece of pottery—or did the clay-body itself melt?"

Burleigh nodded.

"And second, I want to know—if the glass is melt from the original pottery—what kind of temperatures and conditions would be required to melt it to that extent, without reducing the entire sherd to a little puddle of glass?"

Burleigh nodded again.

"And third, I want to know what kind of event could melt the outside face of a piece of pottery and leave the rest, bare millimeters away, untouched."

"We've got the machines," Burleigh said, "and if there are answers to your questions, we'll try to get to the bottom of them."

Over the next few days Burleigh sliced off small cubes of the sherd and prepared them by encasing them in a plastic matrix that would allow them be buffed completely flat and then coated with carbon atoms. The preliminaries done, Dr. C and Danette drove down early one morning to meet Burleigh at the U.S. Geological Survey Laboratory on the campus of New Mexico Tech. There the two scientists met with the geologist and technicians who operated the half-million-dollar Cameca SX-100 microprobe. This high-tech microscope shoots an electron stream through materials, revealing not only structure but also the chemical formula of the target source.

Burleigh handed one of the prepared samples to geochemist Nelia Dunbar, who proceeded to place it in a little compartment inside the SX-100. "What's this material?" she asked.

Dr. C and Dr. Burleigh looked at each other. Somewhat reluctantly, Dr. C produced the greenish sherd from a small, white, padded box. Written on the "normal" side in black permanent ink was its registration number: HO.5-6.UB.21W.7.367, giving the precise in situ location of the clinker: Hammam Object; Season 2005–2006; Area U, Field B; Square 21W; Locus 7; Accession Number 367. Dr. C removed it from the box and handed it to Dunbar.

"Nice piece of trinitite," she said. "Where did you get it?"

"Turn it over," said Dr. C, making little circles in the air with his forefinger.

"Oh, it's pottery," she observed aloud, eyebrows raised. "Where did this come from?"

Again the two men looked at each other.

Dr. C laughed. "Just do the tests," he grinned. "We supply the stuff, you supply the analysis!"

It was hardly a mystery, since the records accompanying the test read, "Tall el-Hammam Excavation Project, Jordan."

Dr. C, Danette, and Burleigh stayed with the USGS scientists for about two of the twelve hours of extensive testing.

(Later, walking around on the university grounds, Dr. C learned why it was that Dunbar and the technicians were so familiar with trinitite. New Mexico Tech has a world-class geological museum on campus with displays of all manner of rocks and minerals, including some fine examples of trinitite. As soon as Dr. C saw the green glass with

On the left is an MB2 pottery sherd from Tall el-Hammam, the surface of which is melted into glass with both carbon and calcium separation typical of trinitite, the two smaller pieces on the right.

tiny white inclusions caused by elemental calcium separation under extreme heat, and the flecks of black carbon separation scattered on their surfaces, Dr. C knew that what they'd found meters underground at Tall el-Hammam was a dead ringer for trinitite.)

"What would you call it? Sodomite?" He chuckled quietly to Danette. "I don't think that'll fly!"

The melt effect on HO.5-6.UB.21W.7.367 wasn't produced by any normal means, Dr. C thought. And indeed, the microprobe showed that while the green glass and the clay pottery beneath it didn't look the same, they had the identical chemical analysis. It was conclusive: nothing foreign had dripped onto the surface of the clay. Instead, the outside surface of the sherd had, itself, become molten, then instantly cooled.

In the lab, Dunbar paid special attention to the middle of the sherd section, shooting the electron beam through what looked on the screen to be a clear globule. A minute sand grain in reality, its magnified appearance made it seem immense and detailed.

"See this?" she asked. Dr. C, Danette, and Burleigh all nodded. "It's a zircon. Now, zircons are normally angular crystals, like salt crystals."

"But this one looks more like a bubble," Danette observed.

Dr. Dunbar explained, "That's because it got hot enough just to lose its angularity, then the heat dissipated and it stayed like this. A little spheroid."

"What kind of temperature does it take to do that?" Dr. C asked. "I mean, it's halfway through the clay-body almost an eighth of an inch away from the surface melt."

Dunbar wrinkled her brow. "Not precisely sure in this case. But it would have to be at least two thousand degrees Fahrenheit at the zircon location." She squinted her eyes and looked closely at the screen. "Actually, the external air temperature would've had to be a lot higher than that, because ceramic material isn't a good conductor of heat, but it reached to the depth of the zircon to the tune of two thousand degrees. But what has me puzzled isn't necessarily the heat that produced it. What's interesting is how the melt didn't go deeper into the sherd."

Burleigh rubbed his chin. "So the heat was intense enough to melt the clay surface into glass, but dissipated quickly so that only the surface of the sherd was affected."

"Yes," she said. "A burst of heat, then a quick drop in temperature."

Dr. C ran through all the scenarios that he knew from Levantine archaeology.

"Could this have happened in a room or closed space like a brick structure?" he asked, thinking of his experience at Bethsaida—corners of a gateway that heat liquefied and that ran down the wall several inches. When archaeologists found the "clinkers," as they called the resulting "melted" surfaces, they knew they were seeing the effect of something that had burned for a good bit of time, fanned into superheated frenzy by a furious wind or upward draft.

"No," Dunbar answered. "There may be ways to get the heat to that temperature, but not under any normal conditions, and not to cool it down instantaneously. It would've been a pool of glass on the floor, and taken quite a while to cool down."

"And that minuscule lapping of the glass just barely over the edge of the break—that says the glass froze in mid-melt, before it even had time to flow barely one or two millimeters," Dr. C interjected.

"Right," she replied.

Dr. C thought of another possible scenario. "What if the unbroken jar was subjected to a blast of heat—say, near a door to an intensely hot, burning room that suddenly burst open—the surface began to melt, then the jar exploded and the broken pieces were instantly dowsed by the cool liquid inside the vessel?"

"Maybe," she said. "But that wouldn't explain the calcium and carbon separation. An intensely burning room could only get to about sixteen hundred, maybe eighteen hundred degrees for a while, but not for long. And even a sudden burst of heat at that temperature wouldn't be enough to melt a pottery surface unless it was sustained for a good bit of time. Tough to do. The temps just aren't high enough. And the elemental separation is a problem, like I said. Remember, that zircon away from the glass at the surface had to get to at least two thousand degrees Fahrenheit. Just not possible in a burning room even with a lot of fuel."

"How about in a kiln?" asked Burleigh. "Or smelting process?"

Dr. C knew ancient pottery was fired between 900 to 1200 degrees Fahrenheit. Far too cool. Smelting copper required the skillful use of bellows to bring the temperature up to 1800 degrees or so. Iron? Dr. C wondered. About the same.

"Same problem with any man-made, low-tech fire," one technician said. "Durative heat. No way to dissipate the heat so that it didn't affect the whole sherd. It was a flash of something and then suddenly much cooler."

Everyone in the room stared at the zircon bubble on the monitor.

Dunbar broke the silence as she moved the electron beam from the zircon to the glass at the surface with the joystick. She increased the resolution. "Look at the molecular structure of the glass near the surface. Only a couple of things can do that," she explained. "One is volcanic magma spewed into cold air or water and cooled instantly." The group stared at the screen. "This makes me think of that—very few crystals. This is the typical 'quench texture' of volcanic glasses." She knew this well: magma was her specialty.

"But this isn't volcanic material," she continued. "Materially, chemically, it's kaolin, made from clayey soil or silt and sand. It's about half silica. I called it trinitite when I first saw it because it looks exactly like the melted surface material at the Trinity Site. They detonated it in an area covered with a lot of sand, and most of the trinitite we see from there still has grains of virgin sand sticking to it, the silica that didn't melt. It was a heat flash and instant cooling." She pointed to the surface glass hugely magnified on the screen. "Just like that."

"Could lightning do this?" asked Dr. C. "I think it's called fulgurite."

"Possible, but it usually looks quite different," Dunbar clarified. "A lot of times it looks like fossilized tree roots, but it's where the lightning hits the sand and melts these tubular fingers through it. But you have to cut it open to see the green glass. It's like this," she said, pointing to the sherd, "but inside out."

"But the best match is trinitite?" Dr. C asked.

"Across the board, yes. Visually, materially, chemically—it's the same result."

"The required heat index and duration would have to be similar to that resulting in trinitite, correct?" Dr. C asked.

"In order to get two similar results, theoretically similar conditions would have to exist. Correct," responded Dunbar.

At the end of the testing process, Dunbar provided Dr. C with a digital copy of the results, and a printout of the data with annotated photographs taken by the microprobe. In layman's terms, the upshot of the analysis is this: its two "parts," pottery and glass, are chemically identical—kaolin. One part, one side, though, had been superheated into glass and then rapidly cooled (in a manner similar to airborne magma becoming volcanic glass), while leaving underlying crystal grains as distinct "bubbles," and the rest unchanged.

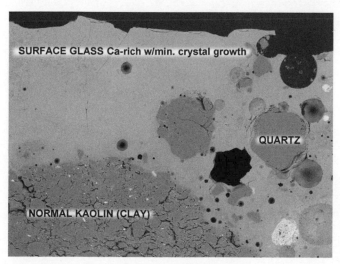

SURFACE GLASS Ca-rich w/min. crystal growth

QUARTZ

NORMAL KAOLIN (CLAY)

Section of MB2 pottery sherd surface melt under Cameca SX-100 microprobe showing glass, mineral "bubbles," and other high-heat features.

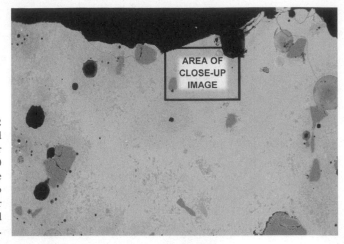

Section of MB2 pottery sherd surface melt under Cameca SX-100 microprobe showing close-up target area for increased magnification.

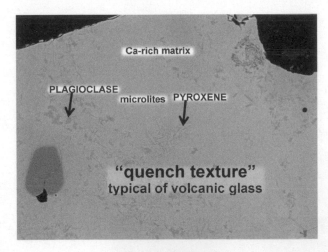

Section of MB2 pottery sherd surface melt under Cameca SX-100 microprobe showing features typical of volcanic glass.

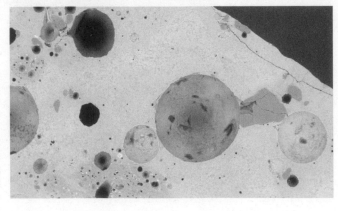

Section of MB2 pottery sherd surface melt under Cameca SX-100 microprobe showing zircons and other crystals as spheroids resulting from high heat and rapid cooling.

It would be several more seasons of excavation before more sherds with these characteristics were found at Tall el-Hammam—a total of five now registered from excavated contexts hundreds of meters apart, four from the lower tall. (The carefully excavated sounding in which Dr. C and his team found the first clinker sherd was full of water each time they proposed reopening it, and keeping an archaeological balk secure when it's soaked is nearly impossible and almost always counterproductive. So, for safety, the square was recently backfilled.)

In addition, at several places within five miles of the tall, pieces of greenish desert glass have been found, documented, and cataloged. Like the desert glass of western Egypt, these are not geological in origin, but something else altogether.

Such glass, also called "impact glass," is the result of particular kinds of cosmic-penetration events. They can be any varieties of sizable meteors, asteroids, or comet fragments that—whether as so-called craterless airbursts or as crater-producing impacts—create extremely high temperatures within their impact zones. The temperatures generated by these events gener-ally exceed those of nuclear ex-

Desert glass (melted silica sand) from near Tall el-Hammam. The melting of sand into lumps of glass is a phenomenon typical of "cosmic airbursts" over areas where sand is surface-exposed.

plosions. For comparison, at 150 to 200 feet from the core of a nuclear detonation the temperature rises to over 18,000 degrees Fahrenheit. Ground temperatures of typical aerial detonations—such as those over Japan—typically reach 11,000 degrees Fahrenheit.

In locations with silica sand or other silica-based materials, impact glass can result. However, the explosive dynamics of these kinds of cosmic impacts prevents the formation of a simple layer of glass, as even the force of craterless impacts—consisting of a kind of debris-plasma superheated by the speed of penetration through earth's atmosphere—tends to severely disrupt the affected surface area. And that's an understatement.

What would have been the effect of that kind of destructive force and superheat on mudbrick buildings and human bodies? Dr. C. wondered. He thought of the documentaries he'd seen, the reading he'd done, on the physical effects of atomic bombs on Hiroshima and Nagasaki. Some of the people who were in direct line of exposure to those blasts, witnesses later reported, simply vaporized in an instant. There would be no documenting vaporized bodies if there had been any at Tall el-Hammam, no proof they ever existed.

Others at the Japanese detonation sites were superheated and their bodies exploded into thousands of pieces. Still others who were shadowed by buildings or other objects survived the catastrophic blast in its first instants but were thrown around by its impact, or died later from radiation poisoning.

But the atomic bomb wasn't the focus of Dr. C's thought. He didn't want to incite the unfettered imaginations of those he called the "pseudoscientific Internet Web-wackos" who'd already speculated that the ancient Egyptians must have used nuclear weapons because of the desert glass found in King Tut's tomb. He wanted no part of that kind of nonsense. But he did want to consider events in nature—not wrought by human hands and minds—that might offer reasonable scientific explanations of what may have terminated Kikkar civilization.

He pondered that piece of desert glass in one of the most famous pieces of jewelry in the world, the pectoral of Tutankhamun. Examinations of the green material found in western Egypt had led scientists like Mark Boslough of Sandia National Laboratories to conclude that some sort of quick, superlatively hot event had occurred in the air over the desert there in unrecorded history, converting exposed sand into chunks of the rare, greenish substance so prized by pharaohs. "For twenty seconds," Boslough says, "the resulting fireball would have been hot enough to melt quartz on the ground, creating the glass that can still be found in the desert."

Dr. C thought of Meteor Crater in Arizona and the greenish glass that formed around that area when the massive heavenly object struck the silica-laden desert. But no one had witnessed that event, either. And there were no craters near Tall el-Hammam.

Without an atomic bomb to create such an effect, says the latest research in astro- and impact physics, the blame would have to fall on a meteor or other midair event producing heat so intense and fleeting that it could melt just the surfaces of the inanimate things exposed to it.

Aside from the heat of these phenomena, the sheer force would be horrific—unimaginable force.

Siberia, he thought. Tunguska, Siberia, 1908. An entire forest, more than one thousand square miles, with 80 million stark, incinerated trees flattened like spilled toothpicks.

EIGHT

The Death of Sodom

THE FAMOUS CITIES OF THE KIKKAR AND ALL THAT SUR-rounded them met a sudden and catastrophic end. Text and ground both testify to the fact. The only written record we have of their sudden disappearance from life in the region describes something so horrific, so violent that many scholars have suspected the account of their destruction to be fictional or, at best, the indelible residual memory of some powerful geological phenomenon, perhaps from the prehistoric past.

The historical geology of the Kikkar doesn't lend itself to such a thing—at least not for any time frame that would correspond with human civilization. Although geological explanations are thin, highly speculative, and contrary to the fundamental language of the text itself, there *are* well-studied physical phenomena of cosmic origin that could account for both the archaeological facts on the ground and the description of the event preserved in Genesis 19.

From a biblical point of view, only the causation is without question: deliberate and divine retribution. But the physics of the event is where the controversy should properly enter the scientific arena. Often the speculation regarding the exact nature of Sodom's destruction stretches the grammatical boundaries of the biblical text to the breaking point and beyond. That makes it all the more important to know exactly what the text says—

and doesn't say. If the Genesis story authentically preserves a phenomeno-logical ("as the ancients saw it") description of a real, civilization-smashing Kikkar disaster, then we can compare that language with what relevant scientific disciplines—like impact physics—have to say about such things. We can also compare the observations from actual events and the predictions of scientific models with what's found in the archaeology of the Kikkar.

From the triad of ancient text, cosmic science, and archaeology, it may be possible to catch a reasonable glimpse of the event that snuffed out life in the Land of the Kikkar so long ago.

Thus it's important to clarify what the Bible actually says about the destruction of Sodom and Gomorrah, Admah and Zeboiim, and the Land of the Kikkar.

Key Biblical Indicators of Destruction

THE FOLLOWING BIBLICAL DATA POINTS are drawn from passages that deal specifically with the destruction of the Cities of the Kikkar. Key indicators from the book of Genesis deal specifically with the destruction of the Cities of the Kikkar:

"Swept Away" (19:15, 17)

THE DIVINE MESSENGER TELLS LOT and his family of the imminent annihilation of their city and that they must escape Sodom lest they "be swept away" when the city is punished. The Hebrew term for "swept away" is *sph,* which almost invariably involves "dramatic change or removal." While *sph* does not necessarily imply that whatever is "swept away" will cease to exist entirely without any visible residue, it does generally indicate a comprehensive removal or destruction.

"Then the LORD Rained Down Burning Sulfur on Sodom and Gomorrah—from the LORD out of the Heavens" (19:24).

THERE ARE TWO HEBREW TERMS used here in a doublet: "sulfur and fire," a fact that isn't made clear in some translations, including the New International Version.

First of all, the consecutive construction of the two terms does not at all imply that "fire" or "burning" can or should be taken as a modifier of "sulfur." Indeed, the two nouns should probably be considered distinct because the pairing of the two terms does not necessarily, or even normally, mean "burning sulfur."

Here's why. The word translated as "sulfur" is *gopriyt*. Used seven times in the Old Testament, *gopriyt* is itself often understood as "burning sulfur," although that idea is mostly inferred from traditional imagination rather than the basic meaning of the word—and because the nominative of *gopriyt* "denotes an inflammable material of which lightning was held to consist" (Ezekiel 38:22), according to linguist J. A. Naude.

We can't attribute a specific chemical meaning to the term, at least not in any modern, scientific sense.

Thus, while *gopriyt* can refer to the naturally occurring element sulfur, its range of meaning is by no means confined to that, especially when the substance proceeds from a heavenward direction. If it does indeed refer to the essence of lightning, its range of meaning is much wider. It's entirely possible that the application of the term to chemical sulfur, which is yellow in its solid, crystalline state, is a secondary semantic referent—the primary referent being the yellow glow of fire, lightning, or even the sun.

Some translations of the Bible use the term "brimstone" to render the word *gopriyt,* taking their cue from the Masoretic scribes who first "pointed" the Hebrew text. However, *gopriyt* does not have an inherent, biblical connection to the idea of the English etymology of "burning rock" that brimstone conveys.

The word for "fire" is *'esh*. Simply put, *'esh* can refer to "fire" of all kinds and descriptions, from sparks to cooking fires, from lightning to sunlight.

Let's clarify what the text actually says and what it does not say. It says that whatever came from a heavenward direction to destroy Sodom and Gomorrah was a fiery phenomenon emitting (yellowish) light. Though the text doesn't specify, we could expect such an event to be accompanied by a thunderous noise. It does not say that the fire consisted of burning sulfur, or that the burning material (gas? particles?) was sulfurous at all (although it certainly could have been).

What it boils down to is fire (*'esh*) and lightning (*gopriyt*) "out of the heavens." *Gopriyt,* like *'esh,* when coming out of the sky, should be translated "lightning": Ezekiel 38:22; Isaiah 30:33; Psalm 11:6; Deuteronomy 29:22–23; Genesis 19:24. All these passages make more sense with *gopriyt* as lightning rather than sulfur.

We do know this: it was full of *gopriyt* and it was on fire.

"Rained Down . . . out of the Heavens" (19:24)

THIS PASSAGE CLEARLY STATES THAT the fiery judgment came from a skyward direction. A Hebrew or Semitic cognate analysis would add nothing to what is plainly communicated by the translation. The implication is that the burning mass penetrated the atmosphere from above the surface of the Kikkar. Whatever it was, it obliterated virtually everything in its target area, perhaps leaving only the foundations of the largest structures.

Many have speculated in the past that such a conflagration would have depended on the existence of flammables such as petroleum, asphalt, and bitumen in the area. However, such a firestorm that could cause the destruction described in the Bible would have carried its own explosive incendiary power, enough, perhaps, to actually melt ordinary sand and other materials given the right conditions.

"Thus He Overthrew Those Cities and the Entire Plain, Destroying All Those Living in the Cities—and Also the Vegetation in the Land" (19:25; see also 19:29)

MUCH HAS BEEN MADE OF the term "overthrew." The Hebrew word, *hpk,* has a range of meanings, including "turn, overturn, destroy, change."

With reference to what happened to the Cities of the Kikkar, some scholars have literalized the meaning of the related Akkadian term, *abaku,* meaning "to overturn" or "turn upside down," to suggest that Sodom and Gomorrah were "overturned" as the result of a geological event that buried them under a layer of earth. While I wouldn't categorically reject such an interpretation on lexical grounds, it would be just about the only such usage among dozens in the Hebrew Scriptures. In such a context, the actual meaning is probably more like Akkadian *abiktu,* which denotes "defeat" or "decisive defeat, massacre, carnage."

"The Entire Plain" (19:25)

IF THE "ENTIRE KIKKAR" WAS overthrown, then the area affected was not only that portion lying east of the Jordan River, but also that portion of the Kikkar west of the river, namely Jericho and its environs. Although the western Kikkar was not the primary target of destruction, it's reasonable to assume that it may have suffered serious collateral damage.

"All Those Living in the Cities" (19:25)

THE FIERY CATASTROPHE KILLED ALL the inhabitants of the Cities of the Kikkar. But is it possible that people living outside the city walls could have survived? This seems doubtful, since even the vegetation of the region was burned up. The animals as well probably would not have survived.

"The Vegetation in the Land" (19:25)

THE HEBREW WORD TRANSLATED "VEGETATION," *tsemakh,* is interesting because it doesn't refer just to plant life, but more specifically to the growth part of a plant such as the shoot or bud. (For example, it's distinguished from *siakh,* used earlier in Genesis for "seed-bearing plant," "green plant," and "plant of the field.") So it's possible that the destruction of the vegetation (*tsemakh*) of the Kikkar consisted of the burning and/or scorching of new annual growth but not necessarily a complete extermination of the flora all over the area. If this be the case, nomadic and seminomadic peoples, who needed pasture for their flocks, could have soon reinhabited the area in the postconflagration era. On the other hand, *tsemakh* may simply refer to "crops." So, the biblical language would also allow the possibility that the destruction was so catastrophic that it took decades or centuries for the area to recover sufficiently to support agriculture once again.

"[Abraham] Looked Down [from the Area of Hebron] Toward Sodom and Gomorrah, Toward All the Land of the Plain, and He Saw Dense Smoke Rising from the Land, Like Smoke from a Furnace" (19:28)

ABRAHAM, FROM SOME VANTAGE POINT (probably) east of the Hebron vicinity, was able to see a huge, dense column of smoke rising from the area of destruction, which could have been as large as four hundred square kilometers or more. Smoke from such a calamity may have been visible at distances much greater than from Hebron (about forty-five miles to the southwest).

"Dense Smoke . . . Like Smoke from a Furnace" (19:28)

THE IDEA OF "DENSE" SMOKE is read into the Hebrew term (*qtr*) by some translators, but isn't actually a feature of it. The Akkadian *qataru* carries the meaning "to smoke . . . blacken with smoke . . . be blackened, darkened," "rise, billow," and "make an incense offering"; but, like the equivalent Hebrew word, it has nothing to say about the density, color (other than its sooty, darkened nature), or other noteworthy features of the smoke. That it was "like smoke from a furnace" (Heb. *kibshan*) may indicate the familiar columnar pattern of smoke that rose from ancient pottery kilns or smelting furnaces.

A Summary of Destruction Indicators from the Biblical Text

THUS THE BIBLICAL TEXT'S PHENOMENOLOGICAL details provide valuable information about the nature and scope of the destruction of the Cities of the Kikkar. In summary, here are the apparent facts derived from the language of destruction in the Genesis record of Sodom and Gomorrah, enlightened by the known physical effects of such phenomena:

1. Regardless of its point of origin, the fiery matrix that rained down upon the Cities of the Kikkar descended from the heavens, that is, through the atmosphere above the Kikkar.

2. When the burning mass struck the surface of the Kikkar, it caused the region's cities and vegetation to burst into flames, possibly even blowing ("sweeping") the cities' mudbrick structures off their stone foundations with a powerful shock wave.

3. The thunderous firestorm was so concentrated that the inhabitants of the Kikkar were unable to escape death. The description of the fire and *gopriyt* make it logical that some people were vaporized. Some burned or were asphyxiated from breathing smoke or superheated air. Others were

killed by the concussion effect of the blast, or trauma caused by disintegrating objects such as stone and brick. Such a matrix traveling through earth's atmosphere at an extremely high velocity, and its impact, would also produce immense electromagnetic discharges—lightning, *gopriyt*.

4. In the aftermath, a great column of smoke and disintegrated debris, probably as much as fifteen to twenty kilometers in diameter, rose from the burning, scorched land and was easily visible from locations such as Hebron forty-five miles away.

5. The Cities of the Kikkar were catastrophically destroyed, or "overturned." They were left in utter ruin, if not partially or entirely removed from the visible realm of existence. The entire Land of the Kikkar suffered an ecological disaster that may have required centuries of recovery before it could once again support permanent urban populations.

A Possible Scenario for the Destruction Event

WHAT I'M ABOUT TO DESCRIBE here for comparison with the destruction language of the biblical text isn't science fiction. Cosmic impact phenomena are, in a manner of speaking, routine for planet earth. Such impacts make up one of the most well-studied and modeled set of phenomena in astrophysics. While the precise composition and origin of the objects that cause such events aren't always known, there are enough observable data from impacts scattered around the globe to give scientists a good idea of the physical forces—a concert of material, mass, velocity, and trajectory—behind their catastrophic reality.

As is the case with many stories in the Bible, Genesis is almost terse in its description of the destruction event of Sodom and the Cities of the Kikkar. While it's presented as a custom-designed and unique supernatural event, it's also true that it had many natural, physical features (in the same way lightning is used in 2 Samuel 22:15 to rout enemies). As a matter of fact, most conjecture about what happened in the Kikkar of the Jordan when Sodom and the Cities of the Plain were destroyed has to do with elements of nature. One of the most popular theories is that an earthquake released gases that ignited, as already mentioned.

Investigating "similar" events in earth's history isn't a denial of the miraculous. In fact, being able to scientifically document other such instances brings the Bible out of its supposed status as a fable and into its proper place as an accurate representation of the events it describes. Indeed, the Sodom impact event isn't described as something like "the breath of God" or "lightning from God's fingertips," but simply as a physical fireball with all the heat and smoke that real cosmic fireballs create. And if it really happened, its aftermath is open to scientific investigation.

Given the specifics we have in the Bible about the destruction event of Sodom—fire and *gopriyt* from the skies that destroyed life in the Kikkar and caused a colossal column of smoke that was visible for long distances—looking for the aftereffects of similar phenomena provides solid ground for a theory of what may have happened in the Kikkar in the days of Abraham.

My colleague Dr. John Witte Moore and I have collated substantial research from other scientists who believe that asteroid and comet fragments striking the earth (or exploding in midair) may be responsible for some significant and otherwise inexplicable changes in the history of the earth.

Annually, we can see with the unaided eye the delightful "meteor showers" that are fragments of comets; however, when a large chunk of a comet actually collides with the earth, it's usually catastrophic. Moore describes "huge explosions with blasts of hot air similar to nuclear blasts . . . followed by fire, great winds, and the ejection of huge quantities of debris into the atmosphere" that could result in "nuclear winter" scenarios.

Moore, following the research of several notable scientists, thinks that comet strikes in the Near East vicinity could explain, for example, how, prior to the Sodom incident, the Early Bronze Age came to such a precipitous and mysterious end. (Recall also the famous impact that many scientists believe caused the extinction of the dinosaurs.) But during a period when comet activity was high for centuries, there must have been smaller strikes, perhaps some of which could properly be classified as "airbursts."

Citing the example of Tunguska, Siberia, Moore describes what happens when a meteoric object consumes itself just above the ground before impact: "Such an airburst creates a huge explosion with considerable damage to the area below and, more importantly, it might leave no debris or evidence of the nature of the event."

Moore continues: "If it was an airburst, such as the strike at Tunguska, there might be no dramatic physical evidence of the event such as a crater. The findings on the ground, however, might still provide clues. First, the air blast would level all standing objects in the vicinity [the wide-scale leveling of the trees was essentially the only finding at Tunguska]. Such an occurrence over an ancient city would have the effect of blasting all habitation off the top of a tall with the possible exception of the larger foundations and walls. Data consistent with such a scenario appear in the excavation reports of both Tall Nimrin and Tall el-Hammam on the Jordan Disk. The nature of archaeological debris around these sites could suggest such an event. At any rate, an airburst would account for the area becoming a 'wasteland' for hundreds of years, as Numbers 21:20 describes."

The research of Sandia physicist Mark Boslough on airburst events describes their killer potential. While he has used Sandia's Red Storm supercomputer to simulate what happens in such impacts, evidence in Tunguska and Egypt demonstrate, says Boslough, that "atmospheric explosions could create fireballs that would be large enough and hot enough to fuse surface materials to glass much like the first atomic explosion generated green glass at the Trinity site in 1945."

Clues to airburst events might also include actual cometary or asteroid debris scattered around impact sites. For example, rare elements like

iridium and osmium can indicate the presence of comet residues. However, decades of intensive research at the Tunguska impact site have
failed to produce any elemental or molecular "smoking" gun. So the
"what" remains a mystery, even if the result is clear. And if scientists can't
tell what toasted Tunguska in 1908, then perhaps we shouldn't be sur-
prised if we never discover what exactly incinerated the eastern Kikkar
nearly four thousand years ago. That "what" may also remain a mystery,
even though its civilization-ending result is abundantly clear.

So What Happened to the Kikkar?

WITH THE DYNAMICS OF EXPLOSIVE airbursts firmly on the table of
hard science—

And with the MB2 incendiary demise of Tall el-Hammam and its
neighboring Cities of the Kikkar established in the archaeological record—

And with the phenomenological language of Genesis 19 describing
the fiery, cosmic destruction of the Land of the Kikkar in the time of
Abraham—

It's now possible to superimpose these three data sets and observe
points of correspondence, to tell the story afresh, looking not only
through Abraham's eyes, but also through the eyes of the physicist and
the archaeologist (see Destruction Comparison Chart).

A harmony of perspectives reinforces the reality of that final, fateful
day when the Bronze Age ended untimely on the eastern Kikkar, circa
1650 BCE.

But first, we shouldn't lose sight of the biblical story amid the flash of
mere cosmic explosions. According to the Genesis text, the destruction
event of Sodom and the other cities didn't simply coincide with a natural
phenomenon. It was predicted by Yahweh, who controlled comets, and
his warning of coming events was a manifestation of his friendship with

Abraham, the openness of friends with each other. It was as much about protection as it was prediction:

> Then Yahweh said, "Shall I hide from Abraham what I am about to do? Abraham will surely become a great and powerful nation, and all nations on earth will be blessed through him. For I have chosen him, so that he will direct his children and his household after him to keep the way of Yahweh by doing what is right and just, so that Yahweh will bring about for Abraham what he has promised him." (Genesis 18:17–19; translation amended by Collins.)

Before 1908, people saw only the aftereffects of cosmic collisions with the earth in places like Meteor Crater, Arizona. There an enormous bowl in the sand, three-fourths of a mile in diameter, stands as mute witness to what happens when a celestial fragment hits the earth.

But as already noted, in recorded history as recently as 1908 over a remote area in Siberia, a comet chunk or small asteroid disintegrated in midair, never actually reaching the ground in solid form, nevertheless devastating the area. We have the eyewitness accounts of what happened there. As far away as London, the night sky lit up bright enough to read a newspaper. Even today, more than a hundred years later, the trunks of trees flattened by the force of the explosion still lie like toothpicks scattered on the forest floor, which is still recovering from the trauma.

Tall el-Hammam and its Kikkar kingdom suffered, I believe, a similar fate. But whereas such a cosmic event flattened 1,500 square miles of forest near Tunguska, the area of the Kikkar was much more concentrated, between five hundred and eight hundred square miles.

The day after Yahweh told Abraham that he was going to destroy an entire culture because of its wickedness, he did what he said he would do.

One moment the sun was rising, casting its rays onto the immense walls of the fortified city of Sodom. Inside, as in all the Cities of the Kikkar, people were going about their own self-centered and indulgent lives.

Perhaps some had breakfast, while others had hangovers. Yet others, still with the taste of dissipation in their mouths, rose and thought of what they could do to advance their lifestyles and their influence. Men and women alike looked to what they saw as the security and inevitability of a new day, the thought that their city walls and their riches and their king protected them.

Without any warning, the light of the sun paled in comparison with a greater, blinding light in the sky, accompanied by the kineticism of the same kinds of electromagnetic charges documented thousands of years later by photographs of atomic blasts. There was a single moment when the light and heat from the sky incinerated everything they reached.

Sand melted into glass. Parts of pottery vessels, directly exposed in courtyards or on rooftops, became like trinitite. All exposed life either vaporized or, if protected from the direct blast, was torn apart, limb from limb, branch from tree, gates and arms and legs from their sockets.

Perhaps, and most probably, no space fragment hit the earth, only the superheated molecular debris and earth atmosphere as the object exploded and disintegrated on entry. The plasma-like matrix formed a fireball so consuming, so voracious, that it even consumed itself.

And with the instantaneous blast came a destructive, thunderous shock wave that boomed out from the impact at an oblique angle, ripping loose materials from agricultural fields and living surfaces, and literally knocking cities off their foundations, tearing mudbricks from their hidden base stones, reducing them in the concussive crush to mere dust in the blink of an eye.

The cooler surrounding air rushed into the superheated impact zone, then spiraled heavenward with violent, tornadic motion, as the columnar vacuum of space, stretched down by the object's near-instantaneous penetration of the earth's atmosphere, collapsed.

The event, as superexplosive airbursts do, aspirated the very atmosphere upward in a shaft of smoke and debris that plumed above the atmosphere in an enormous black vortex. Growing from the ominous pillar of destruction, a spreading mushroom cloud discharged white-hot, gesticulant fingers of lightning, warning off distant observers whose gaze was transfixed by the spectacle of death.

In the dust and particles of disintegration—of all that moments before had been the great Land of the Kikkar—Sodom was stretched thin, suspended between earth and heaven. Touching neither.

Two days' journey from Sodom, near the Oaks of Mamre in the district of Hebron, Abraham felt the sound of terror—a violent wind, the deafening applause of thunder. Never before had he heard—this. But he knew what it was. He turned in the direction of Sodom and saw the dense, polluting smoke rising above clouds, above air, beyond sight. Abraham, broker of deals, cutter of covenants, had bargained for every soul in the great city. They were no more.

Within minutes the deafening thunder began to diminish into a low-pitched, rumbling drone. Motion slowed. The upward surge stopped.

Then it began to rain over the Kikkar. Not water, but bits and chunks of heavier debris now falling from the dying vortex—

Fragments of newly formed desert glass.

Fragments of mudbricks and pottery.

Fragments of idols and weapons and people.

And ash falling like a blizzard of black snow.

For one eternal moment the Kikkar held its breath, sucked away from every lung.

And yet no eye ever recorded what went on that day inside the pulverized walls, for every pupil and iris burned up in the blast. There was no time for thought or panic—a mercy, indeed. No one who experienced it survived to tell the story.

The ancient mind didn't know how to process such an awesome sight, how to talk about something that was beyond words, except to say that it was like fire, like lightning, like sulfur, like the waves of heat and distortion of sight such as the smoke blast from an opened furnace door produced. Something you turned away from, or it destroyed you, too.

Perhaps the resultant fires smoldered for days, for weeks, or even like Gehenna for months. No one knows for how long the judgment of Yahweh rained down the dust of what had been the city, and the ashes of what had been its people and its possessions, upon the ruins of Sodom, to form a layer so silent, so grim, that no one would approach it for dozens of generations, for hundreds of years, for the greater part of a millennium.

Sodom. The city whose name was whispered in fear, in dread, in threat, in curse until it became part of all vocabularies, the stuff of all nightmares, the dust and ash of all fears.

Evidence Is Evidence

T HROUGH THE YEARS, TRINITY SOUTHWEST UNIVERSITY has been blessed with the input and participation of world-class scholars who have offered a unique perspective. Among them is Dr. John W. Oller Jr., whose impressive lifetime body of work has concentrated on theories of linguistics and sign systems in general. Specifically, his teachings on a specific aspect, the "true narrative representation," or TNR, have rippled through the scholarship of the university. He asserts that the Bible is a true narrative representation of the events and people it portrays—a profound claim from an academician who breathes the rarefied air of the upper echelons of higher linguistic scholarship.

"In all TNRs, relative to the facts portrayed the words do not demand any more nor less than the facts deliver, and the facts do not contain anything inconsistent with the words. Therefore, the words are *exactly* as true as they claim, forever," says Oller.

Using the framework of TNR, Trinity professor Dr. Peter Briggs developed and applied a criterial screen in which he identified the site of Khirbet el-Maqatir as the biblical Ai described in the book of Joshua; just as our excavation has used a similar screen of indicators in the Bible to identify Tall el-Hammam as Sodom.

In spite of its limitations and shortcomings, this book has attempted to present a true narrative representation of the discovery of Sodom, in a manner that reflects the true narrative representational nature of the source of the site's history, the Bible.

The existence of a significant Middle Bronze Age city at Tall el-Hammam is now confirmed beyond any doubt. In terms of the biblical Sodom criteria, it's in the right place, at the right time, with all the right stuff. If this isn't Sodom, then I guess we'll have to jettison most other biblical city identifications, because in many ways this evidence is geographically and archaeologically superior to most of those (see tables in Appendix C). Evidence is evidence.

Of course, my findings remain controversial because they counter more than a century of conflicting theories. I understand and appreciate critiques of my work, though it's sometimes annoying to have to re-address criticisms that I've laid to rest time and time again. But that goes with the territory. Whether they agree with me or not, fellow archaeologists and biblical scholars have learned that I don't run from even the toughest questions. In fact, I welcome them.

This research has hardly taken place in a scholastic vacuum: for years I've taken every phase of my writing on the subject and emailed it to dozens of top scholars, inviting their critical review of my ideas. Many have engaged with helpful interactions—people like Anson Rainey, David Maltsberger, Israel Finkelstein, Amihai Mazar, Leen Ritmeyer, Thomas Schaub, William Fulco, Steve Ortiz, Aren Maeir, David Noel Freedman, Ziad al-Saad, James Tabor, Alan Millard, and a number of others.

I want to know what other scholars think because iron sharpens iron. I'm grateful for scholars who actually take the time to become familiar enough with the overall subject, including my views and research, to speak meaningfully about it, as did the highly respected and recently deceased professor Anson Rainey. We corresponded before his final illness, and I'd just sent him a copy of some of my latest ideas arising from our excavations at Tall el-Hammam the day he went to the hospital, never to recover.

Over the years Rainey responded graciously and often instantaneously by email to discuss the location of Sodom and the Cities of the Plain. He regarded my "Kikkar argument" as the crux of the issue, agreeing even to the extent of stating that he wanted to amend his treatment of Sodom's location in his masterful atlas, *The Sacred Bridge,* to reflect a proper understanding of what we both accepted as a formal geographical construct demarcating the thirty-kilometer-diameter, circular alluvial plain of the Jordan immediately north of the Dead Sea as "the Kikkar."

To be fair, I'd never say that Anson—while he agreed with me completely about the Kikkar—thought that Tall el-Hammam was biblical Sodom, per se. Specifically, he believed that Tall el-Hammam was likely the gargantuan and easily visible pile of ancient ruins that gave rise to the etiological stories about Sodom.

Types of Opposing Views

CRITICISMS AGAINST MY IDENTIFICATION OF Tall el-Hammam as Sodom have come in six basic flavors: (1) a priori denial; (2) etiological legend; (3) cultural memory; (4) historical kernel; (5) wrong location; and (6) wrong time.

These opposing views, as voiced by some of the excellent scholars who've either spoken with me or written concerning them, deserve consideration. My disagreement with them regarding the reality and location of Sodom and the Cities of the Plain does not diminish in any way my high regard for their scholarship. I value the important contributions that these scholars make to the discipline of Levantine archaeology—even biblical archaeology—and ancient Near Eastern studies.

1. A Priori Denial

This view dismisses outright the historicity of the Sodom narratives, asserting that the Cities of the

Plain never existed in physical reality. And if Sodom and Gomorrah were purely mythical, why waste time looking for them?

The principal adherent of this view is William Dever (professor emeritus, University of Arizona), long recognized as the American patriarch of Syro-Palestinian archaeology. Dr. Dever has been my guest lecturer at two Trinity Southwest University archaeological symposia, and we get along famously. However, he's always assured me that everything about the Sodom tales is purely mythological. One year at the American Schools of Oriental Research (ASOR), while I was standing near a big display poster titled "Tall el-Hammam/Sodom," Bill came over and said good-naturedly, "Enjoy it, because this is as close as you'll ever get to Sodom!"

In 2007, our excavation at Tall el-Hammam and my search for Sodom were featured in an article on the front page of the *Wall Street Journal*. In that article Dever aimed the following criticism at me: "No responsible scholar goes out with a trowel in one hand and a Bible in the other."

In spite of my appreciation for his personality and expertise, consider the irony: even Dever can't avoid using the Bible when he maintains, for instance, that the famous six-chambered, Iron Age gate at Tel Gezer in Israel is "Solomonic." Is not the Bible the *only* ancient source for our knowledge of King Solomon?

My response to Dever and other "anti-Textualists" in the academic community is this: no responsible scholar excavating in the Levant goes out *without* a trowel in one hand and the best extant ancient texts, including the Bible, in the other.

2. Etiological Legend

Those who take this tack contend that the Sodom
narratives are nonhistorical at their root. They would say
that the story of Yahweh's wrath against the Cities of the
Plain was fabricated as "pious fiction" by Israelite and/
or Judahite priests who, after the ninth century BCE,
wanted to explain the existence of the many piles of ruins
on the eastern Kikkar, particularly Tall el-Hammam.
Prominent scholars in this category are Rainey and
I. Finkelstein.

Although this view dismisses the Sodom narratives
as historical, it concedes that the textual geography of
Sodom is based on actual locations, sites, and topography.
Indeed, both Professor Rainey and Professor Finkelstein
have supported the logic behind my contention that
the Kikkar of the Jordan is located at the north end of
the Dead Sea. For this I'm grateful.

3. Cultural Memory

This view asserts that a widespread calamitous event or
series of events occurred in the southern Levant—or
across the entire Levant—the memory of which lingered
in lore until an ethnic group appropriated it as specific
to themselves. Thus, this view would say, the Israelites
incorporated legends about an ancient disaster into
their national myth of origins, the Torah. Noteworthy
archaeologists T. Schaub, A. Mazar, and B. Porter lean
in this direction.

Three years ago I delivered a lecture at the Friends
of Archaeology and History of Jordan in Amman.
At the end of that presentation I asked, "Could Tall

el-Hammam be biblical Sodom?" Then I provided some observations to support that identification.

In the question-and-answer session following the lecture, Dr. Porter, who is director of the American Center of Oriental Research, Amman, countered my statement that ancient Near Eastern writers, including the writer of the Sodom tales, *never* invented fictitious geographies.

"You should never say 'never'—it's unscientific," she protested. Point well taken. But I'm still waiting for someone to supply an example of a fabricated geography from an ancient Near Eastern source—and also the criteria whereby one might determine that it's fictitious.

Though adherents of this view reject the historicity of the patriarchal narratives, they too see common ground on which to discuss the physical reality behind the Sodom geography in the mind of the Genesis writer(s).

4. Historical Kernel

More precise than "cultural memory," this view contends that a specific catastrophic, civilization-ending event struck the Kikkar of the Jordan during the Bronze Age, from which strands of "Sodom" myths arose that were eventually woven into the ancestral tales of the Israelites. Many fine scholars, including W. Fulco and D. Maltsberger, hold some form of this view.

I've had extensive discussions on the subject of Sodom's location with both Fulco (National Endowment for the Humanities Distinguished Professor of Ancient Mediterranean Studies, Loyola Marymount University) and Maltsberger (Associate Professor of Old Testament and Archaeology, Baptist University of the Americas). Both have extensive archaeological experience and expertise they've graciously lent to the Tall el-Hammam Excavation Project: Fulco, analysis; and Maltsberger, field staff. Though I direct the project, these fine scholars, with their astute criticisms and helpful research, know they don't have to agree with me on any of my conclusions about Sodom.

The sticking point of discussion is the historical authenticity of the patriarchal narratives. Nonetheless, the issue of Sodom's geography remains a fruitful topic of discussion in this arena as well.

Response to the First Four Opposing Views

I CONTEND THAT THE IDENTIFICATION of Sodom—or any other ancient city—must be based on a solid scientific approach, with the following requisite components:

a. Analyze ancient texts in order to extract embedded geographical and chronological data.

b. Analyze the relevant textual language for specificity. (That is, is the language "literal," formulaic, hyperbolic, phenomenological?)

c. Assess both known and unknown geographical quanta from extracted textual geo-data.

d. Assemble a theoretical map, working from the known geo-data (fixed locations or reasonable assumptions) to the unknown geo-data using rigorous logic.

e. Analyze the chronological (occupational) parameters suggested (or required) by the relevant texts. The chronological "ballpark" must become part of the geo-data set.

f. Analyze the relevant physical data from archaeology, geology, paleoclimatology, paleobotany/biology, and other disciplines.

g. Assess the points of correspondence and/or departure between the theoretical text-map and the physical data from the proposed location(s).

This must be done systematically, meticulously, and without preconceived ideas or biases. Then you've got to be willing to go where the evidence leads you. Let the text talk. Let the geography talk. Let the archaeology talk. Let all the lines of inquiry bring their data to the table, then compare it all, and see where the chips fall.

In writing the history of the ancient Near East, all relevant texts must be mined for their historical and geographical information, with the oldest texts (those in closest chronological proximity to the historical period in question) receiving methodological priority.

With regard to geography, ancient writers didn't have any need to concoct fictions. They wanted to explain what they saw, the landscapes they knew, the places they'd experienced—mostly firsthand. Whether the characters and events recorded by the Genesis writer(s) are fact or fiction, their stories are layered over a real-world geography with which they were intimately familiar.

Further, whether the Genesis stories were written during the Bronze Age (maximalist view) or the late Iron Age (minimalist view), their characters traverse known terrain—with actual cities, towns, and villages, whether thriving or in ruins.

Thus, no matter how you slice it, the biblical geography— including Sodom and the Cities of the Kikkar—is a fact-based geography, not a mythical construct.

This is the approach I used to locate biblical Sodom at Tall el-Hammam. I've followed the procedural points outlined above, relentlessly. I still do. And the evidence continues to convince me that I'm right.

Other Opposing Views

THE REMAINING TYPES OF OPPOSITION to the identification of Tall el-Hammam as Sodom fall into two categories:

5. Wrong Location

Adherents to this view would concur that the Sodom tales are based on actual historical events, but would assert that the location of the Cities of the Plain is in the southern Dead Sea area, not in the north. B. G. Wood is the most prominent archaeologist espousing this view.

I have a deep appreciation for Dr. Wood, on whose Khirbet el-Maqatir Excavation staff I served for six seasons, from 1995 to 2000. We both value the relationship between the biblical text and archaeology, and he's been a significant influence on my approach to biblical archaeology.

Nonetheless, Wood wrote a lengthy critique of my views, printed in *Bible and Spade* magazine (published by the Associates for Biblical Research), and I enthusiastically responded. My paper in response to his criticisms is considered by many to be an effective refutation of the southern Sodom viewpoint with Bab edh-Dhra as Sodom.

Like Wood, most adherents of the southern Sodom view accept the historical authenticity of the patriarchal narratives, with which I heartily agree—and, I think, for good scientific reasons. However, on the same scientific grounds, the southern Sodom view has no evidence whatsoever in favor of it—textual, geographical, archaeological, climatological, or otherwise. By contrast, the northern view is supported by these and other lines of evidence.

6. Wrong Time

This point of view accepts the Sodom saga as real history, but assigns a pre–Middle Bronze Age date to Abraham. By employing a literal interpretation of the patriarchal life spans and chronological numbers, it calculates that Sodom's destruction in the time of Abraham occurred in the twenty-first or twentieth century BCE. Wood also holds this as axiomatic when dealing with the identification of Sodom.

A deep respect for the biblical record, which I share, leads Wood and others to regard my honorific-formulaic approach to many of the biblical numbers as erroneous. So be it. But I'm in good company with W. F. Albright, G. E. Wright, K. A. Kitchen, S. Ortiz, and a host of other scholars whose approach to Bronze Age biblical chronology is based on historical synchronisms, not an intractable affirmation of the literalness of patriarchal life spans and associated numbers. For these scholars and for me, historical synchronicity and cultural specificity (which are also part of the biblical record) demand that Abraham, Isaac, Jacob, and Joseph be placed only in the narrow time window of the Middle Bronze Age.

Perhaps there's no such thing as a perfect theory. Reaching my conclusions about the identity of Sodom has been a tough personal journey. I once believed Sodom and Gomorrah were in the south Dead Sea area, at Bab edh-Dhra and Numeira. I taught it. I took people there on tours. In the 1990s I was even a "talking head" in a prime-time television documentary supporting that view.

But then I was confronted with two issues that any serious investigator of the Sodom issue must consider: the text of Genesis 13 and the archaeology of Bab edh-Dhra and Numeira.

Continuing Scholarship and Recognition of the Tall el-Hammam Excavation Project

WE NOW ENTER OUR SECOND decade of fieldwork in the Tall el-Hammam Excavation Project. When we began, archaeologists and historians knew relatively little about the eastern Jordan Disk, and far less about Tall el-Hammam. Our initial five seasons of excavation at this remarkable site were conducted in relative obscurity, even though during that time TeHEP was one of the larger working excavations in Jordan.

However, the director general of the Jordan Department of Antiquities stated in January 2011 that TeHEP had become one of the most important excavations in the Hashemite Kingdom of Jordan, and perhaps one of the most significant archaeological discoveries of all time— Sodom.

Every year since 2007, papers about the excavations at Tall el-Hammam have been presented at the annual meetings of ASOR and the Near East Archaeological Society. In 2009 the first major preliminary report on the TeHEP appeared in the *Annual of the Department of Antiquities of Jordan* (*ADAJ*). Since then, three additional reports have appeared in *ADAJ*. In the summer of 2010, I was invited to deliver a paper on our excavations at the eleventh triennial International Conference on the History and Archaeology of Jordan, held in Paris—a presentation received with much interest and enthusiasm. Over the past several years, articles about Tall el-Hammam and the discovery of biblical Sodom have appeared in magazines and newspapers the world over.

Hardly a week goes by that some scholar doesn't call or email to request permission to use our research and archaeological data in an article, paper, or book. I've just completed an article titled "Sodom and the Cities of the Plain" for a new Bible dictionary, and a feature article for the magazine *Biblical Archaeology Review*, focusing on Tall el-Hammam. At least three additional articles about the Tall el-Hammam excavations appeared in scientific journals in 2012 alone.

In the summer of 2011, the excavation was the subject of a documentary—filmed in Jordan—about the discovery of Sodom at Tall el-Hammam, produced for the National Geographic Channel. The Society of Biblical Literature asked TeHEP to provide a three-hour session on archaeology and the Bible based on the excavations at Tall el-Hammam for its 2011 international (London) and national (San Francisco) meetings, which received warm and lively receptions. My presentations at universities, colleges, and seminaries all over the United States have led to many invitations for repeat visits to provide updates on the progress of our project.

We've also signed a new ten-year Joint Scientific Project Agreement between Trinity Southwest University and the Jordan Department of Antiquities extending TeHEP through Season Sixteen (2020).

While this is only the tip of the iceberg, it provides a glimpse of the growing impact of the Tall el-Hammam Excavation Project and resultant avenues of research on the disciplines of archaeological and biblical scholarship. Indeed, the Sodom issue is only a tiny corner of a very large archaeological investigation opening up a new world of understanding regarding more than four thousand years of life and civilization on the ancient Kikkar of the Jordan.

Going On

ARE THERE THINGS THAT I still struggle with regarding the Sodom identification, things that don't seem to line up? Sure. A little something here, a little something there. My experience at Tall el-Hammam tells me that such things usually get resolved sooner or later. But the big things are solid: Right place. Right time. Right stuff.

The geography of Genesis is the crux, the essential key. The Bible says that Sodom existed, and in a mappable place. It had certain characteristics of size and features, and left evidences of its demise. Not only that, but the Bible tracks Sodom in history from before the Tower of Babel to the time of Abraham to its perpetually ruined condition, one so overt and so terrifying that people have used it ever since to illustrate the power of God over space, time, energy, and human intellect and will.

If, in the cold reality of the twenty-first century, something long regarded as "mythical" can be proved to be historically present in the very dirt of a massive mound in the Hashemite Kingdom of Jordan, then would not intellectual honesty require that the Bible itself be given a fresh, new look as a true narrative representation on its own terms?

Oller points out the implications of this: "If the Bible is true, since it extends from creation to the end of time, it must be the basis for all TNRs without exception. If each of them is connected to space-time, and the Bible covers all of it, all of them are connected to the Bible. If the Bible is true, all proofs must be consistent with it."

The excavation, from the moment it first emerged as an idea in a modest Israeli hotel room over a decade ago, has been a combination of rigorous scholarship and sheer, roller-coaster joy. This book records both, and is Dr. Scott's and my best effort to provide a true narrative representation of the search for biblical Sodom.

We haven't discovered a city-limits sign at Tall el-Hammam yet, but I'll say it myself, based on its own literal mound of evidence:

Welcome to Sodom.

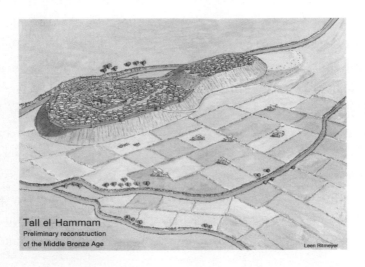

Tall el Hammam
Preliminary reconstruction
of the Middle Bronze Age   Leen Ritmeyer

The Generations of Jacob and the Four Hundred Years of Genesis 15

BY COMPARING GENESIS 15:13–16 AND EXODUS 12:40 IN THE Hebrew Masoretic Text (MT), many have adopted an Israelite sojourn in Egypt of around four hundred years—from the time of Jacob to the Exodus. While the Septuagint (LXX) versions, the Samaritan Pentateuch (SP), the apostle Paul, and the historian Josephus all indicate that the approximately 400 number stretches from the time of Abraham to the giving of the Law at Sinai, a close examination of the MT's own internal chronology also supports this fact. The Genesis 15 passage makes it clear that, after the Israelites' arrival in Egypt, they would later exit their Nile Delta home and return to Canaan in the fourth generation:

> Then Yahweh said to him, "Know for certain that your descendants will be strangers in a country not their own [first, in Canaan], and they will be enslaved and mistreated [second, in Egypt] four hundred years [total for Canaan and Egypt]. But I will punish the nation they serve as slaves [Egypt], and afterward they will come out with great possessions. . . . In the fourth generation your

descendants will come back here [to Canaan from Egypt]. . . ."
[my brackets]

THESE FOUR GENERATIONS ARE CLEARLY seen in the MT's patriarchal chronology, recorded in 1 Chronicles 1–8, where the descendants of
Jacob's twelve sons are delineated. What you must recognize is that this
passage requires only that *parts* of four generations live in Egypt. Jacob,
his twelve sons, and many grandsons were the first "generation" to enter
Egypt (Genesis 46:8–27). Then there were Jacob's great-grandsons, then
great-great-grandsons, then great-great-great-grandsons who were born
in Egypt. So, the Exodus would occur "in the fourth generation" belonging
to Jacob's great(x 3)-grandsons. And that's exactly how it works in the 1
Chronicles 1–8 lists of Jacob's descendants. I won't cite from each of them,
as three examples will suffice.

The first example involves a descendant of Jacob famous in the
Exodus-Conquest narratives for stealing treasures from Jericho that were
"under the ban" (Joshua 7): Achan (or Achar). The genealogy from Jacob
(Israel) to Achar(n) goes like this (1 Chronicles 2:1–7 in parallel with
Joshua 7:16–18):

Israel (Jacob) → Judah → Zerah › Zimri → Carmi → Achar
[Achan], "who brought trouble on Israel by violating the ban on
taking devoted things"

THREE GENERATIONS ENTERED EGYPT TOGETHER, including
Jacob, Judah, and Zerah (Genesis 46:12)—the first generation in Goshen. In Egypt, Zerah had a son, Zimri—generation two. Zimri had a son,
Carmi—generation three. Carmi had a son, Achar [Achan]—generation
four. Thus Achan departed Egypt with Joshua, "in the fourth generation,"
exactly as Genesis 15:16 states.

(Note from Joshua 7:17 that the reference to "Zimri" being "taken"
cannot mean that Achan's grandfather was still alive—for all the previous

Israelite generations before Joshua and Achan were made to die in the "wandering" and not allowed to cross over the Jordan, according to Deuteronomy 1:34–40, 2:14–16. "Zimri" simply refers to his living descendants.)

The second example is the line of ancestors leading from Jacob up to the famous Israelite spy, Caleb (Genesis 46:12; 1 Chronicles 2:3–9, 18, 4:1, 15). Because there's an unstated connection between Caleb son of Hezron and Caleb son of Jephunneh, it's possible that Jephunneh was the son of the earlier Caleb, or perhaps there was an intermediate, unnamed ancestor. However, the clear six-generation sequence from Jacob to Achan, above, argues strongly against an eight-generation sequence from Jacob to Caleb, since Achan and Caleb were post-Exodus contemporaries. The generations from Jacob to Caleb look like this:

Israel (Jacob) → Judah → Perez → Hezron → Caleb → ? → Jephunneh → Caleb

ACCOMPANYING JACOB TO EGYPT WERE son Judah, grandson Perez, and great-grandson Hezron (Genesis 46:12)—the first generation in Goshen. In Egypt, Hezron had a son, Caleb—generation two. Caleb (likely) had a son, Jephunneh—generation three. Jephunneh had a son, Caleb—generation four. Thus Caleb departed Egypt "in the fourth generation," precisely in line with Genesis 15:16.

A third genealogical sequence is worth examining—that of Jacob through Joshua. At first glance, the configuration of 1 Chronicles 7:20–26 seems to suggest at least thirteen and as many as nineteen generations from Jacob to Joshua:

Israel (Jacob) → Joseph → Ephraim → Beriah → Rephah → Resheph → Telah → Tahan → Ladan → Ammihud → Elishama → Nun → Joshua (Hoshea)

OR PERHAPS

> Israel (Jacob) → Joseph → Ephraim → Shuthelah → Bered →
> Tahath → Eleadah → Tahath → Zabad → Shuthelah → Rephah
> → Resheph → Telah → Tahan → Ladan → Ammihud → Elishama
> → Nun → Joshua (Hoshea)

BUT THIS LOOKS WAY OUT of synch with the Genesis 15:16 "in the fourth generation" seen in the previous two examples. The answer to this little genealogical dilemma may lie in the formula "*and* so-and-so his son" in contrast with "so-and-so his son." It could very well be that all the individuals named after Shuthelah with the "*and* so-and-so his son" formula in 1 Chronicles 7:20 belong to Ephraim directly, as does his son, Shuthelah, who appears without the "and" at the beginning of the list of sons because of his *sequential* tie to the descendants named in verse 26 who also appear without the "and" formula.

But if the sequence of names carrying the "*and* so-and-so his son" formula are all equally sons of Ephraim, then why are there two Shuthelahs and two Tahaths? The answer to this question may simply lie in the fact that ancient Hebrew was written without vowels; therefore, it's quite possible that each was pointed ("voweled") differently. And even the consonants *shin* (s or sh) and *tav* (t or th) could have had different vocal values in each instance of what appears in English as the same name. Or, in the case of Shuthelah in 7:20, one might theorize that the "and-*less*" "so-and-so" formula is simply a "section tag" marking him as one of the mainline descendants along with the five "and-*less*" designees in 7:26. This approach is made feasible by the fact that Shuthelah's name is, then, repeated at the end of the list of Ephraim's sons in verse 21. With this in mind, it makes sense that the list of Ephraim's sons (vv. 20–21) is immediately followed by the story of his sons Ezer and Elead, who died untimely deaths.

This suggests that the four names included in 1 Chronicles 7:25 after Ezer and Elead are, likewise, directly sons of Ephraim, all having the "*and* so-and-so his son" formula found in verses 20 and 21. By contrast, the names of the five descendants beginning in verse 26 have the same "and-less" (anarthrous) formula as Shuthelah in verse 20—"so-and-so" or "so-and-so his son" without the article—identifying them as the actual patriarchs leading forward from Ephraim in succession. This same *no-article* formula is used in the "Kings of Judah" lineage of 1 Chronicles 3:10–16, which is sequential. But in the listing of the sons of David in verses 5–9, each has the "and" except the first one, signifying that they all belong to the same category.

It's also worth noting that the "*and* so-and-so his son" formula of 7:20–21, 25 is unique among the several generational formulas of the first eight chapters of 1 Chronicles, which was obviously pieced together from genealogical sources that used a range of different sequencing formulas, most being anarthrous—"father of . . . ," "sons born were . . . ," "wife who bore him . . . ," ". . . his firstborn," "descendants of . . . ," "son of . . . ," "the son of . . . ," "sons of . . . ," "the sons of . . . ," ". . .his son." In other words, for 1 Chronicles 7:20–26, *only* the names listed without an article (the "and-*less*" ones) are sequential, or generational. Thus the actual sequence from Jacob through Joshua is this:

Israel (Jacob) → Joseph → Ephraim → Shuthelah → Ladan → Ammihud → Elishama → Nun → Joshua (Hoshea)

WHEN JACOB ARRIVED IN EGYPT, his son Joseph and grandson Ephraim were already living there (Genesis 46:20)—Israel's first generation in Goshen. In Egypt, Ephraim had a son, Shuthelah—generation two. Shuthelah had a son, Laden—generation three. Laden had a son, Ammihud—generation four. Ammihud had a son, Elishama—generation five. Elishama had a son, Nun—generation six. Nun had a son, Joshua, Moses's eventual replacement and great military strategist—generation seven.

But in this sequence from Jacob to Joshua we still have seven generations in Egypt, not four, as was the case with Jacob-Achan and Jacob-Caleb. However, since Joshua was a contemporary of Achan and Caleb

(Caleb was a close companion of Joshua), reason (not to mention the biblical text!) requires that they exit Egypt at the same time, "in the fourth generation" of Genesis 15:16. This merely requires that Ammihud, Joshua's great-grandfather, still be (even barely) alive at the time of the Exodus.

By way of conclusion, the time allotted for Israel's sojourn in Egypt to the fourth generation (Genesis 15:16) is either 215 years (short sojourn) or 430 years (long sojourn) as allowed in Exodus 12:40—the same four-hundred-year block of time predicted in Genesis 15:13. Both the 400 and the 430 are divided into two pieces: (1) Abram to Jacob (time in Canaan) and (2) Jacob to Exodus (time in Egypt). One thing's for sure: they did come out of Egypt in the fourth generation. That's abundantly clear from the MT genealogies recorded in Genesis 46 and 1 Chronicles 1–8—and you don't need anything close to four hundred years to do that (even four formulaic generations of forty years each requires only 160 years). In this light, the 215 figure is much better. Indeed, 430 years really makes no sense at all, especially in light of the LXX, SP, Paul, and Josephus. And if one considers the entire numerical structure of the biblical patriarchs to be honorific/formulaic, then the actual, physical time frame from Abraham to Jacob and Jacob to Exodus can be shortened significantly, even dramatically.

Historical Synchronisms and Cultural Specificities Limiting the Date Range of Abraham Through Joseph to the First Half of the Second Millennium— the Middle Bronze Age—Between 1900 and 1540 BCE

K. A. Kitchen's Patriarchal Ballpark

(Based on K. A. Kitchen, *On the Reliability of the Old Testament* [Grand Rapids, MI: Eerdmans, 2003], pp. 313–72, hereinafter *OROT.*)

1. WIDE SCOPE OF TRAVEL. Transhumant groups "ranged far and wide in the early second millennium. . . . Pastoralists were not the only travelers across the Near East. . . . Official envoys, merchant caravans . . . We have lists of stopping places and transit times, effectively itineraries, for such routes." (*OROT* 316–17)

2. LONG-DISTANCE MARRIAGES. "Just as we have those wealthy sheikhs Abraham and Isaac sending off to their relatives in Nahor or Harran to obtain brides for Isaac and Jacob, so in the early second millennium we also find Shamsi-Adad I of Assyria securing in marriage Beltum, daughter of Ishkhi-Adad king of Qatna, for his son, Yasmah-Adad, Assyrian king of Mari across a similar span of distance. . . ." There are numerous other examples. (*OROT* 318)

3. TRAVEL TO EGYPT FROM CANAAN. Just as Abraham went into Egypt because of famine, such travel is well-known from the first half of the second millennium. "When the Egyptian courtier Sinuhe fled Egypt for Canaan at the death of Amenemhat I, circa 1944 B.C., he was rescued from dying of thirst by a local tribal pastoralist 'who had been in Egypt.'" It is clear that Semitic Asiatics frequented Egypt's Nile Delta region, interacting with its kings, for "during the Twelfth to Fifteenth Dynasties (ca. 1970–1540), the Egyptian kings (Twelfth/Thirteenth Dynasties) had an East Delta residence at Ro-waty (ruins of Ezbet-Rushdy), near Avaris (center of the god Seth), which in turn the Hyksos rulers (Fifteenth Dynasty) used as their East Delta base. Before the twentieth century B.C., no such arrangement is known; and again, there was no royal residence there during the Eighteenth Dynasty. . . ." (*OROT* 318–19)

4. WIDE POLITICAL HORIZONS. The story of a collision between a four-king coalition and a five-king coalition as described in Genesis 14 has elements stretching across almost the entire Near Eastern landscape. But it is clear that "from circa 2000 to 1750 (1650 at the extreme), we have the one and only period during which extensive power alliances were

common in Mesopotamia and with its neighbors. . . . What is more, it is *only* in this particular period (2000–1700) that the eastern realm of Elam intervened extensively in the politics of Mesopotamia—with its armies—and sent its envoys far west into Syria to Qatna. Never again did Elam follow such wide-reaching policies." (*OROT* 320–21, Kitchen's italics)

5. NIGHTTIME ATTACKS AND RELIGIOUS CONCLUSIONS TO WAR. Abraham's guerrilla-style attack against Kedorlaomer and his subsequent ceremonial rendezvous with Melchizedek of Salem are perfectly consistent with a second millennium context. "*Nighttime attacks* (as in Gen. 14:15) in ancient Near Eastern warfare are very well attested. . . . The *religious conclusion to a campaign,* whether Yakhdun-lim's or Abraham's, was always the natural climax, as can be seen from innumerable examples. . . ." (*OROT* 322)

6. TREATIES AND COVENANTS. Treaties and covenants from the period between 2000 and 1500 BCE are structurally distinct from those of the third millennium and last half of the second millennium BCE. "There is a consistent format: deities are listed as witnesses, by whom oath is taken; then the stipulations; and finally (in complete versions) curses against infraction. . . . This format is wholly distinct from those current both in the third millennium and in the middle and late second millennium, and later." The several man-to-man covenants forged by Abraham in the book of Genesis fit only this early second millennium design. (*OROT* 323)

7. SLAVERY AT WHAT PRICE? During the eighteenth and seventeenth centuries BCE, the price of slaves was

averaging about twenty shekels of silver. "This is the average price (expressed as one-third of a mina) in the laws of Hammurabi and in real-life transactions at Mari (exactly) and in other Old Babylonian documents (within a 15–30 shekel range, averaging 22 shekels). Before this period slaves were cheaper, and after it they steadily got dearer, as inflation did its work." (*OROT* 344)

8. A CHRONOLOGICAL "BALLPARK" FOR THE PATRIARCHS. Having assessed numerous lines of evidence from across the Near East spanning the third and second millennia BCE, Kitchen concludes that "the overall period circa 1900–1600 (2000–1500 at the outermost limits)" is the only tenable placement of Abraham through Joseph. "The overall date of about 1900–1600 for Abraham to Joseph is consistent also with the internal data. . . . Their life spans and birth dates are high; a minimal chronology would allow for possible inflation of these figures in tradition [formulaic-honorific values], while keeping the overall profile [chronological "ballpark"]. This result goes well with that from the external data, such that it is wholly reasonable to speak, once more, of a 'patriarchal age' in biblical terms, but on a far sounder basis than was formerly the case." (*OROT* 358–59, Collins's brackets)

9. KITCHEN'S CONCLUSION. "We are compelled, once and for all, to throw out Wellhausen's bold claim that the patriarchs were merely a glorified mirage of/from the Hebrew monarchy period. For such a view there is not a particle of supporting factual evidence, and the whole of the foregoing indicative background material [only sketched at here] is solidly against it. It should be clear, finally, that

the main features of the patriarchal narratives either fit specifically into the first half of the second millennium or are consistent with such a dating; some features common to that epoch and to later periods clearly must be taken with the early-second-millennium horizon." (*OROT* 371–72, Collins's brackets)

How Are Biblical Cities and Towns Identified and Placed on Bible Maps?

IDENTIFYING A PARTICULAR ARCHAEOLOGICAL SITE as a biblical city or town isn't always easy. Sometimes the modern Arabic (toponym) preserves the basic sound or letters of the ancient name—as modern el-Jib = ancient Gibeon. But most of the time this isn't the case. Then you might hope to find some kind of inscription in an excavation that gives the name of the city or a known king or other identifying feature. But that's very rare.

In most instances, biblical locations are identified by using the geographical "markers" for a given city or town preserved in the Old Testament books. Such geo-markers (or geo-criteria) can be as simple as "beyond Jordan" or "on the coast" or "east of Jerusalem" or "at the foot of Mount Pisgah." Others like "in the time of Joshua" or "in the time of Solomon" suggest "ballpark" occupational dates that should be present at a given site. Still others suggest identifying features like "fortified" or "burned."

By piecing together the geographical and chronological hints, we can identify sites either positively or tentatively. The more indicators there are—and the more detailed they are—the easier it is to find a biblical site or to assign a biblical name to an archaeological site.

The Biblical Site ID Chart lists ancient sites with their biblical names, and whether they're identified by textual geography or inscriptions. You can easily see that very few sites have identifications based on inscription. Most are identified solely by studying their biblical geography. Some have only a few textual indicators, such as Arad with three. Others like Shechem (with twelve) and Jerusalem (with eighteen) have many more, and thus are easier to identify. Note that the geo-criteria "champion" is Sodom, with twenty-five. This makes it interesting to consider that Arad appears on most OT maps, while Sodom rarely appears, and then almost always with a question mark.

Based on the sheer number of geographical indicators for Sodom in Genesis, it ought to be relatively easy to find. In fact, it was. By following the textual geography of Genesis, most nineteenth-century explorer-scholars located it in the same general area as I do. Beyond that they didn't have archaeological science to fine-tune their choices. We do.

The Geoparameters Chart gives the passages from the biblical text establishing geographical and chronological criteria for each site.

Maps and Charts

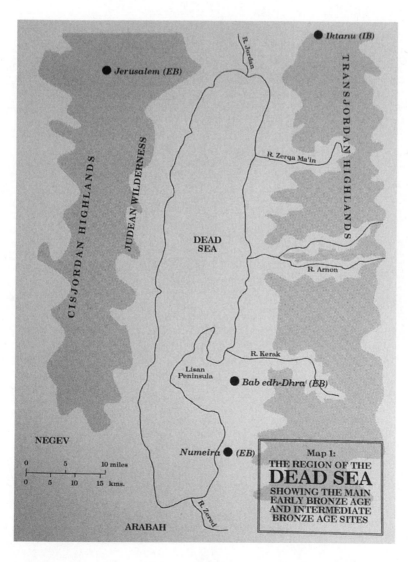

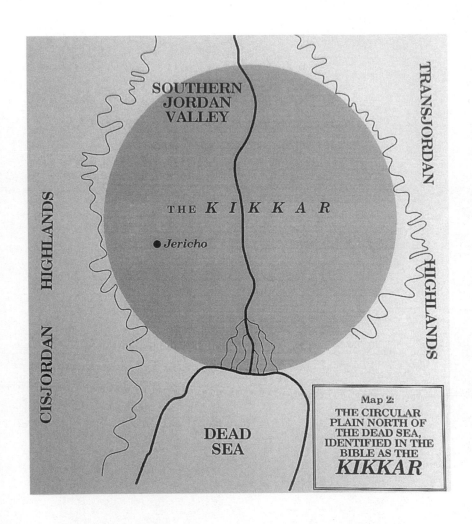

Map 2:
THE CIRCULAR
PLAIN NORTH OF
THE DEAD SEA,
IDENTIFIED IN THE
BIBLE AS THE
KIKKAR

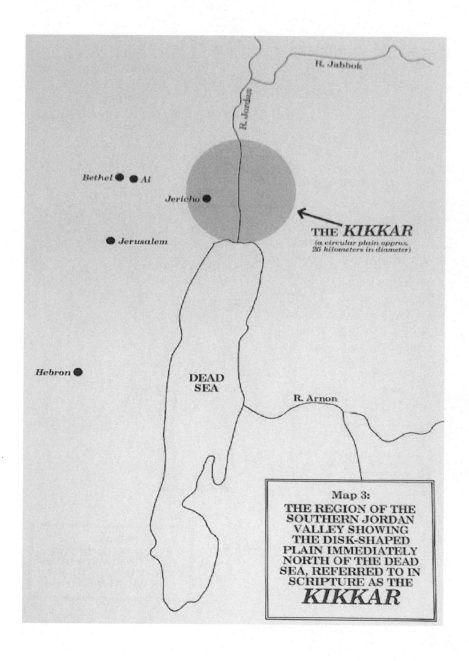

R. Jabbok

R. Jordan

Bethel ● ● Ai

Jericho ●

← THE *KIKKAR*
(a circular plain approx.
26 kilometers in diameter)

● Jerusalem

Hebron ●

DEAD
SEA

R. Arnon

Map 3:
THE REGION OF THE
SOUTHERN JORDAN
VALLEY SHOWING
THE DISK-SHAPED
PLAIN IMMEDIATELY
NORTH OF THE DEAD
SEA, REFERRED TO IN
SCRIPTURE AS THE
KIKKAR

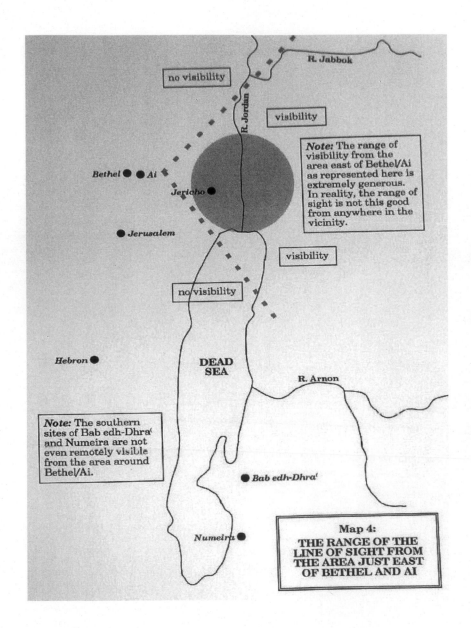

no visibility

R. Jabbok

visibility

R. Jordan

Note: The range of visibility from the area east of Bethel/Ai as represented here is extremely generous. In reality, the range of sight is not this good from anywhere in the vicinity.

Bethel ● ● Ai

Jericho ●

● Jerusalem

visibility

no visibility

Hebron ●

DEAD SEA

R. Arnon

Note: The southern sites of Bab edh-Dhraʿ and Numeira are not even remotely visible from the area around Bethel/Ai.

● Bab edh-Dhraʿ

Numeira ●

Map 4:
THE RANGE OF THE LINE OF SIGHT FROM THE AREA JUST EAST OF BETHEL AND AI

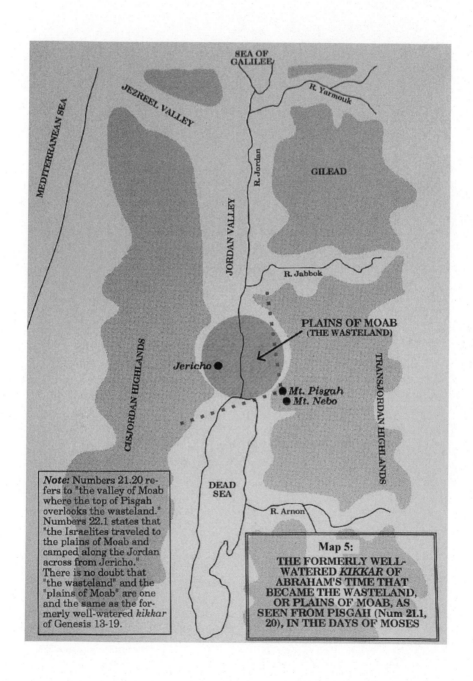

SEA OF
GALILEE

MEDITERRANEAN SEA

JEZREEL VALLEY

R. Yarmouk

R. Jordan

GILEAD

JORDAN VALLEY

R. Jabbok

PLAINS OF MOAB
(THE WASTELAND)

Jericho ●

CISJORDAN HIGHLANDS

● Mt. Pisgah
● Mt. Nebo

TRANSJORDAN HIGHLANDS

Note: Numbers 21.20 re-
fers to "the valley of Moab where the top of Pisgah
overlooks the wasteland."
Numbers 22.1 states that
"the Israelites traveled to
the plains of Moab and
camped along the Jordan
across from Jericho."
There is no doubt that
"the wasteland" and the
"plains of Moab" are one
and the same as the for-
merly well-watered *kikkar*
of Genesis 13-19.

DEAD
SEA

R. Arnon

Map 5:
THE FORMERLY WELL-
WATERED *KIKKAR* OF
ABRAHAM'S TIME THAT
BECAME THE WASTELAND,
OR PLAINS OF MOAB, AS
SEEN FROM PISGAH (Num 21.1,
20), IN THE DAYS OF MOSES

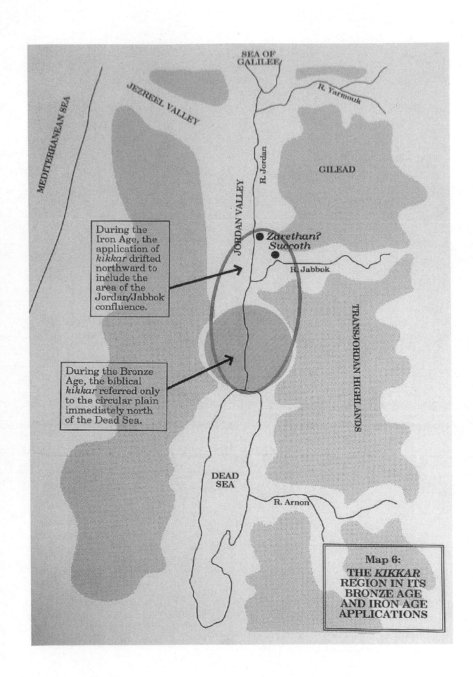

During the Iron Age, the application of *kikkar* drifted northward to include the area of the Jordan/Jabbok confluence.

During the Bronze Age, the biblical *kikkar* referred only to the circular plain immediately north of the Dead Sea.

Map 6:
THE *KIKKAR* REGION IN ITS BRONZE AGE AND IRON AGE APPLICATIONS

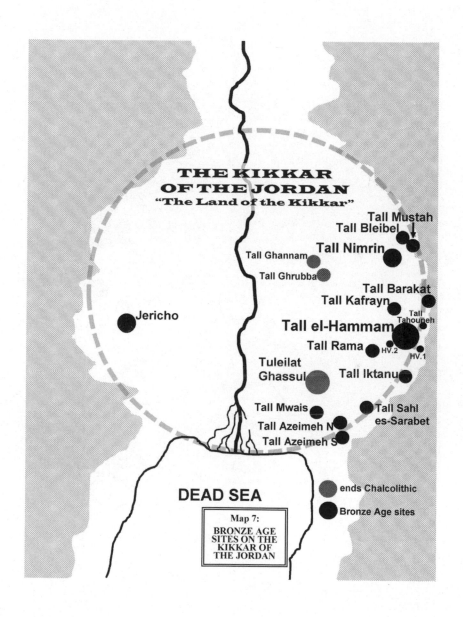

THE KIKKAR
OF THE JORDAN
"The Land of the Kikkar"

Tall Mustah
Tall Bleibel
Tall Nimrin
Tall Ghannam
Tall Ghrubba
Tall Barakat
Tall Kafrayn
Tall Tahouneh
Jericho
Tall el-Hammam
Tall Rama
HV.2
HV.1
Tuleilat Ghassul
Tall Iktanu
Tall Mwais
Tall Sahl es-Sarabet
Tall Azeimeh N
Tall Azeimeh S

DEAD SEA

ends Chalcolithic
Bronze Age sites

Map 7:
BRONZE AGE
SITES ON THE
KIKKAR OF
THE JORDAN

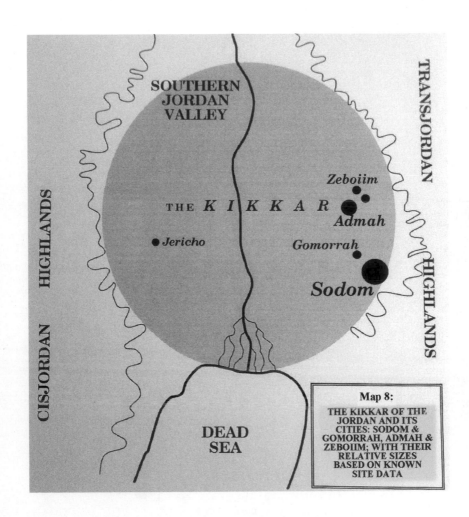

Map 8:

THE KIKKAR OF THE JORDAN AND ITS CITIES: SODOM & GOMORRAH, ADMAH & ZEBOIIM; WITH THEIR RELATIVE SIZES BASED ON KNOWN SITE DATA

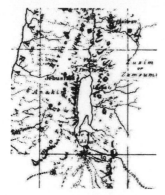

Bible map influenced by
explorer-scholars Clark and Grove,
published in the 1860s, showing the
"Plain of the Five Cities" at
the north end of the Dead Sea.

Clark-Grove 1860s Map

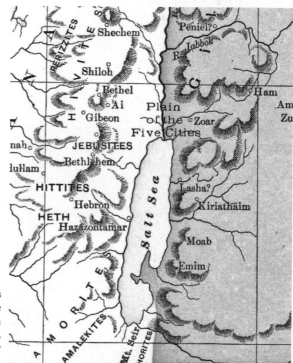

Bible map from the 1880s
with the "Plain of the Five
Cities" above the northern
end of the Dead Sea,
influenced by
explorer-scholar Thomson.

Bible 1880s Map

Bible map in a late-nineteenth-century edition of *Smith's Bible Dictionary* showing the "Plain of the Five Cities" north of the Dead Sea.

Smith-Grove Map

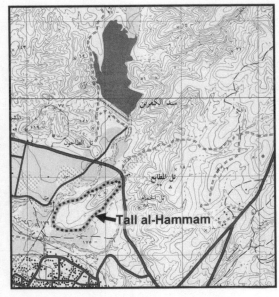

Modern Jordanian geophysical survey map showing the location of Tall el-Hammam just south of the Kafrayn reservoir (dark gray mass, top center). Note the steep, rising terrain of the Transjordan Highlands to the east and north of the road passing at the eastern foot of Tall el-Hammam. Hammam itself sits on the eastern edge of the plain of the southern Jordan Valley, the Kikkar.

Hammam Vicinity Map

Archaeological Ages	
Late Neolithic	6600–4600 BCE
Chalcolithic	4600–3600 BCE
Early Bronze 1	3600–3000 BCE
Early Bronze 2	3000–2700 BCE
Early Bronze 3	2700–2350 BCE
Intermediate Bronze	2350–2000 BCE (formerly EB IV–MB I)
Middle Bronze 1	2000–1800 BCE (formerly MB II A)
Middle Bronze 2	1800–1540 BCE (formerly MB II B–C)
Late Bronze 1	1540–1400 BCE
Late Bronze 2	1400–1200 BCE
Iron 1	1200–1000 BCE
Iron 2	1000–586 BCE
Iron 3	586–332 BCE
Hellenistic	332–63 BCE
Early Roman	63 BCE–135 CE

Destruction Comparison Chart

Phenomenon	Textual Data	Archaeological Data, T. Hammam	Airburst Data
Cosmic origin	yes	consistent w/ data	yes
Fireball	strongly implied	consistent w/ data	yes
Consuming heat	strongly implied	consistent w/ data	yes
Super-temps inside impact zone	implied	consistent w/ data	yes
Some sand and silica-based materials melted into glass	not stated	physical evidence exists	yes
Intense electro-magnetic discharges	yes	undetermined	yes
Human and animal life in impact zone terminated	yes	implied by 700-year occupational hiatus	yes

Phenomenon	Textual Data	Archaeological Data, T. Hammam	Airburst Data
Plant life in impact zone obliterated	yes	implied by 700-year occupational hiatus	yes
Powerful shock wave flattens standing objects, demolishes structures	strongly implied	physical evidence exists	yes
Disintegrated and loose materials caught up in "exit" vortex	implied	undeterminable	yes
Smoke and debris column visible from distant locations	yes	undeterminable	yes
Target area uninhabitable for considerable time	strongly implied	consistent w/ data	yes

(Continued)

Destruction Comparison Chart *(Continued)*

Phenomenon	Textual Data	Archaeological Data, T. Hammam	Airburst Data
"Curse" lore of surrounding peoples reinforces long abandonment of the impact zone	Implied	consistent w/ data	yes

Biblical Site ID Chart

Modern Site Name*	Biblical Site Identification	ID Based on Textual Geography†	ID Based on Primary Inscription‡	ID Based on Secondary Inscription§
et-Tell	Ai (Abram)	yes: 4 criteria	no	no
Khirbet el-Maqatir	Ai (Joshua)	yes: 12 criteria	no	no
Tell 'Arad	Arad	yes: 3 criteria	no	no
Khirbet 'Ara'ir	Aroer	yes: 4 criteria	no	no
Tel Ashdod	Ashdod	yes: 7 criteria	no	no
Ashkelon	Ashkelon	yes: 4 criteria	no	no
Tell Zakariya	Azekah	yes: 8 criteria	no	no
Tell es-Saba'	Beersheba	yes: 7 criteria	no	no
Tell el-Husn	Beth-Shean	yes: 7 criteria	no	no
Tel Beth-Shemesh	Beth Shemesh	yes: 8 criteria	no	no

(Continued)

Biblical Site ID Chart *(Continued)*

Modern Site Name*	Biblical Site Identification	ID Based on Textual Geography[†]	ID Based on Primary Inscription[‡]	ID Based on Secondary Inscription[§]
Beitin	Bethel	yes: 6 criteria	no	no
Tell el-Qadi	Dan	yes: 7 criteria	no	yes
Dhiban	Dibon	yes: 8 criteria	no	no
Khirbet el-Burj	Dor	yes: 5 criteria	no	no
Tel Dothan	Dothan	yes: 3 criteria	no	no
Tel Miqne	Ekron	yes: 8 criteria	yes	no
Tel Zafit	Gath	yes: 6 criteria	no	no
Tell 'Azza	Gaza	yes: 8 criteria	no	no
et-Tell	Geshur	yes: 7 criteria	no	no
Tell el-Jazari	Gezer	yes: 6 criteria	no	yes

Modern Site Name*	Biblical Site Identification	ID Based on Textual Geography[†]	ID Based on Primary Inscription[‡]	ID Based on Secondary Inscription[§]
el-Jib	Gibeon	yes: 8 criteria	no	yes
Tell el-Qedah	Hazor	yes: 7 criteria	no	yes
Tell Rumeideh	Hebron	yes: 10 criteria	no	yes
Tell Hesban	Heshbon	yes: 6 criteria	no	no
Khirbet el-Yarmuk	Jarmuth	yes: 3 criteria	no	no
Tell es-Sultan	Jericho	yes: 10 criteria	no	no
Jerusalem	Jerusalem	yes: 18 criteria	no	yes
Tel Jezreel	Jezreel	yes: 9 criteria	no	no
Tel Yoqne'am	Jokneam	yes: 5 criteria	no	no
Yafa el-'Atiqa	Joppa	yes: 7 criteria	no	no
Tell el-Qudeirat	Kedesh Barnea	yes: 7 criteria	no	no

(Continued)

Biblical Site ID Chart *(Continued)*

Modern Site Name*	Biblical Site Identification	ID Based on Textual Geography†	ID Based on Primary Inscription‡	ID Based on Secondary Inscription§
Tell ed-Duweir	Lachish	yes: 7 criteria	yes (?)	no
Tel Megiddo	Megiddo	yes: 7 criteria	no	no
Tell Sandah-anna	Mareshah	yes: 4 criteria	no	no
Amman	Rabbath-Ammon	yes: 8 criteria	no	no
Samaria	Samaria	yes: 5 criteria	no	no
Tell Balatah	Shechem	yes: 12 criteria	no	no
Sailun	Shiloh	yes: 7 criteria	no	no
Tall el-Hammam	Sodom	yes: 25 criteria	no	no
Tell Ta'annek	Taanach	yes: 7 criteria	no	no
Tel Batash	Timnah	yes: 9 criteria	no	no

* It is impossible to determine if Arabic toponyms reflect actual ancient designations or merely reflect later traditions (assumptions) by Byzantine and Islamic geographers who speculated about the locations of biblical sites. Hebrew toponyms are simply modern adaptations of biblical site names.

† Such textual geographies are found in the Old Testament, but also found occasionally in Egyptian and Mesopotamian documents and inscriptions. Late sources (Josephus, Eusebius, etc.) can also be helpful. Biblical data are often more detailed, and are used here to determine the number of known geographical criteria available for a given site.

‡ For Old Testament sites, a primary inscription is one found in situ in a sealed archaeological context, specifically providing the name of the site in question. Further, the inscription must date from the Old Testament period, i.e., either the Bronze Age or Iron Age. It must also be unquestionable as to translation.

§ For Old Testament sites, a secondary inscription is one found in situ in a reasonable archaeological context, naming the site, but originating from a later period (say, the Hellenistic, Roman, or Byzantine periods), or a Bronze Age or Iron Age inscription providing the name of a ruler, official, or resident known to have been associated with that particular site in the biblical record.

Geoparameters Chart

Biblical Site	Geographical Criteria Derived from the Biblical Text˙	Number of Geo-Criteria
Ai (Abram)	(1) Early Bronze Age, occupied, Gen 10; (2) means "the ruin," so was likely unoccupied during this Middle Bronze Age narrative, Gen 12/13; (3) east of and near Bethel, Gen 12:8; (4) vicinity overlooks the Kikkar of the southern Jordan Valley, Gen 13:10.	4
Ai (Joshua)	(1) Late Bronze Age, Josh; (2) Iron Age 3, Ezra 2:28, Neh 7:32 (3) up from and not far from Jericho, Josh 7:2; (4) east of Bethel; (5) small, Josh 7:3, 10:2; (6) fortified, Josh 7:5; (7) stone quarry or "heap" nearby en route to Jericho, Josh 7:5; (8) hilly terrain to the east en route to Jericho, Josh 7:5; (9) deep valley to immediate SW, Josh 8:4,12; (10) gate on north side, Josh 8:11; (11) shallow valley to the north side, Josh 8:11,14; (12) destroyed by fire, Josh 8:28.	12
Arad	(1) Late Bronze Age, Num, Josh, Judg; (2) Iron Age 1–2, 1 Chron; (3) in the Negev, Num 21:1.	3

Biblical Site	Geographical Criteria Derived from the Biblical Text*	Number of Geo-Criteria
Aroer	(1) Late Bronze Age, Num, Deut, Josh, Judg; (2) Iron Age 1–2, 1&2 Sam, 2 Kings, 1 Chron, Isa, Jer; (3) southern border town of the Amorites and Reuben/Gad, Num 32:34, Josh 12:2, 13:16; (4) on the north rim of the Arnon Gorge, Deut 2:36, 3:12.	4
Ashdod	(1) Late Bronze Age, Josh; (2) Iron Age 1–2, 1 Sam, 2 Chron; (3) Iron Age 3, Neh; (4) in Philistia, Josh 13:3; (5) west of Ekron, Josh 15:46; (6) near the Mediterranean coast, Josh 15:47; (7) smaller IA† towns nearby, 2 Chron 26:6.	7
Ashkelon	(1) Late Bronze Age, Josh, Judg; (2) Iron Age 1–2, 1&2 Sam, Jer, Amos; (3) Iron Age 3, Neh, Zech; (4) in Philistia, Josh 13:3; on the Mediterranean coast, Jer 47:7.	4
Azekah	(1) Late Bronze Age, Josh; (2) Iron Age 1–2, 1 Sam, 2 Chron, Jer; (3) Iron Age 3, Neh; (4) down from Beth Horon along the same road, Josh 10:10; (5) in the western foothills, Josh 15:33–36; (6) near Socoh, 1 Sam 17:1; (7) adjacent to the Elah Valley, 1 Sam 17:1–3; (8) with surrounding settlements not far from Lachish, Neh 11:30, Jer 34:7.	8

(Continues to page 296)

Biblical Site	Geographical Criteria Derived from the Biblical Text	Number of Geo-Criteria
Beersheba	(1) Middle Bronze Age, Gen 21; (2) Late Bronze Age, Josh, Judg; (3) Iron Age 1–2, 1&2 Sam, 1&2 Kings, 1&2 Chron, Amos; (4) Iron 2I, Neh; (5) in a desert area, Gen 21:14; (6) in the Negev adjacent to Philistia, Gen 21:33–34, 2 Sam 24:7; (7) in the territory of Judah, Josh 19:1–6.	7
Beth–Shean	(1) Late Bronze Age, Josh, Judg; (2) Iron Age 1–2, 1&2 Sam, 1 Kings, 1 Chron; (3) in the territory of Manassah, Josh 17:10–16; (4) controlled by Canaanites, Josh 17:16, Judg 1:27; (5) IA stronghold of the Philistines near Mount Gilboa, 1 Sam 31:7–10; (6) close to Jabesh Gilead, 1 Sam 31:11–13; (7) next to Zarethan below Jezreel, 1 Kings 4:12; (8) east end of the Jezreel Valley at the Jordan Valley, 1 Chron 7:29.	8
Beth Shemesh	(1) Late Bronze Age, Josh, Judg; (2) Iron Age 1–2, 1 Sam, 1&2 Kings, 1&2 Chron; (3) south of Mount Jearim, east of Timnah, Josh 15: 10–11; (4) in the territory of Judah, Josh 21:9–16, 2 Kings 14:11; (5) up the road east of Ekron, 1 Sam 6:1–16; (6) near Kiriath Jearim, 1 Sam 6:21.	6

Biblical Site	Geographical Criteria Derived from the Biblical Text	Number of Geo-Criteria
Bethel	(1) Middle Bronze Age, Gen 12; (2) Late Bronze Age, Josh, Judg; (3) Iron Age 1–2, 1 Sam, 1&2 Kings, 1&2 Chron, Jer, Hos, Amos; (4) Iron Age 3, Ezra, Neh, Zech; (5) west of Ai, Gen 12:8; (6) not far from Shechem, Gen 35:3–4; (7) in Canaan, Gen 35:6; (8) deep valley to the east, Josh 8:9; (9) in the hill country, Josh 16:1; (10) in the Benjamin tribal allotment, Josh 18:21–24.	10
Dan	(1) Middle Bronze Age, Gen 14; (2) Late Bronze Age, Deut, Josh, Judg; (3) Iron Age 1–2, 1&2 Sam, 1&2 Kings, 1&2 Chron, Jer, Amos; (4) Iron Age 3, Ezek; (5) in Bashan, Deut 33:22; (6) in a valley near Beth Rehob, Judg 18:28; (7) a northern border city of Israel, 2 Kings 10:29.	7

Biblical Site	Geographical Criteria Derived from the Biblical Text*	Number of Geo-Criteria
Dibon	(1) Late Bronze Age, Num, Josh; (2) Iron Age 2, Isa, Jer; (3) Iron Age 3, Neh; (4) in the territory of Moab (then the Amorites) in Transjordan, Num 21:29–30; (5) in the territory of Gad, Num 32:34–36; (6) north of the border of Moab (Arnon Gorge), Num 33:44–45; (7) generally south of Nebo, Num 33:46–48; (8) on the Medeba Plateau, Josh 13:9–21.	8
Dor	(1) Late Bronze Age, Josh, Judg; (2) Iron Age 1–2, 1 Kings, 1 Chron; (3) on the Canaanite western extremity, Josh 11:2; (4) in the territory of Manasseh, Josh 17:11; (5) on the western extremity of the Jezreel Valley corridor, Judg 1:27.	5
Dothan	(1) Middle Bronze Age, Gen 37; (2) Iron Age 2, 2 Kings; (3) not far and probably north from Shechem, Gen 37:14–17.	3

Biblical Site	Geographical Criteria Derived from the Biblical Text*	Number of Geo-Criteria
Ekron	(1) Late Bronze Age, Josh, Judg; (2) Iron Age 1–2, 1 Sam, 2 Kings, Jer, Amos; Zeph (3) Iron Age 3, Zech; (4) a northernmost territory of the Philistines, Josh 13:3; (5) a northern marker of the Judah territory on the Philistine Plain, Josh 15:11–12; (6) east of Ashdod, Josh 15:46; (7) down the valley west of Beth Shemesh, 1 Sam 5:10–6:16; (8) a fortified city, 1 Sam 17:52.	8
Gath	(1) Late Bronze Age, Josh; (2) Iron Age 1–2, 1&2 Sam, 1&2 Kings, 1&2 Chron, Amos, Mic; (3) in Philistia, Josh 13:3; (4) a fortified city, 1 Sam 17:52, 2 Chron 26:5; (5) west of the Elah Valley, 1 Sam 17:2–52; (6) in the territory of Judah, 2 Chron 11:5–10.	6

Biblical Site	Geographical Criteria Derived from the Biblical Text	Number of Geo-Criteria
Gaza	(1) Early Bronze Age/Intermediate Bronze Age, Gen 10; (2) Late Bronze Age, Deut, Josh, Judg; (3) Iron Age 1–2, 1 Sam, 1&2 Kings, Jer, Amos, Zeph; (4) Iron Age 3, Zech; (5) western, coastal extremity of the Canaanite clans, Gen 10; (6) coastal city settled by Caphtorites, a sea people, Deut 2:23; (7) a Philistine city, Josh 13:3; (8) in Judahite territory, Judg 1:18; (8) a fortified city, Amos 1:7.	8
Geshur (Zer/Zed)	(1) Late Bronze Age, Josh; (2) Iron Age 1–2, 2 Sam, 1 Chron; (3) borders Bashan, Josh 12:5; (4) in the Israelite Transjordan tribal allotment, Josh 13:11; (5) remained Geshurite through most of its history, Josh 13:13; (6) one of the fortified cities of the fishermen, Zer, on the north side of Lake Kinneret, Josh 19:35–38; (7) orientation to northern kingdoms, 1 Chron 2:23.	7

Biblical Site	Geographical Criteria Derived from the Biblical Text*	Number of Geo-Criteria
Gezer	(1) Late Bronze Age, Josh, Judg; (2) Iron Age 1–2, 2 Sam, 1 Kings, 1 Chron; (3) in the Shephelah, Josh 16:3; (4) in the territory of Ephraim, Josh 16:10; (5) remained significantly Canaanite until Iron 2, Judg 1:29, 1 Kings 9:16; (6) rebuilt by Solomon, 1 Kings 9:15.	6
Gibeon	(1) Late Bronze Age, Josh; (2) Iron Age 2, 2 Sam, 1 Kings, 1&2 Chron, Isa, Jer; (3) Iron Age 3, Neh; (4) not far from Jericho or Ai, Josh 9:3; (5) larger than Ai, Josh 10:2; (6) in the Benjamin allotment, Josh 18:21–28; (7) location of a famous great rock and/or high place, 2 Sam 20:8, 1 Kings 3:4; (8) location of a great pool/cistern, Jer 41:12.	8
Hazor	(1) Late Bronze Age, Josh, Judg; (2) Iron Age 1–2, 1&2 Sam, 1&2 Kings, Jer; (3) Iron Age 3, Neh; (4) a very large and influential city, Josh 11:10; (5) burned by Joshua, Josh 11:11; (6) rebuilt by Solomon, 1 Kings 9:15; (7) a northern city in the Kinneret region, 2 Kings 15:29.	7

Biblical Site	Geographical Criteria Derived from the Biblical Text	Number of Geo-Criteria
Hebron	(1) Middle Bronze Age, Gen; (2) Late Bronze Age, Exod, Num, Josh, Judg; (3) Iron Age 1–2, 1&2 Sam, 1 Kings, 1&2 Chron; (4) in Canaan, Gen 23:2; (5) associated with a significant valley, Gen 37:14; (6) north of the Negev, Num 13:22; (7) in the hill country of Judah, Josh 11:21; (8) "faced" by a hill, Judg 16:3; (9) surrounded by satellite towns, 2 Sam 2:3; (10) an "overnight" march from Bethlehem, 2 Sam 2:32.	10
Heshbon	(1) Late Bronze Age, Num, Deut, Josh, Judg; (2) Iron Age 1–2, 1 Chron, S of S, Isa, Jer; (3) Iron Age 3, Neh; (4) Amorite city with surrounding settlements on the Medeba Plateau, Num 21:25, Josh 13:16–17; (5) north of the Arnon Gorge, south of the Jabbok River, Deut 2:24, Josh 12:2; (6) an Israelite tribal allotment, Deut 29:7–8.	6
Jarmuth	(1) Late Bronze Age, Josh; (2) Iron Age 3, Neh; (3) in or near the western foothills of the central hill country, Josh 10:3–5, 15:33–36.	3

Biblical Site	Geographical Criteria Derived from the Biblical Text	Number of Geo-Criteria
Jericho	(1) Late Bronze Age, Num, Deut, Josh; (2) Iron Age 1–2, 2 Sam, 1&2 Kings, 1&2 Chron, Jer; (3) Iron Age 3, Ezra, Neh; (4) west of the Jordan River across from the Plains of Moab, Num 22:1, 26:2,63; (5) closely associated with the Jordan River, Num 34:15; (6) in Canaan on the opposite side of the Jordan from Mount Nebo, Deut 32:49; (7) the City of Palms on the western Kikkar, Deut 34:2; (8) a fortified city, Josh 6:1; (9) local springs, Josh 16:1; (10) a tall mound, Josh 18:12.	10

Biblical Site	Geographical Criteria Derived from the Biblical Text*	Number of Geo-Criteria
Jerusalem	(1) Middle Bronze Age, Gen 14; (2) Late Bronze Age, Josh, Judg; (3) Iron Age 1–2, 1&2 Sam, 1&2 Kings, 1&2 Chron, Psa, Eccl, S of S, Isa, Jer, Lam; (4) Iron Age 3, Ezra, Neh, Esth, Ezek, Dan, etc.; (5) west of, and in close proximity to, Sodom, for Sodom's king Bera accompanies Abram to visit Melchizedek in the King's Valley east of Salem, Gen 14:17–24; (6) a hill country city-state, Josh 10:1–5; (7) valley of Ben Hinnom to the immediate south, Josh 15:8; (8) in the Benjamin tribal allotment, Josh 18:21–28; (9) a fortified city in the IA, 1 Kings 3:1, 9:15; (10) a notable hill to the east, 1 Kings 11:7; (11) multiple IA gates, 2 Kings 14:13; (12) aquaducts and pools/reservoirs, 2 Kings 18:17; (13) next to the Kidron Valley, 2 Kings 23:4,6; (14) Babylonian siege works built around it, 2 Kings 25:1; (15) adjacent to Mount Moriah, 2 Chron 3:1; (16); IA II gate towers, 2 Chron 26:9; (17) fiery destruction by the Babylonians, 2 Chron 39:19; (18) rebuilt in IA III, Ezra, Neh.	18

Biblical Site	Geographical Criteria Derived from the Biblical Text*	Number of Geo-Criteria
Jezreel	(1) Late Bronze Age, Josh, Judg; (2) Iron Age 1–2, 1&2 Sam, 1&2 Kings, 1&2 Chron, Hos; (3) adjacent to the hill country, Josh 15:56; (4) associated with the Valley of Jezreel, Josh 17:16; (5) in the Issachar tribal allotment, Josh 19:17–18; (6) a local spring, 1 Sam 29:2; (7) near Beth Shean and Zarethan near the eastern half of the Jezreel Valley, 1 Kings 4:12; (8) fortified, 1 Kings 21:23; (9) a notable tower, 2 Kings 9:16.	9
Jokneam	(1) Late Bronze Age, Josh; (2) Iron Age 1–2, 1 Chron; (3) in/near Carmel, Josh 12:22; (4) near a notable ravine/wadi, Josh 19:11; (5) in the Zebulun tribal allotment, Josh 21:34.	5
Joppa	(1) Late Bronze Age, Josh; (2) Iron Age 2, 2 Chron, Jon; (3) Iron Age 3, Ezra; (4) in the original coastal tribal allotment of Dan, Josh 19:40–48; (5) a Mediterranean port city, 2 Chron 2:16, Ezra 3:7, Jon 1:3.	5

Biblical Site	Geographical Criteria Derived from the Biblical Text*	Number of Geo-Criteria
Kedesh Barnea (Kedesh)	(1) Middle Bronze Age, Gen; (2) Late Bronze Age, Num, Deut, Josh, Judg; (3) in the Desert of Paran/Zin, Gen 14:7, Num 13:26, 20:1, 34:4, Deut 1:19; (4) in the Negev, Gen 20:1; (5) via the Mount Seir road, eleven days from Horeb, Deut 1:1; (6) on the edge of Edomite territory, Num 20:14–16; (7) a place of springs, Num 27:14.	7
Lachish	(1) Late Bronze Age, Josh; (2) Iron Age 2, 2 Kings, 2 Chron, Isa, Jer, Mic; (3) Iron Age 3, Neh; (4) in/near the southern hill country, Josh 10:3–5,31; (5) not far from Eglon, Josh 10:34; (6) in the western foothills of the Judahite tribal allotment, Josh 15:21–39; (7) fortified, refurbished by Rehoboam, 2 Chron 11:5–10.	7
Mareshah	(1) Late Bronze Age, Josh; (2) Iron Age 1–2, 1&2 Chron, Mic; (3) in the south/west hills of the Judah tribal allotment, Josh 15:21–44; (4) in/near the Valley of Zephathah, 2 Chron 14:10.	4

Biblical Site	Geographical Criteria Derived from the Biblical Text*	Number of Geo-Criteria
Megiddo	(1) Late Bronze Age, Josh, Judg; (2) Iron Age 1–2, 1&2 Kings, 1&2 Chron; (3) Iron Age 3, Zech; (4) in the Manasseh tribal allotment, Jezreel Plain corridor, Josh 17:11, 2 Chron 35:22; (5) associated settlements, Josh 17:11; (6) major water source, Judg 5:19; (7) rebuilt/fortified by Solomon, 1 Kings 9:15.	7
Rabbah–Ammon	(1) Late Bronze Age, Deut, Josh; (2) Iron Age 1–2, 2 Sam, 1 Chron, Jer; Amos; (3) Iron Age 3, Ezek; (4) principal Ammonite city, Deut 3:11; (5) near Aorer, Josh 13:25; (6) notable water supply, 2 Sam 12:27; (7) destroyed by Joab, 1 Chron 20:1; (8) fortified, Amos 1:4.	8
Samaria	(1) Iron Age 2, 1&2 Kings, 2 Chron, Isa, Jer, Hos, Amos, Oba, Mic; (2) Iron Age 3, Ezra, Neh, Ezek; (3) founded by king Omri of Israel in the Samaria region, 1 Kings 16:24; (4) built on a hill, 1 Kings 16:24; (5) fortified, 1 Kings 22:10, 2 Kings 7:1.	5

Biblical Site	Geographical Criteria Derived from the Biblical Text˙	Number of Geo-Criteria
Shechem	(1) Middle Bronze Age, Gen; (2) Late Bronze Age, Num, Josh, Judg; (3) Iron Age 1–2, 1 Kings, 1&2 Chron, Psa, Jer, Hos; (4) in the Canaan hill country, Gen 12:6, 33:18; (5) fortified, Gen 34:20; (6) in the Manasseh tribal allotment, Josh 17:7; (7) in the hill country of Ephraim, Josh 20;7; (8) between Mount Ebal and Mount Gerizim, Deut 11:29, Josh 24:1–27; (9) a notable tower, Judg 9:46; (10) N/S road between Bethel and Shechem, Judg 21:19; (11) IA II fortification, 1 Kings 12:25; (12) associated villages, 1 Chron 7:28.	12
Shiloh	(1) Late Bronze Age, Josh, Judg; (2) Iron Age 1–2, 1 Sam, 1 Kings, Jer; (3) in the Ephraim hill country tribal allotment, Josh 16:5–8; (4) in Canaan, Josh 21:2, Judg 21:12; (5) north of Bethel, Judg 21:19; (6) east of the Bethel/ Shechem road, Judg 21:19; (7) south of Lebonah, Judg 21:19.	7

Biblical Site	Geographical Criteria Derived from the Biblical Text'	Number of Geo-Criteria
Sodom	(1) Early Bronze Age/Intermediate Bronze Age, Gen 10; (2) Middle Bronze Age, Gen 13–19; (3) city and associates never mentioned again as living cities, and general area unoccupied for several centuries, Num 21:20; (4) in league with at least five nearby, named cities, Gen 10:19; (5) marks the eastern extent of the Canaanite clans in the Rift Valley, Gen 10:19; (6) likely the southernmost and principal city in a formulaic S-to-N trade route configuration, with Lasha = Laish/Dan, Gen 10:19; (7) in a doublet with Gomorrah, signifying close proximity to that town, Gen 13:10, 14:10–11, 18:20, 19:24,28; (8) the other "doublet," Admah/Zeboiim, at a farther distance than Gomorrah, likely to the north, with the plural Zeboiim probably representing two or more towns in very close proximity, Gen 10:19ff; (9) in Transjordan, out of traditional Canaan, Gen 13:12; (10) in an area visible from the environs of Bethel/Ai W/NW above Jericho, Gen 13:3–4,10; (11) in or immediately adjacent to the eastern alluvial Kikkar of the Jordan River north of the Dead Sea,	25

Biblical Site	Geographical Criteria Derived from the Biblical Text*	Number of Geo-Criteria
Sodom (*continued*)	Gen 13:10–12; (12) in a flat, disk-shaped area entirely visible from the plateau near Bethel/Ai, Gen 13:10; (13) in a grouping of at least five cities on the eastern Kikkar, Gen 1019, 13:12; (14) In a notably well-watered area, Gen 13:10; (15) in an area watered by a major river as in Eden and Egypt, Gen 13:10; (16) in close proximity to the annual inundation of the Jordan River, analogous to that in Egypt, Gen 13:10; (17) in an eastward direction from Bethel/Ai, Gen 13:11; (18) as far as it was possible to go on the Kikkar before mounting into the Transjordan Plateau, Gen 13:12; (19) north of Zoar, Gen 13:10; (20) the largest of the Kikkar cities, always first in the group list, and the only one ever mentioned by itself, Gen 10:19, 13:12–19:29; (21) north of Hazazon Tamar/En Gedi, Gen 14:5–12; (22) Kikkar coalition army engages Kedorlaomer near the Dead Sea north of Hazazon Tamar/En Gedi attempting to thwart Kedorlaomer's northern advance toward Sodom and Gomorrah on the eastern Jordan Disk north of the Dead Sea, Gen 14:7–12; (23) battle survivor escapes	25

Biblical Site	Geographical Criteria Derived from the Biblical Text*	Number of Geo-Criteria
Sodom (*continued*)	to warn Abram at nearby Hebron, just west of En Gedi, Gen 14:13; (24) in relatively close proximity to Jerusalem, as Sodom's king Bera meets Abram in the Valley of Shaveh east of Jerusalem, then accompanies him to visit Melchizedek, Gen 14:17–24; (25) subject to fiery destruction along with the associated Cities of the Plain during the MBA, Gen 19:24–29.	25
Taanach	(1) Late Bronze Age, Josh, Judg; (2) Iron Age 1–2, 1 Kings, 1 Chron; (3) in/near the Jezreel Valley corridor, Josh 17:11; (4) in the Manasseh tribal allotment, Josh 21:25, Judg 1:27; (5) near the waters of Megiddo, Judg 5:19; (6) likely close to Megiddo, 1 Kings 4:12; (7) associated villages, 1 Chron 7:29.	7

Biblical Site	Geographical Criteria Derived from the Biblical Text*	Number of Geo-Criteria
Timnah	(1) Middle Bronze Age, Gen; (2) Late Bronze Age, Josh, Judg; (3) Iron 2, 2 Chron; (4) near Beth Shemesh, Josh 15:10; (5) in the Judah tribal allotment, in the western foothills, Josh 15:21,48–57; (6) in the original Danite allotment, Josh 19:40–48; (7) near Zorah of Samson, Judg 14:1–2; (8) down the valley from Zorah, Judg 13:2, 14:5; (9) near Philistine territory, 2 Chron 28:17–18.	9

© Copyright 2008 by Steven Collins.

* One chronological criterion is always included based on a face-value assessment of the biblical chronology. One criterion is assigned for each general archaeological period during which a city/town is said to have been occupied according to the biblical text. For example, if a site is included in the Joshua narrative (Late Bronze Age), one geo-criterion is assigned. If the same site is mentioned during the reign of Solomon (Iron 2), another geo-criterion is assigned. Further, if it is specifically stated or implied that a site was unoccupied during a given archaeological period, another geo-criterion is assigned.

† IA = Iron Age

Bibliography

ONE: Down from the Jordan's Source: The Setting for Sodom

Aharoni, Y. *The Land of the Bible: A Historical Geography*. Philadelphia: Westminster, 1979.

Collins, S. *The Search for Sodom and Gomorrah: A Scientific Application of Dialogical Methodology in Determining Material Correspondence between Archaeological Data and Biblical Narrative*. Albuquerque, NM: Trinity Southwest University Press, 2011.

Dornemann, R. H. *The Archaeology of the Transjordan in the Bronze and Iron Ages*. Milwaukee: Milwaukee Public Museum, 1983.

Dorsey, D. *The Roads and Highways of Ancient Israel*. Baltimore: Johns Hopkins University Press, 1991.

MacDonald, B. *East of the Jordan: Territories and Sites of the Hebrew Scriptures*. Boston: American Schools of Oriental Research, 2000.

Mazar, A. *Archaeology of the Land of the Bible*. New York: Doubleday, 1990.

Rainey, A. F., and R. S. Notley. *The Sacred Bridge*. Jerusalem: Carta, 2006.

Wright, G. E. *Biblical Archaeology*. Philadelphia: Westminster, 1960.

BACKSTORY: Dr. C's Dilemma

Albright, W. F. "The Archaeological Results of an Expedition to Moab and the Dead Sea," *Bulletin of the American Schools of Oriental Research* 14 (1924): 2–12.

Ben-Tor, A. *The Archaeology of Ancient Israel*. New Haven: Yale University Press, 1992.

Collins, S. *The Search for Sodom and Gomorrah: A Scientific Application of Dialogical Methodology in Determining Material Correspondence between Archaeological Data and Biblical Narrative*. Albuquerque, NM: Trinity Southwest University Press, 2011.

Finkelstein, I. "From Sherds to History." *Israel Exploration Journal* 48 (1998): 120–31 (based on a 1996 *Eretz Israel* article by Finkelstein published in Hebrew as "The Settlement History of the Transjordan Plateau in the Light of Survey Data").

Howard, D. M., Jr. "Sodom and Gomorrah Revisited," *Journal of the Evangelical Theological Society* 27 (1984): 385–400.

MacDonald, B. *East of the Jordan: Territories and Sites of the Hebrew Scriptures.* Boston: American Schools of Oriental Research, 2000.

Rainey, A. F., and R. S. Notley. *The Sacred Bridge.* Jerusalem: Carta, 2006.

Rast, W. E. "Bab edh-Dhra'." In D. N. Freedman, ed., *The Anchor Bible Dictionary.* New York: Doubleday, 1993.

Wright, G. E. *Biblical Archaeology.* Philadelphia: Westminster, 1960.

TWO: Coming to Tall el-Hammam

Aharoni, Y. *The Land of the Bible: A Historical Geography.* Philadelphia: Westminster, 1979.

Collins, S. *The Search for Sodom and Gomorrah: A Scientific Application of Dialogical Methodology in Determining Material Correspondence between Archaeological Data and Biblical Narrative.* Albuquerque, NM: Trinity Southwest University Press, 2011.

Dornemann, R. H. *The Archaeology of the Transjordan in the Bronze and Iron Ages.* Milwaukee: Milwaukee Public Museum, 1983.

Dorsey, D. *The Roads and Highways of Ancient Israel.* Baltimore: Johns Hopkins University Press, 1991.

Falconer, S. E. "The Middle Bronze Age." In R. B. Adams, ed., *Jordan: An Archaeological Reader,* 263–80. London: Equinox, 2008.

Ibrahim, M., K. Yassine, and J. A. Sauer. "The East Jordan Valley Survey 1975" (Parts 1 and 2). In K. Yassine, ed., *The Archaeology of Jordan: Essays and Reports*, 159–207. Amman: Department of Archaeology, University of Jordan, 1988.

Khouri, R. G. *The Antiquities of the Jordan Rift Valley*. Amman: Al Kutba, 1988.

Leonard, A. "The Jordan Valley Survey, 1953: Some Unpublished Soundings Conducted by James Mellaart." *Annual of the American Schools of Oriental Research*, vol. 50. Winona Lake, IN: Eisenbrauns, 1992.

MacDonald, B. *East of the Jordan: Territories and Sites of the Hebrew Scriptures*. Boston: American Schools of Oriental Research, 2000.

THREE: The Chronicles of the Kikkar

Adams, R. B., ed. *Jordan: An Archaeological Reader*. London: Equinox Publishing Ltd., 2008.

Albright, W. F. "The Jordan Valley in the Bronze Age." *Annual of the American Schools of Oriental Research* 1924–25, vol. 6, 13–74. New Haven: Yale University Press, 1926.

Aljarrah, H. This most thorough study of the Ar-Rawda Dolmen Field is yet to be published. The information has been provided by Mr. Aljarrah to the authors of this report for inclusion in the Tall el-Hammam database.

Amiran, R. *Early Arad: The Chalcolithic Settlement and Early Bronze City.* Jerusalem: Israel Exploration Society, 1978.

Astour, M. C. "Chedorlaomer." In D. N. Freedman, ed., *The Anchor Bible Dictionary*, vol. 1, 893–95. New York: Doubleday, 1992.

Collins, S. *The Search for Sodom and Gomorrah: A Scientific Application of Dialogical Methodology in Determining Material Correspondence between Archaeological Data and Biblical Narrative.* Albuquerque, NM: Trinity Southwest University Press, 2011.

Falconer, S. E. "The Middle Bronze Age." In R. B. Adams, ed., *Jordan: An Archaeological Reader*, 263–80. London: Equinox, 2008.

Falconer, S. E., P. L. Fall, and J. E. Jones. "Life at the Foundation of Bronze Age Civilization: Agrarian Villages in the Jordan Valley." In T. E. Levy, P. M. Michèle Daviau, R. W. Younker, and M. Shaer, eds., *Crossing Jordan: North American Contributions to the Archaeology of Jordan*, 261–68. London: Equinox, 2007.

Finkelstein, I., and R. Gophna. "Settlement, Demographic and Economic Patterns in the Highlands of Palestine in the Chalcolithic and Early Bronze Periods and the Beginning of Urbanism." *Bulletin of the American Schools of Oriental Research* 289 (1993): 1–22.

Hadas, G. "Dead Sea Sailing Routes During the Herodian Period." *Bulletin of the Anglo-Israel Archaeological Society* 26 (2008): 31–36.

Harrison, T. "Early Bronze Age Social Organization as Reflected in Burial Patterns from the Southern Levant." In S. R. Wolff, ed., *Studies in the Archaeology of Israel and Neighbouring Lands in Memory of Douglas L. Esse*, 215–36. Chicago: Oriental Institute of the University of Chicago, 2001.

———. "Shifting Patterns of Settlement in the Highlands of Central Jordan during the Early Bronze Age." *Bulletin of the American Schools of Oriental Research* 306 (1997) 1–38.

Krahmalkov, C. R. "Exodus Itinerary Confirmed by Egyptian Evidence." *Biblical Archaeology Review* 20.5 (1994): 54–62.

Lemche, N. P. *Prelude to Israel's Past.* Peabody, MA: Hendrickson, 1998.

MacDonald, B. *East of the Jordan: Territories and Sites of the Hebrew Scriptures.* Boston: American Schools of Oriental Research, 2000.

Mazar, A. *Archaeology of the Land of the Bible.* New York: Doubleday, 1990.

Moran, W. L. *The Amarna Letters.* Baltimore: Johns Hopkins University Press, 1992.

Prag, K. "The Dead Sea Dolmens: Death and the Landscape." In S. Campbell and A. Green, eds., *The Archaeology of Death in the Ancient Near East*, 75–84. Oxford: Oxbow Monograph 51, 1995.

Rainey, A. F., and R. S. Notley. *The Sacred Bridge.* Jerusalem: Carta, 2006.

Schath, K., S. Collins, and H. Aljarrah. "The Excavation of an Undisturbed Demi-Dolmen and Insights from the Ḥammām Megalithic Field, 2011 Season." *Annual of the Department of Antiquities of Jordan* 55 (2011).

Simons, J. *The Geographical and Topographical Texts of the Old Testament.* Leiden: Brill, 1959.

―――. *Handbook for the Study of Topographical Lists Relating to Western Asia.* Leiden: Brill, 1937.

Waterhouse, S. D. "Who Are the Habiru of the Amarna Letters?" *Journal of the Adventist Theological Society* 12.1 (2001): 31–42.

Yadin, Y. *The Art of Warfare in Biblical Lands*, vol. 1. New York: McGraw-Hill, 1963.

FOUR: Warlords and Destruction:
The Bible and the Backstory

Broshi, M., and R. Gophna. "Middle Bronze Age II Palestine: Its Settlements and Population." *Bulletin of the American Schools of Oriental Research* 261 (1986): 73–90.

Collins, S. *The Search for Sodom and Gomorrah: A Scientific Application of Dialogical Methodology in Determining Material Correspondence between Archaeological Data and Biblical Narrative.* Albuquerque, NM: Trinity Southwest University Press, 2011.

Falconer, S. E. "The Middle Bronze Age." In R. B. Adams, ed., *Jordan: An Archaeological Reader*, 263–80. London: Equinox, 2008.

Gabriel, R. A., and K. S. Metz. *A Short History of War: The Evolution of Warfare and Weapons, Professional Readings in Military Strategy*, no. 5. Carlisle Barracks: Strategic Studies Institute, 1992, available at http://www.au.af.mil/au/awc/awcgate/gabrmetz/gabr003a.htm.

MacDonald, B. *East of the Jordan: Territories and Sites of the Hebrew Scriptures*. Boston: American Schools of Oriental Research, 2000.

Mazar, A. *Archaeology of the Land of the Bible*. New York: Doubleday, 1990.

Moran, W. L. *The Amarna Letters*. Baltimore: Johns Hopkins University Press, 1992.

Rainey, A. F., and R. S. Notley. *The Sacred Bridge*. Jerusalem: Carta, 2006.

Waterhouse, S. D. "Who are the Habiru of the Amarna Letters?" *Journal of the Adventist Theological Society* 12.1 (2001): 31–42.

Yadin, Y. *The Art of Warfare in Biblical Lands*, vol. 1. New York: McGraw-Hill, 1963.

BACKSTORY: Dr. C's Search

Briggs, P. "Testing the Factuality of the Conquest of Ai Narrative in the Book of Joshua." Institute of Archaeology & Biblical History Academic Monograph Series AR-2 (2004), available at http://www.representationalresearch.com/pdfs/factualitypaper12apr04.pdf.

Broshi, M., and R. Gophna. "Middle Bronze Age II Palestine: Its Settlements and Population." *Bulletin of the American Schools of Oriental Research* 261 (1986): 73–90.

Chang-Ho, C., and J. K. Lee. "The Survey in the Regions of 'Iraq al-Amir and Wadi al-Kafrayn, 2000." *Annual of the Department of Antiquities of Jordan* 46 (2002): 179–95.

Collins, S. *The Search for Sodom and Gomorrah: A Scientific Application of Dialogical Methodology in Determining Material Correspondence between Archaeological Data and Biblical Narrative.* Albuquerque, NM: Trinity Southwest University Press, 2011.

Falconer, S. E. "The Middle Bronze Age." In R. B. Adams, ed., *Jordan: An Archaeological Reader*, 263–80. London: Equinox, 2008.

Finkelstein, I. "From Sherds to History." *Israel Exploration Journal* 48 (1998): 120–31 (based on a 1996 *Eretz Israel* article by Finkelstein published in Hebrew as "The Settlement History of the Transjordan Plateau in the Light of Survey Data").

Flanagan, J. W., D. W. McCreery, and K. N. Yassine. "Tall Nimrin: Preliminary Report on the 1995 Excavation and Geological Survey." *Annual of the Department of Antiquities of Jordan* 40 (1996): 271–92.

————. "Tell Nimrin: Preliminary Report on the 1993 Season." *Annual of the Department of Antiquities of Jordan* 38 (1994): 205–44.

Glueck, N. "Exploration in Eastern Palestine." *Annual of the American Schools of Oriental Research*, vols. 18–19 for 1937–39. New Haven: American Schools of Oriental Research, 1939.

Ibrahim, M., K. Yassine, and J. A. Sauer. "The East Jordan Valley Survey 1975" (Parts 1 and 2). In K. Yassine, ed., *The Archaeology of Jordan: Essays and Reports*, 159–207. Amman: Department of Archaeology, University of Jordan, 1988.

Khouri, R. G. *The Antiquities of the Jordan Rift Valley*. Amman: Al Kutba, 1988.

Leonard, A. "The Jordan Valley Survey, 1953: Some Unpublished Soundings Conducted by James Mellaart." *Annual of the American Schools of Oriental Research*, vol. 50. Winona Lake, IN: Eisenbrauns, 1992.

MacDonald, B. *East of the Jordan: Territories and Sites of the Hebrew Scriptures*. Boston: American Schools of Oriental Research, 2000.

Mazar, A. *Archaeology of the Land of the Bible*. New York: Doubleday, 1990.

Prag, K. "Preliminary Report on the Excavations at Tell Iktānū and Tell al-Hammam, Jordan, 1990." *Levant* 23 (1991): 55–66.

Rast, W. E. "Bab edh-Dhra'." In D. N. Freedman, ed., *The Anchor Bible Dictionary*. New York: Doubleday, 1993.

Richard, S., ed. *Near Eastern Archaeology: A Reader.* Winona Lake, IN: Eisenbrauns, 2003.

Wood, B. G. "The Discovery of the Sin Cities of Sodom and Gomorrah." *Bible and Spade* 12.3 (1999): 67–80.

Wright, G. E. *Biblical Archaeology.* Philadelphia: Westminster, 1960.

FIVE: Right Place: Centuries of Seeking Sodom

Avner, U., and I. Carmi. "Settlement Patterns in the Southern Levant Deserts during the 6th–3rd Millennia BC, a Revision based on C14 Dating." *Radiocarbon* 43 (2001): 1203–16.

Briggs, P. "Testing the Factuality of the Conquest of Ai Narrative in the Book of Joshua." Institute of Archaeology & Biblical History Academic Monograph Series AR-2 (2004), available at http://www .representationalresearch.com/pdfs/factualitypaper12apr04.pdf.

Brown, F., S. R. Driver, and C. A. Briggs. *A Hebrew and English Lexicon of the Old Testament.* Oxford: Clarendon, 1975.

Chang-Ho, C., and J. K. Lee. "The Survey in the Regions of 'Iraq al-Amir and Wadi al-Kafrayn, 2000." *Annual of the Department of Antiquities of Jordan* 46 (2002): 179–95.

Collins, S. "A Response to Bryant G. Wood's Critique of Collins' Northern Sodom Theory." In S. Collins, ed., *The Search for Sodom and Gomorrah*, 217–52. Albuquerque, NM: Trinity Southwest University Press, 2011.

————. "Rethinking the Location of Zoar: An Exercise in Biblical Geography." *Biblical Research Bulletin* 6.3 (2006): 1–5.

————. *The Search for Sodom and Gomorrah: A Scientific Application of Dialogical Methodology in Determining Material Correspondence between Archaeological Data and Biblical Narrative*. Albuquerque, NM: Trinity Southwest University Press, 2011.

————. "Sodom: The Discovery of a Lost City." *Bible and Spade* 20.3 (2007): 70–77.

Collins, S., and H. Aljarrah. "The Tall el-Hammam Excavation Project: End of Season Activity Report—Season Six: 2011 Excavation, Exploration, and Survey." Filed with the Department of Antiquities of Jordan, January 26, 2011.

————. "Tall al-Hammam Season Six, 2011: Excavation, Survey, Interpretations and Insights." *Annual of the Department of Antiquities of Jordan* 55 (2011): 581–608.

Collins, S., and Y. Eylayyan. "The Tall el-Hammam Excavation Project: End of Season Activity Report—Season Seven: 2012 Excavation, Exploration, and Survey." Filed with the Department of Antiquities of Jordan, February 2012.

Collins, S., K. Hamdan, and G. Byers. "Tall al-Ḥammām: Preliminary Report on Four Seasons of Excavation (2006–2009)." *Annual of the Department of Antiquities of Jordan* 53 (2009): 385–414.

Culver, R. D. "Zoar." In *The Zondervan Pictorial Encyclopedia of the Bible*. Grand Rapids. MI: Zondervan, 1976.

Domeris, W. R., and R. S. Hess. "ככר" In W. A. VanGemeren, ed., *New International Dictionary of Old Testament Theology and Exegesis*, vol. 2, 636–37. Grand Rapids, MI: Zondervan, 1997.

Dorsey, D. *The Roads and Highways of Ancient Israel*. Baltimore: Johns Hopkins University Press, 1991.

Finkelstein, I., and R. Gophna. "Settlement, Demographic and Economic Patterns in the Highlands of Palestine in the Chalcolithic and Early Bronze Periods and the Beginning of Urbanism." *Bulletin of the American Schools of Oriental Research* 289 (1993): 1–22.

Holladay, W., ed. *A Concise Hebrew and Aramaic Lexicon of the Old Testament*. Grand Rapids, MI: Eerdmans, 1988.

Howard, D. M., Jr. "Sodom and Gomorrah Revisited," *Journal of the Evangelical Theological Society* 27 (1984): 385–400.

Koehler, L., and W. Baumgartner, eds. *Lexicon in Veteris Testamenti Libros: A Dictionary of the Hebrew Old Testament in English and German*. Leiden: Brill, 1985.

MacDonald, B. *East of the Jordan: Territories and Sites of the Hebrew Scriptures*. Boston: American Schools of Oriental Research, 2000.

Morgan, Carl E. "The Geography of Kedorlaomer's Campaign in Genesis 14 and Its Bearing on the Location of Sodom." In S. Collins, ed., *The Search for Sodom and Gomorrah: A Scientific Application of Dialogical Methodology in Determining Material Correspondence between Archaeological Data and Biblical Narrative*, 415–91. Albuquerque, NM: Trinity Southwest University Press, 2011.

Neev, D., and K. O. Emery. *The Destruction of Sodom and Gomorrah, and Jericho: Geological, Climatological, and Archaeological Background*. New York: Oxford University Press, 1995.

Prag, K. "Water Strategies in the Iktānū Region of Jordan." *Studies in the History and Archaeology of Jordan* 9 (2007): 405–12.

Rainey, A. F., and R. S. Notley. *The Sacred Bridge*. Jerusalem: Carta, 2006.

Rast, W. E. "Bab edh-Dhra'." In D. N. Freedman, ed., *The Anchor Bible Dictionary*. New York: Doubleday, 1993.

―――. "Bab edh-Dhra and the Origin of the Sodom Saga." In L. G. Perdue, L. E. Toombs, and G. L. Johnson, eds., *Archaeology and Biblical Interpretation: Essays in Memory of D. G. Rose*. Atlanta: John Knox Press, 1987.

Schaub, R. T., and M. S. Chesson. "Life in the Earliest Walled Towns on the Dead Sea Plain: Bab edh-Dhra' and an-Numayra." In T. E. Levy, P. M. Michèle Daviau, R. W. Younker, and M. Shaer, eds., *Crossing

Jordan: North American Contributions to the Archaeology of Jordan, 245–52. London: Equinox, 2007.

Thomson, W. M. *The Land and the Book: Southern Palestine and Jerusalem*. New York: Harper & Brothers, 1882.

Tristram, H. B. *The Land of Moab: Travels and Discoveries on the East Side of the Dead Sea and the Jordan*, 2nd ed. Piscataway, NJ: Gorgias Press, 1874.

VanGemeren, W. A., ed. *New International Dictionary of Old Testament Theology and Exegesis*. 5 vols. Grand Rapids, MI: Zondervan, 1997.

van Hattem, W. C. "Once Again: Sodom and Gomorrah." *Biblical Archaeology* 44 (1981): 87–92

Wood, B. G. "The Discovery of the Sin Cities of Sodom and Gomorrah." *Bible and Spade* 12.3 (1999): 67–80.

———. "Locating Sodom: A Critique of the Northern Proposal." *Bible and Spade* 20.3 (2007): 78–84.

Wright, G. E. *Biblical Archaeology*. Philadelphia: Westminster, 1960.

———, ed. *The Westminster Historical Atlas to the Bible*. Philadelphia: Westminster, 1956.

SIX: Right Time: Finding the Ballpark

Avner, U., and I. Carmi. "Settlement Patterns in the Southern Levant Deserts during the 6th–3rd Millennia BC, a Revision based on C14 Dating." *Radiocarbon* 43 (2001): 1203–16.

Ben-Tor, A. *The Archaeology of Ancient Israel.* New Haven: Yale University Press, 1992.

Briggs, P. "Testing the Factuality of the Conquest of Ai Narrative in the Book of Joshua." Institute of Archaeology & Biblical History Academic Monograph Series AR-2 (2004), available at http://www.representationalresearch.com/pdfs/factualitypaper12apr04.pdf.

Collins, S. *Let My People Go: Using Historical Synchronisms to Identify the Pharaoh of the Exodus.* Albuquerque, NM: Trinity Southwest University Press, 2005.

———. "A Response to Bryant G. Wood's Critique of Collins' Northern Sodom Theory." In S. Collins, ed., *The Search for Sodom and Gomorrah,* 217–52. Albuquerque, NM: Trinity Southwest University Press, 2011.

———. *The Search for Sodom and Gomorrah: A Scientific Application of Dialogical Methodology in Determining Material Correspondence between Archaeological Data and Biblical Narrative.* Albuquerque, NM: Trinity Southwest University Press, 2011.

———. "Sodom: The Discovery of a Lost City." *Bible and Spade* 20.3 (2007): 70–77.

Collins, S., A. Abu Dayyeh, A. abu-Shmais, G. A. Byers, K. Hamdan, H. Aljarrah, J. Haroun, M. C. Luddeni, and S. McAllister. "The Tall el-Hammam Excavation Project, Season Activity Report, Season Three: 2008 Excavation, Exploration, and Survey." Filed with the Department of Antiquities of Jordan, February 13, 2008.

Collins, S., and H. Aljarrah. "Tall al-Ḥammām Season Six, 2011: Excavation, Survey, Interpretations and Insights." *Annual of the Department of Antiquities of Jordan* 55 (2011): 581–608.

———. "The Tall el-Hammam Excavation Project: End of Season Activity Report—Season Six: 2011 Excavation, Exploration, and Survey," filed with the Department of Antiquities of Jordan January 26, 2011.

Collins, S., G. A. Byers, and M. C. Luddeni. "The Tall el-Hammam Excavation Project, Season Activity Report, Season One: 2005/2006 Probe Excavation and Survey." Filed with the Department of Antiquities of Jordan, January 22, 2006.

Collins, S., G. A. Byers, M. C. Luddeni, and J. W. Moore. "The Tall el-Hammam Excavation Project, Season Activity Report, Season Two: 2006/2007 Excavation and Survey." Filed with the Department of Antiquities of Jordan, February 4, 2007.

Collins, S., and Y. Eylayyan. "The Tall el-Hammam Excavation Project: End of Season Activity Report—Season Seven: 2012 Excavation, Exploration, and Survey." Filed with the Department of Antiquities of Jordan, February 2012.

Collins, S., K. Hamdan, and G. Byers. "Tall al-Ḥammām: Preliminary Report on Four Seasons of Excavation (2006–2009)." *Annual of the Department of Antiquities of Jordan* 53 (2009): 385–414.

Collins, S., K. Hamdan, G. A. Byers, J. Haroun, H. Aljarrah, M. C. Luddeni, S. McAllister, Q. Dasouqi, and A. Abu-Shmais. "The Tall el-Hammam Excavation Project, Season Activity Report, Season Five: 2010 Excavation, Exploration, and Survey." Filed with the Department of Antiquities of Jordan, January 31, 2010.

Collins, S., K. Hamdan, G. A. Byers, J. Haroun, H. Aljarrah, M. C. Luddeni, S. McAllister, Q. Dasouqi, A. Abu-Shmais, and D. Graves. "The Tall el-Hammam Excavation Project, Season Activity Report, Season Four: 2009 Excavation, Exploration, and Survey." Filed with the Department of Antiquities of Jordan, February 27, 2009.

Collins, S., and J. W. Moore. "Abraham and Tall Nimrin: Does the Chronology Work?" In S. Collins, ed., *The Search for Sodom and Gomorrah*, 95–96. Albuquerque, NM: Trinity Southwest University Press, 2011.

Falconer, S. E. "The Middle Bronze Age." In R. B. Adams, ed., *Jordan: An Archaeological Reader*, 263–80. London: Equinox, 2008.

Finkelstein, I., and R. Gophna. "Settlement, Demographic and Economic Patterns in the Highlands of Palestine in the Chalcolithic and Early Bronze Periods and the Beginning of Urbanism." *Bulletin of the American Schools of Oriental Research* 289 (1993): 1–22.

Flanagan, J. W., D. W. McCreery, and K. N. Yassine. "Tall Nimrin: Preliminary Report on the 1995 Excavation and Geological Survey."

Annual of the Department of Antiquities of Jordan 40 (1996): 271–92.

——. "Tell Nimrin: Preliminary Report on the 1993 Season." *Annual of the Department of Antiquities of Jordan* 38 (1994): 205–44.

Frumkin, A., and Y. Elitzur. "The Rise and Fall of the Dead Sea." *Biblical Archaeology Review* 27.6 (November–December 2001): 43–50.

Grimal, N. *A History of Egypt.* Oxford: Oxford University Press, 1992.

Hoffmeier, J. K. *Israel in Egypt: The Evidence for the Authenticity of the Exodus Tradition.* New York: Oxford University Press, 1996.

Kitchen, K. A. *On the Reliability of the Old Testament.* Grand Rapids, MI: Eerdmans, 2003.

——. *Ramesside Inscriptions.* Oxford: Oxford University Press, 1979.

Langgut, D., and F. Neumann. "The Paleo-Climatic History of the Middle Bronze–Iron Age Time Interval: High Resolution Pollen Study of Dead Sea Cores." Paper presented to the 2010 Annual Meeting of the American Schools of Oriental Research.

Mazar, A. *Archaeology of the Land of the Bible.* New York: Doubleday, 1990.

Prag, K. "The Intermediate Early Bronze–Middle Bronze Age: An Interpretation of the Evidence from Transjordan, Syria and Lebanon." *Levant 6* (1974): 69–116.

Rast, W. E. "Bab edh-Dhra'." In D. N. Freedman, ed., *The Anchor Bible Dictionary*. New York: Doubleday, 1993.

Richard, S. L. "The Early Bronze Age: The Rise and Collapse of Urbanism." *Biblical Archaeologist* 50 (1987): 22–43.

Schaub, R. T., and M. S. Chesson. "Life in the Earliest Walled Towns on the Dead Sea Plain: Bab edh-Dhra' and an-Numayra." In T. E. Levy, P. M. Michèle Daviau, R. W. Younker, and M. Shaer, eds., *Crossing Jordan: North American Contributions to the Archaeology of Jordan*, 245–52. London: Equinox, 2007.

Wright, G. E. *Biblical Archaeology*. Philadelphia: Westminster, 1960.

———. "The Discovery of the Sin Cities of Sodom and Gomorrah." *Bible and Spade* 12.3 (1999): 67–80.

———. "Locating Sodom: A Critique of the Northern Proposal." *Bible and Spade* 20.3 (2007): 78–84.

SEVEN: Right Stuff: Agitations, Architecture, and Artifacts

Ben-Tor, A. *The Archaeology of Ancient Israel*. New Haven: Yale University Press, 1992.

Briggs, P. "Testing the Factuality of the Conquest of Ai Narrative in the Book of Joshua." Institute of Archaeology & Biblical History Academic Monograph Series AR-2 (2004), available at http://www.representationalresearch.com/pdfs/factualitypaper12apr04.pdf.

Broshi, M., and R. Gophna. "Middle Bronze Age II Palestine: Its Settlements and Population." *Bulletin of the American Schools of Oriental Research* 261 (1986): 73–90.

Burke, A. A. *"Walled Up to Heaven": The Evolution of Middle Bronze Age Fortification Strategies in the Levant.* Winona Lake, IN: Eisenbrauns, 2008.

Collins, S. *The Search for Sodom and Gomorrah: A Scientific Application of Dialogical Methodology in Determining Material Correspondence between Archaeological Data and Biblical Narrative.* Albuquerque, NM: Trinity Southwest University Press, 2011.

Collins, S., A. Abu Dayyeh, A. Abu-Shmais, G. A. Byers, K. Hamdan, H. Aljarrah, J. Haroun, M. C. Luddeni, and S. McAllister. "The Tall el-Hammam Excavation Project, Season Activity Report, Season Three: 2008 Excavation, Exploration, and Survey." Filed with the Department of Antiquities of Jordan, February 13, 2008.

Collins, S., and H. Aljarrah. "The Tall el-Hammam Excavation Project: End of Season Activity Report—Season Six: 2011 Excavation, Exploration, and Survey." Filed with the Department of Antiquities of Jordan, January 26, 2011.

Collins, S., G. A. Byers, and M. C. Luddeni. "The Tall el-Hammam Excavation Project, Season Activity Report, Season One: 2005/2006 Probe Excavation and Survey." Filed with the Department of Antiquities of Jordan, January 22, 2006.

Collins, S., G. A. Byers, M. C. Luddeni, and J. W. Moore. "The Tall el-

Hammam Excavation Project, Season Activity Report, Season Two: 2006/2007 Excavation and Survey." Filed with the Department of Antiquities of Jordan, February 4, 2007.

Collins, S., and Y. Eylayyan. "The Tall el-Hammam Excavation Project: End of Season Activity Report—Season Seven: 2012 Excavation, Exploration, and Survey." Filed with the Department of Antiquities of Jordan, February 2012.

Collins, S., K. Hamdan, and G. Byers. "Tall al-Ḥammām: Preliminary Report on Four Seasons of Excavation (2006–2009)." *Annual of the Department of Antiquities of Jordan* 53 (2009): 385–414.

Collins, S., K. Hamdan, G. A. Byers, J. Haroun, H. Aljarrah, M. C. Luddeni, S. McAllister, Q. Dasouqi, and A. Abu-Shmais. "The Tall el-Hammam Excavation Project, Season Activity Report, Season Five: 2010 Excavation, Exploration, and Survey." Filed with the Department of Antiquities of Jordan, January 31, 2010.

Collins, S., K. Hamdan, G. A. Byers, J. Haroun, H. Aljarrah, M. C. Luddeni, S. McAllister, Q. Dasouqi, A. Abu-Shmais, and D. Graves. "The Tall el-Hammam Excavation Project, Season Activity Report, Season Four: 2009 Excavation, Exploration, and Survey." Filed with the Department of Antiquities of Jordan, February 27, 2009.

Falconer, S. E., P. L. Fall, and J. E. Jones. "Life at the Foundation of Bronze Age Civilization: Agrarian Villages in the Jordan Valley." In T. E. Levy, P. M. Michèle Daviau, R. W. Younker, and M. Shaer, eds., *Crossing Jordan: North American Contributions to the Archaeology of Jordan*, 261–68. London: Equinox, 2007.

Finkelstein, I. "Middle Bronze Age 'Fortifications': A Reflection of Social Organization and Political Formations." *Tel Aviv* 19 (1992): 201–20.

Flanagan, J. W., D. W. McCreery, and K. N. Yassine. "Tall Nimrin: Preliminary Report on the 1995 Excavation and Geological Survey." *Annual of the Department of Antiquities of Jordan* 40 (1996): 271–92.

———. "Tell Nimrin: Preliminary Report on the 1993 Season." *Annual of the Department of Antiquities of Jordan* 38 (1994): 205–44.

Harris, G. M. and A. P. Beardow. "The Destruction of Sodom and Gomorrah: A Geotechnical Perspective." *Quarterly Journal of Engineering Geology* 28 (1995): 349–62.

Kempinski, A. "Middle and Late Bronze Age Fortifications." In A. Kempinski and R. Reich, eds., *The Architecture of Ancient Israel*, 127–42. Jerusalem: Israel Exploration Society, 1992.

———. "Urbanization and Town Plans in the Middle Bronze Age II." In A. Kempinski and R. Reich, eds., *The Architecture of Ancient Israel*, 121–26. Jerusalem: Israel Exploration Society, 1992.

Kempinski, A., and R. Reich, eds. *The Architecture of Ancient Israel*. Jerusalem: Israel Exploration Society, 1992.

McAllister, S. S. "Middle Bronze Age Fortifications in the Southern Levant: Systems Analysis and Quantitative Survey." Doctoral dissertation, College of Archaeology and Biblical History, Trinity Southwest University, 2009.

Najjar, M. "The Jordan Valley (East Bank) During the Middle Bronze Age in the Light of New Excavations." In M. Zaghloul, K. 'Amr, F. Zayadine, R. Nabeel, and N. Rida Tawfiq, eds., *Studies in the History and Archaeology of Jordan IV*, 149–54. Amman: Department of Antiquities of Jordan, 1992.

Neev, D., and K. O. Emery, *The Destruction of Sodom and Gomorrah, and Jericho: Geological, Climatological, and Archaeological Background.* New York: Oxford University Press, 1995.

Parr, P. J. "The Origin of the Rampart Fortifications of Middle Bronze Age Palestine and Syria." *Zeitschrift des deutschen Palästina-Vereins* 84 (1968): 18–45.

Schaub, R. T. "Mud-Brick Town Walls in the EBI-II Southern Levant and Their Significance for Understanding the Formation of New Social Institutions." In F. al-Khraysheh, R. Harahsheh, Q. Fakhoury, H. Taher, and S. Khouri, eds., *Studies in the History and Archaeology of Jordan IX*, 247–52. Amman: Department of Antiquities of Jordan, 2007.

Schaub, R. T., and M. S. Chesson. "Life in the Earliest Walled Towns on the Dead Sea Plain: Bab edh-Dhra' and an-Numayra." In T. E. Levy, P. M. Michèle Daviau, R. W. Younker, and M. Shaer, eds., *Crossing Jordan: North American Contributions to the Archaeology of Jordan*, 245–52. London: Equinox, 2007.

Warner, D. *The Archaeology of the Canaanite Cult: An Analysis of Canaanite Temples from the Middle and Late Bronze Age in Palestine.* Saarbrücken: VDM Verlag [and] Dr. Müller Aktiengesellschaft, 2008.

Wood, B. G. "The Discovery of the Sin Cities of Sodom and Gomorrah." *Bible and Spade* 12.3 (1999): 67–80.

BACKSTORY: Dr. C's Dream

Broshi, M., and R. Gophna. "Middle Bronze Age II Palestine: Its Settlements and Population." *Bulletin of the American Schools of Oriental Research* 261 (1986): 73–90.

Burke, A. A. *"Walled Up to Heaven": The Evolution of Middle Bronze Age Fortification Strategies in the Levant.* Winona Lake, IN: Eisenbrauns, 2008.

Collins, S. *The Search for Sodom and Gomorrah: A Scientific Application of Dialogical Methodology in Determining Material Correspondence between Archaeological Data and Biblical Narrative.* Albuquerque, NM: Trinity Southwest University Press, 2011.

Collins, S., and H. Aljarrah. "The Tall el-Hammam Excavation Project: End of Season Activity Report—Season Six: 2011 Excavation, Exploration, and Survey." Filed with the Department of Antiquities of Jordan, January 26, 2011.

————. "Tall al-Ḥammām Season Six, 2011: Excavation, Survey, Interpretations and Insights." *Annual of the Department of Antiquities of Jordan* 55 (2011): 581–608.

Collins, S., and Y. Eylayyan. "The Tall el-Hammam Excavation Project: End of Season Activity Report—Season Seven: 2012 Excavation, Exploration, and Survey." Filed with the Department of Antiquities of Jordan, February 2012.

Collins, S., K. Hamdan, and G. Byers. "Tall al-Ḥammām: Preliminary Report on Four Seasons of Excavation (2006–2009)." *Annual of the Department of Antiquities of Jordan* 53 (2009): 385–414.

Finkelstein, I. "Middle Bronze Age 'Fortifications': A Reflection of Social Organization and Political Formations." *Tel Aviv* 19 (1992): 201–20.

Kempinski, A. "Middle and Late Bronze Age Fortifications." In A. Kempinski and R. Reich, eds., *The Architecture of Ancient Israel*, 127–42. Jerusalem: Israel Exploration Society, 1992.

Kempinski, A., and R. Reich, eds. *The Architecture of Ancient Israel*. Jerusalem: Israel Exploration Society, 1992.

McAllister, S. S. "Middle Bronze Age Fortifications in the Southern Levant: Systems Analysis and Quantitative Survey." Doctoral dissertation, College of Archaeology and Biblical History, Trinity Southwest University, 2009.

Najjar, M. "The Jordan Valley (East Bank) During the Middle Bronze Age in the Light of New Excavations." In M. Zaghloul, K. 'Amr, F. Zayadine, R. Nabeel, and N. Rida Tawfiq, eds., *Studies in the History and Archaeology of Jordan IV*, 149–54. Amman: Department of Antiquities of Jordan, 1992.

Parr, P. J. "The Origin of the Rampart Fortifications of Middle Bronze Age Palestine and Syria." *Zeitschrift des deutschen Palästina-Vereins* 84 (1968): 18–45.

Schaub, R. T. "Mud-Brick Town Walls in the EBI-II Southern Levant and Their Significance for Understanding the Formation of New Social Institutions." In F. al-Khraysheh, R. Harahsheh, Q. Fakhoury, H. Taher, and S. Khouri, eds., *Studies in the History and Archaeology of Jordan IX*, 247–52. Amman: Department of Antiquities of Jordan.

BACKSTORY: Tale of the Trinitite

Boslough, M. B. E. "Riddle of the Desert Glass." *Lab News*, Sandia National Laboratories, September 15, 2007.

Boslough, M. B. E., and D. A. Crawford. "Low-Altitude Airbursts and the Impact Threat." Submitted to *Journal of Impact Engineering*, May 2007.

Collins, S. *The Search for Sodom and Gomorrah: A Scientific Application of Dialogical Methodology in Determining Material Correspondence between Archaeological Data and Biblical Narrative.* Albuquerque, NM: Trinity Southwest University Press, 2011.

Collins, S., and H. Aljarrah. "Tall al-Ḥammām Season Six, 2011: Excavation, Survey, Interpretations and Insights." *Annual of the Department of Antiquities of Jordan* 55 (2011): 581–608.

Collins, S., and Y. Eylayyan. "The Tall el-Hammam Excavation Project: End of Season Activity Report—Season Seven: 2012 Excavation, Exploration, and Survey," filed with the Department of Antiquities of Jordan, February 2012.

Collins, S., K. Hamdan, and G. Byers. "Tall al-Ḥammām: Preliminary Report on Four Seasons of Excavation (2006–2009)." *Annual of the Department of Antiquities of Jordan* 53 (2009): 385–414.

Gasperrini, L., E. Bonatti, and G. Longo. "The Tunguska Mystery." *Scientific American* (June 2008): 80–86.

Longo, Giuseppe. "The Tunguska Event." In P. T. Bobrowsky and H. Rickman, eds., *Comet/Asteroid Impacts and Human Society: An Interdisciplinary Approach*. London: Springer Verlag, 2007.

EIGHT: The Death of Sodom

Boslough, M. B. F., and D. A. Crawford. "Low-Altitude Airbursts and the Impact Threat." Submitted to *Journal of Impact Engineering*, May 2007.

Brown, F., S. R. Driver, and C. A. Briggs. *A Hebrew and English Lexicon of the Old Testament*. Oxford: Clarendon, 1975.

Collins, S. *The Search for Sodom and Gomorrah: A Scientific Application of Dialogical Methodology in Determining Material Correspondence between Archaeological Data and Biblical Narrative*. Albuquerque, NM: Trinity Southwest University Press, 2011.

Collins, S., A. Abu Dayyeh, A. Abu-Shmais, G. A. Byers, K. Hamdan, H. Aljarrah, J. Haroun, M. C. Luddeni, and S. McAllister. "The Tall el-Hammam Excavation Project, Season Activity Report, Season Three: 2008 Excavation, Exploration, and Survey." Filed with the Department of Antiquities of Jordan, February 13, 2008.

Collins, S., and H. Aljarrah. "The Tall el-Hammam Excavation Project: End of Season Activity Report—Season Six: 2011 Excavation, Exploration, and Survey." Filed with the Department of Antiquities of Jordan, January 26, 2011.

———. "Tall al-Ḥammām Season Six, 2011: Excavation, Survey, Interpretations and Insights." *Annual of the Department of Antiquities of Jordan* 55 (2011): 581–608.

Collins, S., G. A. Byers, and M. C. Luddeni. "The Tall el-Hammam Excavation Project, Season Activity Report, Season One: 2005/2006 Probe Excavation and Survey." Filed with the Department of Antiquities of Jordan, January 22, 2006.

Collins, S., G. A. Byers, M. C. Luddeni, and J. W. Moore. "The Tall el-Hammam Excavation Project, Season Activity Report, Season Two: 2006/2007 Excavation and Survey." Filed with the Department of Antiquities of Jordan, February 4, 2007.

Collins, S., and Y. Eylayyan. "The Tall el-Hammam Excavation Project: End of Season Activity Report—Season Seven: 2012 Excavation, Exploration, and Survey." Filed with the Department of Antiquities of Jordan, February 2012.

Collins, S., K. Hamdan and G. Byers. "Tall al-Ḥammām: Preliminary Report on Four Seasons of Excavation (2006–2009)." *Annual of the Department of Antiquities of Jordan* 53 (2009): 385–414.

Collins, S., K. Hamdan, G. A. Byers, J. Haroun, H. Aljarrah, M. C. Luddeni, S. McAllister, Q. Dasouqi, and A. Abu-Shmais. "The Tall el-Hammam Excavation Project, Season Activity Report, Season Five:

2010 Excavation, Exploration, and Survey." Filed with the Department of Antiquities of Jordan, January 31, 2010.

Collins, S., K. Hamdan, G. A. Byers, J. Haroun, H. Aljarrah, M. C. Luddeni, S. McAllister, Q. Dasouqi, A. Abu-Shmais, and D. Graves. "The Tall el-Hammam Excavation Project, Season Activity Report, Season Four: 2009 Excavation, Exploration, and Survey." Filed with the Department of Antiquities of Jordan, February 27, 2009.

Els, P. J. J. S. "ספה" In W. A. VanGemeren, ed., *New International Dictionary of Old Testament Theology and Exegesis,* vol. 3, 277–78. Grand Rapids, MI: Zondervan, 1997.

Flanagan, J.W., D.W. McCreery, and K. N. Yassine. "Tell Nimrin: Preliminary Report on the 1993 Season." *Annual of the Department of Antiquities of Jordan* 38 (1994): 205–244.

———."Tell Nimrin: Preliminary Report on the 1995 Excavation and Geological Survey." *Annual of the Department of Antiquities of Jordan* 40 (1996): 271–292.

Frumkin, A., and Y. Elitzur. "The Rise and Fall of the Dead Sea." *Biblical Archaeology Review* 27.6 (November–December 2001): 43–50.

Gasperrini, L., E. Bonatti, and G. Longo. "The Tunguska Mystery." *Scientific American* (June 2008): 80–86.

Holladay, W., ed. *A Concise Hebrew and Aramaic Lexicon of the Old Testament.* Grand Rapids, MI: Eerdmans, 1988.

Koehler, L., and W. Baumgartner, eds. *Lexicon in Veteris Testamenti Libros: A Dictionary of the Hebrew Old Testament in English and German.* Leiden: Brill, 1985.

Longo, G. "The Tunguska Event." In P. T. Bobrowsky and H. Rickman, eds., *Comet/Asteroid Impacts and Human Society: An Interdisciplinary Approach.* London: Springer Verlag, 2007.

Naude, J. "גפרית" In W. A. VanGemeren, ed., *New International Dictionary of Old Testament Theology and Exegesis,* vol. 2, 200–201. Grand Rapids, MI: Zondervan, 1997.

————. " אש " In W. A. VanGemeren, ed., *New International Dictionary of Old Testament Theology and Exegesis,* vol. 1, 532–37. Grand Rapids, MI: Zondervan, 1997.

Neev, D., and K. O. Emery. *The Destruction of Sodom and Gomorrah, and Jericho: Geological, Climatological, and Archaeological Background.* New York: Oxford University Press, 1995.

CONCLUSION: Evidence Is Evidence

Clapp, F. G. "The Site of Sodom and Gomorrah." *American Journal of Archaeology* 40 (1936): 323–44.

Collins, S. "A Response to Bryant G. Wood's Critique of Collins' Northern Sodom Theory." In S. Collins, ed., *The Search for Sodom and Gomorrah: A Scientific Application of Dialogical Methodology in Determining Material Correspondence between Archaeological Data and Biblical Narrative*, 217–52. Albuquerque, NM: Trinity Southwest University Press, 2011.

———. *The Search for Sodom and Gomorrah: A Scientific Application of Dialogical Methodology in Determining Material Correspondence between Archaeological Data and Biblical Narrative*. Albuquerque, NM: Trinity Southwest University Press, 2011.

Collins, S., and H. Aljarrah. "Tall al-Ḥammām Season Six, 2011: Excavation, Survey, Interpretations and Insights." *Annual of the Department of Antiquities of Jordan* 55 (2011): 581–608.

Collins, S., and Y. Eylayyan. "The Tall el-Hammam Excavation Project: End of Season Activity Report—Season Seven: 2012 Excavation, Exploration, and Survey." Filed with the Department of Antiquities of Jordan, February 2012.

Collins, S., K. Hamdan, and G. Byers. "Tall al-Ḥammām: Preliminary Report on Four Seasons of Excavation (2006–2009)." *Annual of the Department of Antiquities of Jordan* 53 (2009): 385–414.

Collins, S., K. Hamdan, G. A. Byers, J. Haroun, H. Aljarrah, M. C. Luddeni, S. McAllister, Q. Dasouqi, and A. abu-Shmais. "The Tall el-Hammam Excavation Project, Season Activity Report, Season Five: 2010 Excavation, Exploration, and Survey." Filed with the Department of Antiquities of Jordan, January 31, 2010.

Falconer, S. E., P. L. Fall, and J. E. Jones. "Life at the Foundation of Bronze Age Civilization: Agrarian Villages in the Jordan Valley." In T. E. Levy, P. M. Michèle Daviau, R. W. Younker, and M. Shaer, eds., *Crossing Jordan: North American Contributions to the Archaeology of Jordan*, 261–68. London: Equinox, 2007.

Finkelstein, I. "From Sherds to History." *Israel Exploration Journal* 48 (1998): 120–31 (based on a 1996 *Eretz Israel* article by Finkelstein published in Hebrew as "The Settlement History of the Transjordan Plateau in the Light of Survey Data").

Frumkin, A., and Y. Elitzur. "The Rise and Fall of the Dead Sea." *Biblical Archaeology Review* 27.6 (November–December 2001): 43–50.

Harland, J. P. "Sodom and Gomorrah." *Biblical Archaeologist* 5 (1942): 17–32.

———. "Sodom and Gomorrah." *Biblical Archaeologist* 6 (1943): 41–54.

Kitchen, K. A. *On the Reliability of the Old Testament*. Grand Rapids, MI: Eerdmans, 2003.

Kreiger, B. *Living Waters: Myth, History, and Politics of the Dead Sea*. New York: Continuum, 1988.

Lemche, N. P. *Prelude to Israel's Past*. Peabody, MA: Hendrickson, 1998.

Neev, D., and K. O. Emery, *The Destruction of Sodom and Gomorrah, and Jericho: Geological, Climatological, and Archaeological Background*. New York: Oxford University Press, 1995.

Rainey, A., and R. S. Notley. *The Sacred Bridge*. Jerusalem: Carta, 2006.

Redford, D. B. *The Wars in Syria and Palestine of Thutmose III: Culture and History of the Ancient World.* Boston: Brill, 2003.

Schaub, R. T., and M. S. Chesson. "Life in the Earliest Walled Towns on the Dead Sea Plain: Bab edh-Dhraʾ and an-Numayra." In T. E. Levy, P. M. Michèle Daviau, R. W. Younker, and M. Shaer, eds., *Crossing Jordan: North American Contributions to the Archaeology of Jordan,* 245–52. London: Equinox, 2007.

Shanks, H. "Have Sodom and Gomorrah Been Found?" *BAR* 6.5 (1980): 26–36.

Von Rad, G. *Genesis.* Philadelphia: Westminster, 1961.

Westermann, C. *Genesis 12–36: A Commentary.* Minneapolis: Augsburg, 1985.

Wood, B. G. "The Discovery of the Sin Cities of Sodom and Gomorrah." *Bible and Spade* 12.3 (1999): 67–80.

———. "Have Sodom and Gomorrah Been Found?" *Bible and Spade* 3 (1974): 65–89.

———. "Locating Sodom: A Critique of the Northern Proposal." *Bible and Spade* 20.3 (2007): 78–84.

———. "Sodom and Gomorrah Update." *Bible and Spade* 6 (1977): 24–30.

———. "Sodom and Gomorrah Update." *Bible and Spade* 12 (1983): 22–33.

Acknowledgments

Mᵧ wɪꜰᴇ, Dᴀɴᴇᴛᴛᴇ—ᴡʜᴏ'ꜱ ᴀɴ ɪɴᴛʀᴇᴘɪᴅ ᴅɪɢɢᴇʀ ɪɴ ʜᴇʀ
own right!—has stood with me throughout my archaeological career, and
provided many excellent ideas and criticisms throughout this book project. To each of the many volunteer diggers and financial supporters of
the Tall el-Hammam Excavation Project (TeHEP) I must say "thank you"
from the bottom of my heart. Without your personal sacrifices and hard
work on behalf of the project, this book would not have been possible.
I owe a deep debt of gratitude to my TeHEP staff and colleagues who,
from the inception of the project, have always gone above and beyond the
call of duty in serving this historic effort—Gary Byers (assistant director) and wife, Gayle; Carroll Kobs (assistant director) and husband, Jeff;
Mike Luddeni (photographer) and wife, Jean. My heartfelt thanks also
go out to the members of our senior staff, without whom the excavation
would quickly plunge into chaos: Carl Morgan (field supervisor), Ginny
Kay Massara (field supervisor; artist), Steve McAllister (area supervisor), David Graves (field supervisor), and Phil Silvia (field supervisor). I
must also recognize the members of our field staff who supervise excavation squares (trenches)—Kennet Schath, Father Chris Craig, Carl Fink,
Brandy Forrest (also director of planning), Walt Pasadag, Jennifer Fair,
Chuck Scott, and Aaron Taylor. There are many who, through seven ex-

cavation seasons, have performed a wide range of services and functions for TeHEP, and to whom I must express sincere appreciation: Daniel Galassini (videographer), David Maltsberger (field consultant), John Leslie (osteologist), John Young (equipment maintenance), Marlene Young (assistant pottery/objects registrar), Lucy Clayton (anthropologist), Heather Reichstadt (conservator), and Bob Mullins (ceramic typologist). I would also like to thank the field archaeologists from the Department of Antiquities of the Hashemite Kingdom of Jordan, who, as members of the TeHEP team, labored with us during our first seven seasons of excavation: Hussein Aljarrah, Adeib Abu-Shmais, Jehad Haroun, Khalil Hamdan, Yazeed Eylayyan, Rami Freihat, Tawfiq Hunaiti (surveyor), and Qutaiba Dasouqi (surveyor). I must also express gratefulness for the assistance and friendship of Ziad Al-Saad, who was director general of the Jordan Department of Antiquities during our sixth season, and who remains a dear colleague and consultant on technical scientific issues. Special thanks go to Leen Ritmeyer, whose unparalleled architectural expertise and masterful artistry have richly enhanced our understanding of a magnificent ancient city, Tall el-Hammam/Sodom. I also wish to recognize Kay Prag, David Burleigh, and John Park for their kind assistance and consultations during the course of our research, explorations, and excavations. I must express profound appreciation for longtime friend and colleague John Moore, who's walked with me in this quest since the first moment I began to take a critical interest in solving the mystery of Sodom's true location. Special thanks to Mike Luddeni, who's the best dig photographer ever, and who took most of the photos in this book. Finally, thank you, Latayne Scott, for your wonderful gift of writing and perseverance through an extreme hardship in order to make this book a reality. May God be exalted!